I0130595

'Reading this fascinating collection, I realized that, finally, we have a book that addresses the complexities of psychoanalysis in Latin America. Focusing on the political, cultural and social specificities of the region, this is an indispensable book that, from a novel and interdisciplinary perspective, fills an important gap existing in the big narratives on psychoanalysis. Its wonderfully crafted chapters question the possibilities and limitations of a psychoanalytic approach to the Latin American multiverse reality. It will become a must read for anyone interested in psychoanalysis and in Latin American culture and politics in general.'

Mariano Ben Plotkin, *researcher at the Centro de Investigaciones Sociales (CONICET) and Professor at the Universidad Nacional de Tres de Febrero*

'Psychoanalysis is here decolonized thanks to intense, unforgettable readings of urgent issues ranging from feminicide violence, to an impossible mourning for the desaparecidos, to melancholy and necropolitics, to decolonized clinical practice with Afro-Brazilians, to the plight of intersex and trans-transvestite children. This fiercely relevant collection shows how psychoanalysis in Latin America and the Caribbean brings about a transformation of race, class, and gender while redrawing the map of transnational psychoanalysis today.'

Patricia Gherovici, *psychoanalyst and author of* Transgender Psychoanalysis: A Lacanian Perspective on Sexual Difference

Psychoanalysis as Social and Political Discourse in Latin America and the Caribbean

A regional, intersectional, and transnational perspective of psychoanalysis in Latin America and the Caribbean that illuminates psychoanalysis's role as social and political discourse through a collection of original interventions in the fields of psychoanalysis, cultural studies, psychology, anthropology, health sciences, history, and philosophy.

The authors contribute to discussions about the applicability of psychoanalytic concepts to reading Latin American and Caribbean sociopolitical phenomena as well as how these regionally specific dimensions challenge and transform traditional psychoanalytic notions. First, the book offers a regional overview of psychoanalysis as a discourse that reflects on the imbrication between the psychic and the sociopolitical. Second, it showcases intersectional perspectives that illuminate psychoanalysis's potentials and limitations in addressing contemporary problematics around race, gender, sexuality, and class. Finally, the book attests to the area's role in advancing psychoanalysis as a transnational discipline.

By providing both a balanced regional overview and an interdisciplinary perspective, the volume will be essential for all psychoanalysts and scholars wanting to understand the place of psychoanalysis in Latin American and Caribbean discourse.

Paola Bohórquez is Assistant Professor, teaching stream, cross-appointed between Woodsworth College and the Faculty of Arts and Science at the University of Toronto. She has published in the *Journal of Intercultural Studies*, *Synthesis*, and *Tusaaji: A Translation Review*, and in the collections *On and Off the Page: Mapping Place in Text and Culture, American Multicultural Studies*, and *La Lingua Spaesata: Il Multilinguismo Oggi*.

Verónica Garibotto is Professor of Latin American literary and cultural studies at the University of Kansas. She is the author of *Crisis y reemergencia: el siglo XIX en la ficción contemporánea de Argentina, Chile y Uruguay* (2015) and *Rethinking Testimonial Cinema in Post-Dictatorship Argentina* (2019), and co-editor, with Jorge Pérez, of *The Latin American Road Movie* (2016).

Psychoanalysis as Social and Political Discourse in Latin America and the Caribbean

Edited by Paola Bohórquez and Verónica Garibotto

Routledge
Taylor & Francis Group

LONDON AND NEW YORK

Cover image: Getty Images/Cesar Okada

First published 2022
by Routledge
4 Park Square, Milton Park, Abingdon, Oxon OX14 4RN

and by Routledge
605 Third Avenue, New York, NY 10158

Routledge is an imprint of the Taylor & Francis Group, an informa business

© 2022 selection and editorial matter, Paola Bohórquez and Verónica Garibotto; individual chapters, the contributors

The right of Paola Bohórquez and Verónica Garibotto to be identified as the authors of the editorial material, and of the authors for their individual chapters, has been asserted in accordance with sections 77 and 78 of the Copyright, Designs and Patents Act 1988.

All rights reserved. No part of this book may be reprinted or reproduced or utilised in any form or by any electronic, mechanical, or other means, now known or hereafter invented, including photocopying and recording, or in any information storage or retrieval system, without permission in writing from the publishers.

Trademark notice: Product or corporate names may be trademarks or registered trademarks, and are used only for identification and explanation without intent to infringe.

British Library Cataloguing-in-Publication Data
A catalogue record for this book is available from the British Library

Library of Congress Cataloging-in-Publication Data
A catalog record has been requested for this book

ISBN: 978-1-032-20983-8 (hbk)
ISBN: 978-1-032-20984-5 (pbk)
ISBN: 978-1-003-26621-1 (ebk)

DOI: 10.4324/9781003266211

Typeset in Times New Roman
by Apex CoVantage, LLC

With gratitude to the philosophers and psychoanalysts who accompanied the passage, in friendship, to this elsewhere.

Contents

Acknowledgments

We are deeply grateful to the many people who made this collection possible. To our contributors, who enthusiastically engaged with us in the fort/da of writing, revision, and translation, we thank you for the always stimulating intellectual exchange. We are immensely thankful to the Department of Spanish and Portuguese at the University of Kansas, and to Woodsworth College Principal, Carol Chin, and Vice-Dean Undergraduate, Randy Boyagoda, at the Faculty of Arts and Science at the University of Toronto for their support and funding. A special thanks to Veronika Brejkaln and Dana Hill for their excellent translation of the contributions submitted in Spanish, and to Seungjoo Lee for her research assistance and careful work on the manuscript design. We would also like to give a special thanks to Hannah Wright and Kate Hawes, from Routledge, for their enthusiasm for this project and for their patience in pandemic times. Finally, our love and gratitude to our partners and children for their support and the time borrowed.

Notes on Contributors

Ricardo Ainslie holds the M.K. Hage Centennial Professorship in Education at the University of Texas at Austin, teaching in the Department of Educational Psychology. He is also the director of the LLILAS-Benson Mexico Center and affiliate faculty at Dell Medical School. He was Adjunct Faculty at the Houston Center for Psychoanalytic Studies (1994–2011) and founding member and past president of the Austin Society for Psychoanalytic Psychology. He is a member of the editorial board for the journals *Psychoanalytic Psychology* and *Psychoanalysis, Culture, and Society.*

Neil Altman is Faculty at the William Allison White Institute and Visiting Faculty at Ambedkar University of Delhi. He is Editor Emeritus of *Psychoanalytic Dialogues*, and the editorial staff of the *Journal of Infant, Child, and Adolescent Psychotherapy*, the *International Journal of Applied Psychoanalytic Studies*, and *the Journal of Child Psychotherapy*. He is the author of *White Privilege: Psychoanalytic Perspectives* (Routledge, 2020), *Psychoanalysis in an Age of Accelerating Cultural Change: Spiritual Globalization* (Routledge, 2015), *The Analyst in the Inner City: Race, Class and Culture through a Psychoanalytic Lens* (Routledge, 2010), and co-author of *Relational Child Psychotherapy* (Other Press, 2002).

Juan Pablo Aranguren-Romero is Associate Professor in the Department of Psychology at the Universidad de Los Andes (Colombia). Since 2016, he coordinates the project *The Ethics of Listening*, focused on understanding the emotional management of the war and the Colombian armed conflict for different professionals who work in this context. Currently, he is a researcher at the project "Transfunéraire – Violences de masse et pratiques funéraires" funded by the ANR (France). Aranguren is author of *Managing Testimony and Administrating Victims* (Palgrave, 2017), *Cuerpos al límite: tortura, subjetividad y memoria en Colombia* (Ediciones Uniandes, 2016), and *Las inscripciones de la guerra en el cuerpo de los jóvenes combatientes* (Ediciones Uniandes, 2011). He is currently finishing the book *The Ethics of Representation*, which addresses the emotional experience of 20 photographers covering the Colombian armed conflict.

Paola Bohórquez is Assistant Professor, teaching stream, cross-appointed between Woodsworth College and the English Language Learning Program in the Faculty of Arts and Science at the University of Toronto, where she teaches writing in the disciplines, translingual composition, and rhetoric. Originally, a psychologist from Universidad de Los Andes (Bogotá) with clinical experience in psychoanalytic-oriented counselling and mental health interventions for victims of social and political violence in Colombia, Bohórquez holds an MA in Psychoanalytic Studies from the New School for Social Research and a PhD in Social and Political Thought from York University (Toronto). Informed by her psychoanalytic training and interdisciplinary scholarly work on the relations between language and identity, translation, and translocality, Bohórquez's current research focuses on pedagogical innovations for teaching critical literacies in multilingual learning contexts. She has published in the *Journal of Intercultural Studies, Synthesis*, and *Tusaaji: A Translation Review*, and in the collections *On and Off the Page: Mapping Place in Text and Culture, American Multicultural Studies, and La Lingua Spaesata: Il Multilinguismo Oggi.*

Jana Evans Braziel is Western Endowed Professor in the Department of Global and Intercultural Studies at Miami University. Braziel is author of five monographs: *"Riding with Death": Vodou Art and Urban Ecology in the Streets of Port-au-Prince* (2017); *Duvalier's Ghosts: Race, Diaspora, and U.S. Imperialism in Haitian Literatures* (2010); *Caribbean Genesis: Jamaica Kincaid and the Writing of New Worlds* (2009); *Artists, Performers, and Black Masculinity in the Haitian Diaspora* (2008); and *Diaspora: An Introduction* (2008). She has also co-edited five edited collections, two special issues of a peer-reviewed academic journal, and published myriad articles and book chapters. Currently, she has several manuscripts in process including a study of the contemporary global refugee crisis.

Juan Nicolás Cardona-Santofimio is a psychotherapist in private practice. He is also an IPA psychoanalyst in training (Sociedad Colombiana de Psicoanálisis, SOCOLPSI) psychologist, and philosopher from the Universidad de Los Andes. He is the author of *Fantasmagorías: un mosaico filosófico sobrenatural* (Fallidos Editores, 2020). His academic interests are focused on analyzing the forms of emotional management of absence in contexts of political violence and armed conflict.

Pablo G. Celis-Castillo is Associate Professor of Spanish at the Department of World Languages and Cultures at Elon University in North Carolina. He is also the coordinator of Elon's Latin American Studies Program. His most recent scholarly work revolves around the visual culture thematically connected to the Peruvian armed conflict of the 1980s and 1990s. He has also published works exploring how contemporary Peruvian narratives negotiate identity and subjectivity in the post-conflict context. His work has appeared in the *Revista Canadiense de Estudios Hispánicos* and in *Transmodernity: Journal of Peripheral Cultural Production of the Luso-Hispanic World*, among others.

Mauricio Clavero Lerena is "Licenciado en Psicología" and "Magíster en Psicología Clínica" (Universidad de la República, Montevideo, Uruguay). Clavero holds a specialization in Psychoanalytic Psychotherapy from the Instituto Universitario de Posgrado (IUPA), Asociación Uruguaya de Psicoterapia Psicoanalítica (AUDEPP) and is a doctoral candidate in Psychology at the Facultad de Psicología y Psicopedagogía, Universidad del Salvador and the Asociación Psicoanalítica Argentina. Clavero is Professor and Academic Director of the Maestría en Psicoterapia Psicoanalítica at the IUPA.

Alejandro Dagfal is the director (and founder) of the Centro Argentino de la Historia del Psicoanálisis, la Psicología y la Psiquiatría at the Biblioteca Nacional de Argentina. He is also an independent researcher at the Consejo Nacional de Investigaciones Científicas y Técnicas de Argentina (CONICET) and a tenured joint professor of History of Psychology at the Facultad de Psicología, Universidad de Buenos Aires. He has lectured in Brazil, Chile, Spain, France, the United States, the UK, Colombia, and Mexico. He has published several papers and books in Spanish, French, English, and Portuguese on the history of psychology and psychoanalysis in the twentieth century. His main interest is the circulation of theories and authors between France, England, the United States, and Argentina and its impact on sociocultural, intellectual, and political contexts. His first book *Entre París y Buenos Aires: la invención del psicólogo* (Paidós, 2009) received the 2011 National Prize of the Ministry of Culture in Argentina.

Verónica Garibotto is Professor of Latin American literary and cultural studies at the University of Kansas. She is the author of *Crisis y reemergencia: el siglo XIX en la ficción contemporánea de Argentina, Chile y Uruguay* (Purdue UP, 2015) and *Rethinking Testimonial Cinema in Post-Dictatorship Argentina* (Indiana UP, 2019), and co-editor, with Jorge Pérez, of *The Latin American Road Movie* (Palgrave Macmillan, 2016). Garibotto has also published several articles in journals such as *Latin American Research Review*, *Revista Iberoamericana*, *Revista de Estudios Hispánicos*, *Journal of Latin American Cultural Studies*, *Latin American Literary Review*, and *Studies in Hispanic Cinemas*. She is currently working on a new book, *Paradoxical Ideologies: an Intersectional View of Argentine Psychoanalytic Culture*.

Oren Gozlan, Psy.D., ABPP, FIPA, is a practicing psychoanalyst, Chair of the Scientific Committee, and faculty member at the Toronto Institute of Psychoanalysis. He is also Faculty at the Toronto Institute of Contemporary Psychoanalysis and at the Canadian Institute for Child and Adolescent Psychoanalytic Psychotherapy, and a member of the IPA committee for Gender Diversity and Sexuality. His book *Transsexuality and the Art of Transitioning: A Lacanian Approach* (Routledge, 2014) won the American Academy and Board of Psychoanalysis's annual book prize. He is also the winner of the Symonds Prize (2016). His edited collection titled *Current Critical Debates in the Field of Transsexual Studies: In Transition* (Routledge, 2018) was nominated for the 2019 Gradiva Award.

Miguel Gutiérrez-Peláez, PhD, is Full Professor of the Center for Psychosocial Studies (CEPSS) and Psychology Program of the Universidad del Rosario (Bogotá, Colombia). Dr. Gutiérrez-Peláez is a psychologist from the Pontificia Universidad Javeriana (PUJ) and obtained his MA in psychoanalysis and PhD in psychology from the Universidad de Buenos Aires (UBA). He is a member of the World Association of Psychoanalysis (AMP) and the New Lacanian School (NEL). He has worked with Colombian soldiers and police officers who fought in war zones, as well as with other persons with psychological difficulties derived from the armed conflict. Gutierrez is the author of *Confusion of Tongues. A Return to Sandor Ferenczi* (Routledge, 2018), *Arte y psicoanálisis. Invenciones (artísticas) inéditas de sujetos singulares* (Universidad del Rosario, 2018, co-edited with Beatriz García Moreno), and *Sandor Ferenczi. A Critical Introduction* (Routledge, 2022, co-authored with Alberto Fergusson).

Horacio Legrás is Professor at the University of California-Irvine, where he teaches courses on Latin American literature and culture, critical theory, visual studies, and film. His primary appointment is in the Spanish and Portuguese departments. He holds associate appointments in the departments of Comparative Literature, European Studies, the Critical Theory Emphases, and the Culture and Theory program. He is the author of *Literature and Subjection. The Economy of Writing and Marginality in Latin America* (2008) and *Culture and Revolution: Violence, Memory and the Making of Modern Mexico* (2016). He has two forthcoming books, *Reality in Question: The Counter-Factual Work of Race, Gender, Ethnicity and the Unconscious in Twentieth-Century Latin America*, and *Lacan and the Question of Reading*.

Claudia dos Reis Motta has a PhD and an MA in Health Sciences (Interactive Processes of Organs and Systems) from the Universidade Federal da Bahia, Brazil, from where she also received her BA in Psychology. She has worked as a psychoanalyst for over 25 years, and is currently a member of Sede Psicanálise. Dr. Motta has published journal articles and book chapters on clinical child and pediatric psychology in Brazil and Portugal. She is the author of *The Speech of Children, Adolescents and Their Parents About Intestinal Dysfunction: Clinical Listening* (currently under consideration by a university press).

Andrés Rabinovich is a PhD candidate in Latin American literary and cultural studies in the Department of Spanish and Portuguese at the University of Kansas. He holds an MA in Latin American literature from the University of Kansas and a BA in Spanish and Italian from Queen's University (Canada). His doctoral dissertation examines the ways in which representations of soccer in Argentine and Brazilian film and narrative between 2003 and 2015 shed light on the cultural impact of neoliberalism. He has presented his research at the Latin American Studies Association—Southern Cone Conference (2017), the

Mid America Conference on Hispanic Literatures (2017), and the American Portuguese Studies Association Conference (2018).

Silvia Rivera-Largacha, PhD, is Assistant Professor of the Medicine Program of the Escuela de Medicina at the Universidad del Rosario (Bogotá, Colombia), where she is member of the Grupo de Estudios Sociales de las Ciencias, las Tecnologías y las Profesiones (GESCTP). Dr. Rivera-Largacha is a psychologist from the Pontificia Universidad Javeriana (PUJ) and obtained her MA in ethnology, sociology, and psychoanalysis from the University Paul Valery (Montpellier III-France) and her PhD in Psychology and Educational Sciences from the Université Catholique de Louvain. She has taught in different universities in Colombia and France. As a clinician, she has worked in psychosocial support offered to humanitarian workers in Colombia. She is the author of various publications in indexed journals and book chapters on issues related to the subjective impact of social policies and health practices interventions in mental health.

Mariano Ruperthuz Honorato is a psychoanalyst at the Sociedad Chilena de Psicoanálisis-ICHPA and an academic researcher at the Universidad Andrés Bello and the Fondo Nacional de Desarrollo y Tecnología (FONDECYT) of the Agencia Nacional de Investigación y Desarrollo (ANID) in Chile. He is doctor in Psychology (Universidad de Chile) and doctor in History (Universidad de Santiago de Chile). He is the author of *Freud y los chilenos: un viaje transnacional (1910–1949)* (Pólvora, 2016) and co-author, with Mariano Ben Plotkin, of *Estimado Dr. Freud. Una historia cultural del psicoanálisis en América Latin*a (Edhasa, 2017). Ruperthuz Honorato is also the president of the Sociedad Chilena de Historia de la Psicología.

Antonio Luciano de Andrade Tosta is Associate Professor of Brazilian Literature and Culture and Interim Director of the Center for Global and International Studies at The University of Kansas. He has a PhD in Comparative Literature and an MA in Portuguese and Brazilian Studies from Brown University. Tosta is the author of *Confluence Narratives: Ethnicity, History, and Nation Making in the Americas* (Bucknell UP, 2016) and co-editor of *Luso American Literature: Writings by Portuguese Speaking Peoples in North America* (Rutgers UP, 2011) and *Brazil* (ABC/Clio, 2015). His areas of research include postcolonial/decolonial theory, immigration, and ethnic and race studies. His publications on hemispheric American literature, film, and music have appeared in several journals and as book chapters in the United States, Brazil, Canada, and England.

Introduction

Beyond the Therapist Couch: Psychoanalysis as Social and Political Discourse in Latin America and the Caribbean

Paola Bohórquez and Verónica Garibotto

On July 15, 2010, thousands of Argentines gathered in front of the National Congress as senators debated, and eventually passed, a federal law of marriage equality. Broadcast live on a big screen, Senator María Eugenia Estenssoro gave the final favorable arguments: "In the great human family there are many systems of kinship, families, and marriages. There is no natural family or natural system . . . as Freud says" (Bravo 114).[1] In the exposition immediately preceding Estenssoro's, Senator Samuel Cabanchik presented a similar idea. He claimed that, after having read several psychoanalytic articles, he was convinced that there was no scientific evidence proving that children raised by same-sex couples had more difficulties than those raised by heterosexual couples (Bravo 69).

The references to psychoanalysis should not be surprising in a country dominated by what Mariano Ben Plotkin calls "a psychoanalytic culture": an entire culture whose metaphors and forms of thinking revolve around the discipline—one of Argentina's distinct features (*Freud en las pampas* 2).[2] In this case, however, the influence was more prominent than usual. Between 2005 (when the Comunidad Homosexual Argentina presented a proposal for a federal law of civil union that developed into the law of marriage equality) and 2010 (the year the latter finally passed), psychoanalysts dominated the public conversation on gender and sexuality. They voiced their specialized opinions on television and radio programs, newspapers, and at the National Congress. Moreover, several psychoanalytic associations, such as the Asociación Psicoanalítica Argentina and the Centro de Investigación y Estudios Clínicos de Córdoba issued collective volumes and journal dossiers on LGBTQIA+ topics aiming at a lay audience (Agrest Wainer and Rotenberg; Zelcer; Ceballos).

Although seemingly a minor event in the broader history of psychoanalysis in Latin America and the Caribbean, the case of the Argentine law of marriage equality points to several features that are specific to the vicissitudes of the discipline in the region: the widespread social and political influence of psychoanalytic discourses; the discipline's role in the creation of categories of identity, such as gender, sexuality, race, and class; and the popular appeal and public circulation

DOI: 10.4324/9781003266211-1

of psychoanalytic thought. Even when more visible in Argentina, these features constitute less a national exception than a regional particularity. In Mexico, for instance, psychoanalysis has informed discourses on criminology since the 1930s, when judge Raúl Carrancá y Trujillo introduced psychoanalytic concepts into the legal profession, paving the way for the discipline to act as a key element in, among other cases, the resolution of León Trotski's assassination in 1940 (Gallo 253). In Peru and Brazil, to name just two of the most paradigmatic examples, Freudomarxist ideals inspired social and revolutionary thought, as seen in José Mariátegui's political interpretations of Peruvian society as early as 1926 and in the Colégio de Psicanálise da Bahia and the Instituto Felix Guattari's calls for action in the midst of Latin America's guerrilla movements of the 1970s (Legrás, "Psychoanalysis in Latin America" n.p.). Freudomarxism has also been a residual, yet founding, discourse of Cuban culture and politics, as evidenced in the works of José Martí and Tomás Gutiérrez Alea (Bosteels 35–55; 107–140). In the last few years, too, psychoanalytic concepts have played a crucial role in intellectual and activist groups and agendas across the region, most notably in transnational feminist movements like #NiUnaMenos and in the recent debates on abortion and trans rights, especially in Uruguay, Chile, and El Salvador.

Taking this regional commonality as a starting point, our volume offers a sociopolitical, intersectional, and transnational perspective of psychoanalysis in Latin America and the Caribbean. Rather than providing a history of the discipline, our book illuminates psychoanalysis's role as social and political discourse through a collection of state-of-the-art interventions in the fields of clinical and theoretical psychoanalysis, cultural studies, psychology, literature, health sciences, history, anthropology, and philosophy. The chapters in the first section explore the applicability of psychoanalytic concepts for reading Latin American and Caribbean sociopolitical phenomena as well as how these regionally specific dimensions challenge and transform traditional psychoanalytic notions. The second section examines psychoanalytic discourses from an intersectional perspective to elucidate the discipline's potential and limitations in addressing contemporary problematics around race, gender, sexuality, and class. Finally, the third section focuses on the popular reception and public circulation of psychoanalysis and acknowledges Latin America and the Caribbean's key role in the configuration of a "transnational system of thought" (Plotkin, "Introduction" 229).

Reading Latin America and the Caribbean: Sociopolitical Perspectives

Psychoanalysis has been an influential discourse in Latin America and the Caribbean at least since the early twentieth century, when it entered the region via pioneers such as Juliano Moreira in Brazil, Germán Greve Schlegel in Chile, Honorio Delgado in Peru, Raúl Carrancá y Trujillo in Mexico, Juan Bautista Montoya in Colombia, and Gonzalo Lafora in Argentina. The history of this influence has generated significant academic attention and has been widely documented both in Latin American and in international circles, especially since 1991, when the appointment of Horacio Etchegoyen as the first Latin American president of the International Psychoanalytical Association (IPA) made the centrality of psychoanalysis in the region even more visible. In 1993, inspired by this recent visibility, Moisés Lemlij and Dana Cáceres published *Psychoanalysis in Latin America* with the intention of "presenting English-speaking audiences with a selection of clinical works by Latin American psychoanalysts" (ix). The volume offers texts on clinical psychoanalysis from Argentina, Chile, Uruguay, Mexico, Venezuela, Brazil, Colombia, and Peru; provides a chronology of the official incorporation of Latin American associations to the IPA; and traces the origins of the discipline in the region to Greve Schlegel's presentation on psychotherapy and anxiety at an international medical conference held in Buenos Aires in 1910. Greve Schlegel's presentation is also the event that marks the public appearance of the discipline in Latin America according to *Truth, Reality, and the Psychoanalyst: Latin American Contributions to Psychoanalysis*, a volume co-edited by Sergio Lewcowicz and Silvia Flechner that covers both early public appearances in Argentina, Peru, Chile, Colombia, Brazil, Uruguay, Mexico, Venezuela, and Paraguay as well as the most recent regional contributions to the field. In a special dossier on Latin America in the journal *Psychoanalysis and History*, however, Plotkin and Jane Russo date this first appearance a decade earlier with Moreira's inclusion of Freud's early writings in the bibliography of the courses he taught at the Faculdade Baiana de Medicina in 1899 (227, 298). Other articles in this same dossier further illuminate the early circulation of psychoanalytic thought, most notably the 1920's exchange of ideas between Spain and Argentina that contributed to the institutionalization of the discipline in the latter country and the reception of psychoanalysis in Chilean medical circles between 1910 and 1940 (Druet 237–251; Ruperthuz Honorato 285–296). The key role of transatlantic connections for the institutionalization of the discipline is also the primary focus of Plotkin and Ruperthuz Honorato's *Estimado Dr. Freud: Una historia cultural del psicoanálisis en América Latina*, a book that carefully traces how Freud's relationship with Latin American intellectuals influenced the discipline and was crucial for its consolidation in the region. Along the same lines, Bruno Bosteels's book *Marx and Freud in Latin America* has provided a most welcome contribution on the relevance of Freudian thought for intellectuals, artists, and writers in Cuba, Argentina, Mexico, and Chile.

Yet, as Horacio Legrás rightly claims, "For a psychoanalytic culture to emerge, a mutual association of esoteric and exoteric forms of propagation was needed" ("Psychoanalysis in Latin America" n.p.). That is, psychoanalysis's powerful influence lied in the discipline's esoteric, internal register as a therapeutic practice whose modalities and techniques require a special kind of expertise as well as an exoteric, public register as social discourse of wide circulation. This latter, exoteric register constitutes our volume's primary object of study. Instead of providing a history of how the discipline's esoteric register arrived and settled in Latin America and the Caribbean—which has already been successfully addressed in the aforementioned contributions—we offer a regional overview of psychoanalysis as a discourse that reflects on the imbrication between the psychic and the sociopolitical registers. Our chapters go beyond psychoanalysis's circulation in the intellectual field to examine its discursive impact on the public register.

Indeed, the extent of such discursive impact and, in particular, the viability of psychoanalysis for understanding Latin American specific sociopolitical realities is the main focus of "Feminicides, Psychoanalysis, and the Status of Social Desire in Our Time," Legrás's own contribution to our volume. Using a Lacanian framework that foregrounds the centrality of the concept of *jouissance* for an ethics of psychoanalysis, Legrás approaches the feminicides in Ciudad Juárez, Mexico, as an instance of "the passage to the (violent) act" characteristic of social (dis) orders caught between an impossible return to an obsolete patriarchal order and a *jouissance* coopted by the logic of market-driven capitalism. In Legrás's view, psychoanalysis can retain its status as social discourse only if it continues to hold fast to *jouissance* as a guarantor of subjective liveability while denouncing its insidious commodification. Drawing also from a Lacanian framework, Andrés Rabinovich's chapter "Staging Desire" rehearses Slavoj Žižek's concept of ideological fantasy to argue that Argentine football (soccer) culture, read as a key popular culture text, effectively stages a return to the Real of desire. Through an analysis of fan behavior at live games, club team identifications, and football coaching philosophies, Rabinovich illustrates the particular articulation of Imaginary and Symbolic investments and identifications that shapes the nation's collective reality and its paths to *jouissance*. In his groundbreaking book, *The Political Unconscious*, Fredric Jameson claims that psychoanalysis developed due to the capitalistic separation of the private and the public spheres, which paved the way for the appearance of "desire" and "sexuality" as individual drives. Since its inception, Jameson argues, psychoanalysis has run the risk of remaining locked within the private realm, unless the individual is decentered in the direction of the collective (61–69). Ernest Gellner raises a similar critique. The chief psychoanalytic goal of individual adjustment leads to political quietism (xv). The discipline's ritualistic, esoteric, and elitist nature makes it a highly individual practice, leading to what he calls "the embourgeoisment of the psyche" (139–149). Legrás and Rabinovich's chapters, however, go against the grain of these capitalistic and bourgeois tendencies: When grounding Lacanian concepts in Argentine and Mexican class and gender realities, they successfully decenter the notion of desire in the direction of the political and the collective.

From a slightly different psychoanalytic perspective—one that is closer to Freudian-inspired conceptions of trauma and mourning—Jana Evans Braziel, Pablo G. Celis-Castillo, Juan Pablo Aranguren-Romero, and Juan Nicolás Cardona-Santofimio also reflect on the imbrication between the psychic and the sociopolitical registers by examining the effects of state-sponsored violence on the recent histories of Latin America and the Caribbean. Braziel explores the space/ place of Titanyen in the Haitian collective imaginary. As a mass burial site of victims of the extrajudicial killings of the Duvalier dictatorship and the military regime of Raoul Cédras, and later on, of the dead bodies of the 2010 earthquake victims, Titanyen comes to represent a stratified sediment of the "ungrievable" victims of necropolitics—expendable and disposable life. Through a lens that intersects Giorgio Agamben's concept of *homo sacer* and psychoanalytic understandings of collective trauma, Braziel offers a reading of Raoul Peck's film *Assistance Mortelle* (2013) as an enactment of mourning rites for the ungrieved victims of state violence and state failure in Haiti. In "A Phantom in the Andes," Celis-Castillo engages in a comparative analysis of Alonso Cueto's novel *La hora azul* (2005) and Renato Cisneros's *La distancia que nos separa* (2015) to propose an "anasemic reading" that deploys Nicolas Abraham and Maria Torok's concept of the transgenerational phantom as a lens to examine the sedimented role of racism in the social dynamics underpinning the Peruvian armed conflict of the 1980s and 1990s. Making parallels with the truth-seeking process undertaken by the Truth and Reconciliation Commission, Celis-Castillo reflects on the limits and failures of the TRC, suggesting that the transgenerational phantom of racism continues to haunt the reconciliation process. The spectral also occupies Aranguren-Romero and Cardona Santofimio's essay on the aporias of "the work of mourning" concerning the Forcibly Disappeared in Latin America. Impunity and absence of justice, the authors argue, prompt the emergence of spectral figures that resist the work of mourning and generate instead melancholic formations and cryptic incorporations of the "non-living-undead" that, in turn, resist silencing and forgetting.

Taken as a whole, the essays in this section show that psychoanalysis is neither just a discipline that sustains therapeutic practices in Latin America and the Caribbean nor just a clinical discourse whose esoteric register permeates the intellectual field, but, above all, a body of thinking that provides a rich theoretical framework for understanding and explaining the region's particular sociopolitical reality. Conversely, the chapters suggest that the specificity of these sociopolitical phenomena demands a reexamination of classic psychoanalytic concepts ("trauma," "mourning," and *"jouissance"*) and opens up new avenues for thinking about collective memory, violence, racism, and desire. As implied in Braziel, Celis-Castillo, and Aranguren-Romero and Cardona Santofimio's contributions, for instance, the traditional, Freudian-based conception of trauma as unwitting reenactment—a conception that, via Cathy Caruth, Shoshana Felman, and Dori Laub, has become the dominant mode of reading the effects of state-sponsored violence in Latin America—is too narrow for understanding the complexity of these effects, particularly when impunity and the lack of recognition of victims—and, often, of the very reality of the crimes—foreclose justice and the collective metabolization of trauma. As these essays suggest, the absence or failure of such mechanisms of "empathic witnessing" (Santer 25) generates particular forms of social disease that eventually sediment into the body politic. Novels such as *La hora azul* and *La distancia que nos separa* and films like *Assistance Mortelle* document such insidious and insistent effects, though neither as unwittingly reenacted occurrences nor as uncontrolled discourses by traumatized subjects. Rather, these narratives self-reflectively foreground their own symptoms when openly representing specific events affecting society. The more conventional conception of trauma, these essays then suggest, needs to be enriched with notions that are able to account for how grief is publicly represented, symbolically acknowledged, and socially worked-through and memorialized. Only such enriched perspective can prevent Latin American and Caribbean state violence from constituting what Dominick LaCapra calls a "founding trauma" (*History* 56; *Writing* 81): a traumatic event that shatters identity yet paradoxically becomes its basis. By the same token, classic notions of transgenerational mourning—usually based on the case of Holocaust survivors—need to be rethought through a Latin American lens. In Latin America and the Caribbean, as these essays also show, the generational distinction is not as straightforward. Crucially, several of the victims of state, parastate, and guerrilla violence are closer to the figure of the specter or the phantom than to that of the survivor. In line with current incursions into "spectropoetics" understood as "the will-to-history in the context of an enforced amnesia" (Demos 14), these contributors explore the potential of the liminal category of the ghostly as a medium of resistance and counter-memory that extricates the disappeared, the NNs, and those buried in unmarked graves from radical annihilation. In productive conversation with the classical concepts of mourning and melancholia, these contributions challenge the ethical imperative to complete the work of mourning and point to culturally situated ways of continuing to hold the ungrieved and the ungrievable. Furthermore, as Legrás, Rabinovich, and Celis-Castillo's contributions compellingly indicate, in order for psychoanalysis to avoid being a master paradigm whereby concepts theorized in the "first world" are merely applied to the "third world"—a critique already raised by scholars such as Antonio Traverso and Mick Broderick (3)—it is necessary for psychoanalytic thought to account for class, race, gender, and national parameters that are unique to Latin American social locations. Rather than generalizing subject formation and omitting differences of class, race, gender, and nationality, Legrás, Rabinovich, and Celis-Castillo's essays ground their views in these categories to illuminate and challenge classic concepts such as *jouissance*, desire, and phantom.

Race, Class, Gender, and Sexuality: Intersectional Perspectives

Although an intersectional perspective that takes into account how psychoanalysis can both be rooted in and create categories of difference such as race, class, gender, and sexuality is of utmost importance for understanding the discipline's sociopolitical implications in Latin America and the Caribbean, it was not until 2019, when Patricia Gherovici and Christopher Christian co-edited *Psychoanalysis in the Barrios: Race, Class, and the Unconscious*, that such perspective gained significant attention in academic circles. A combination of essays by scholars of psychoanalysis and by clinicians who base their therapeutic practices on psychoanalysis, the volume denounces the effects of colonialism on the culture around mental health treatment in the *barrios*, understood as "racialized enclaves that function like sociolinguistic islands inside and outside of the U.S. borders" (2). The collection also explores how psychoanalytic treatment can empower Latin American and LatinX populations and advances a psychoanalytically informed critique that challenges medical diagnoses that ultimately aim to regulate and control LatinX bodies, such as panic attack, Puerto Rican syndrome, psychosis, and autism.

In line with Gherovici and Christian's volume—yet more centered on Latin America and the Caribbean than on the U.S. LatinX context—the essays included in our book draw from a mixture of clinical experiences and theoretical knowledge to showcase intersectional perspectives that illuminate psychoanalysis's potential and limitations in addressing contemporary problematics around race, gender, sexuality, and class. In "In Defense of Psychoanalysis," licensed psychoanalyst Claudia dos Reis Motta and cultural scholar Antonio Luciano de Andrade Tosta argue that psychoanalysis's subversive mission works as a two-way street, both transforming and being transformed by the cultures with which it comes into contact. By looking at the case of Afro-Brazilians who undergo analysis in the city of Salvador, Bahia, their essay proposes that psychoanalysis works through language to unsettle a predetermined fate to which one has been subjected through their personal history and that of their racial group.

Grounded in psychoanalytic and postcolonial theories, the chapter analyzes case studies from the local community and ultimately shows that psychoanalysis mobilizes articulations between the individual and the collective, dialectically and reciprocally, creating a subversive dialogue with the local culture(s). In "Psychoanalysis in Colombia," Silvia Rivera-Largacha and Miguel Gutiérrez-Peláez draw from their clinical experiences working with actors and victims of sociopolitical violence in the country to illuminate how various forms of violence—domestic, gendered, social, and political—sediment in the psychic lives of those who have been structurally excluded from the nation-building project. Posing the exclusion of the radical Other as the thread that holds together all these violences, the article suggests that psychoanalysis can help counteract segregation and misrecognition through the value of singularity. Also borrowing from his own clinical practice, in this case with gender nonconforming patients, Oren Gozlan advances a reading of Lucía Puenzo's *XXY* (Argentina, 2007) that underscores the film's staging of ambiguity, liminality, and uncertainty as inherent tensions in the always unpredictable unfolding of gender identification. Gozlan's essay draws a parallel between the audience's and the analyst's struggle with "the need to know," and claims that the film offers a compelling illustration of what it means to hold a space of waiting not saturated by fantasies of origin or anxiety over the future.

"Oppressive practices"—says Vivian May—"can be hidden in plain view or subtly embedded in liberatory frameworks or political strategies: central to intersectional analyses and applications, then, is pursuing its invitation to think beyond (or against the grain of) familiar boundaries or categories, to perceive sites of omission, and to consider their meanings and implications" (4). An intersectional view of psychoanalytic discourses suggests that the discipline can constitute a

liberatory framework yet, at the same time, open the path for oppressive practices. In other words, psychoanalytic discourses can sometimes illuminate how
categories of difference create exclusion, as seen in Rivera-Largacha, Gutiérrez-
Peláez, and Gozlan's essays. They are sometimes able to unsettle narratives of
marginalization—as in the case of the Afro-Brazilians studied by dos Reis Motta
and Tosta. But they can also reinforce ideologies that result in interlocking forms
of oppression. During Argentina's dictatorship, for instance, the military "appropriated portions of psychoanalytic discourse for their own purposes" (Plotkin and
Damousi xx). In the more recent context of the feminist movements across the
region, psychoanalysis-based narratives of desire, trauma, and motherhood both
fueled arguments in favor of decriminalizing abortion and have also been grounded
in racialized and classist notions of gender and sexuality whereby white, upper-
middle-class women universalize their own experiences yet paradoxically continue
to silence the voices of historically marginalized gestating persons. Undoing psychoanalytic discourses from an intersectional perspective—and thinking beyond
(or against the grain of) familiar boundaries or categories—can thus be a vital
step toward constructing a more egalitarian view of Latin American and Caribbean societies. Mauricio Clavero's contribution to our volume, "Trans-transvestite
Childhoods: Considerations for an Out-of-Closet Psychoanalysis in Argentina and
Uruguay," takes an important step in that direction and frames the rethinking of
sexual diversity as an epistemological problem that compels psychoanalysis to
revisit its metapsychological foundations in light of new and yet unthought gender
subjectifications. Driven by the question of how to respond to the forms of psychic suffering effected by the biopolitical devise of the closet, Clavero proposes
to approach trans-transvestite childhoods as *existenciaries*: a process of becoming
which, in contrast to identity, is open to temporality and contingency.

The essays in this second section, then, offer a critical examination of the discipline's social and political implications. Rather than taking for granted psychoanalysis's role as a progressive discourse that allows for social, political, and
individual emancipation, the chapters provide an overarching perspective of the
discipline's articulations with race, gender, sexuality, and class and thus further
our understanding of the (often paradoxical) links between psychoanalysis and
intersectionality.

Popular Reception and Public Circulation:
Transnational Perspectives

"The history of psychoanalysis in Latin America"—say Lemlij and Cáceres—"is
inextricably linked to European and North American psychoanalysis" (xxv). First,
the latter are the original sources of the psychoanalytic tradition. Second, European psychoanalysts were the ones who migrated to Latin America and influenced
the region's thoughts. Third, European and U.S.-trained psychoanalysts founded
the first Latin American associations. Therefore, Lemlij and Cáceres conclude:
"The development of Latin American psychoanalytic thought has been for several

years more influenced by the European and North American psychoanalytic movements than by its own regional developments" (xxv).

These observations—included in a volume that, as mentioned earlier, aimed to undo this unilateral influence and bring English-speaking audiences into closer contact with the Latin American tradition—allude to broader questions that are crucial for our book: Does psychoanalysis in Latin America and the Caribbean constitute a form of neocolonialism? Does the popularity of the discipline in the region perpetuate the global hierarchy via a neocolonial cultural rhetoric—that is, via psychoanalytic concepts that interpret Latin American and Caribbean societies through the eyes of foreign, more powerful societies? Do concepts theorized in the so-called first world (i.e., trauma, acting out, and the Oedipus complex) apply equally to the so-called third world? Are Latin American and Caribbean psycho-analysts and scholars of psychoanalysis participating in a kind of "autoethnogra-phy": "in which colonized subjects undertake to represent themselves in ways that *engage with* the colonizer's terms" (Pratt 9, emphasis in the original)?

Several of the essays included in the first and second sections hint at negative answers for each of these questions when revisiting classic psychoanalytic notions through particular regional and national lenses. The chapters in the third section continue and deepen this line of thought. They break away from a derivative view of the discipline that reinforces an ethnocentric, subalternizing perspective that relegates Latin America and the Caribbean to the role of passive consumers of European and U.S. theories. Veering from this top-down approach, they engage in a decentering perspective of the history of psychoanalysis in Latin America and the Caribbean that illuminates how psychoanalytic discourses are shaped and reconfigured through dynamic dialogues across borders, disciplines, and social classes and that acknowledges the region's contribution to the creation of psy-choanalysis as a transnational system of thought.

In "Anarchists, Socialists, Communists, and Freudians," Ruperthuz Honorato offers a reading of working-class historiographical records and publications span-ning from the 1920s to the 1950s demonstrating how Chilean anarchists, social-ists, and communists received, transformed, and appropriated Freudian theories and concepts to respond to the mental health challenges and emancipatory aspi-rations of the working class in Chile. Through a "history of below" approach, Ruperthuz Honorato illuminates a neglected portion in the history of the early reception of psychoanalysis that emphasizes working-class people's resistance to hegemonic readings of psychoanalysis, thus calling into question their role as passive receivers of elitist ideas. In "The Early Expansion of Psychoanalysis in Latin America. The Key Role of the Argentine *Revista de Psicoanálisis*," Alejan-dro Dagfal traces the deliberate and farsighted mechanisms and strategies imple-mented by the founders of the Asociación Psicoanalítica Argentina (APA) in order to position it as a continental authority in Freudian and post-Freudian discourses and practices. With a methodological approach that focuses on the dissemination materials published in the *Revista's* early years, Dagfal documents the complex forms of institutional, scholarly, and pedagogical sociability through which the

Revista contributed to the APA's consolidation and prestigious international presence. Finally, in "A Voice Behind the Curtain," Ricardo Ainslie and Neil Altman engage in archival research of the consultative exchanges between U.S. anthropologist Oscar Lewis and the founding members of the Asociación Mexicana de Psicoanálisis to trace the influence of Mexican psychoanalysis in shaping Lewis's views on anthropology and on the controversial concept of the culture of poverty. Shedding light on this previously unknown collaboration, Ainslie and Altman argue, calls attention to mainstream psychoanalysis's inattention to the psychological dimensions of poverty, points to potential theoretical and methodological innovations in exploring the impact of social context on psychological identity, and alludes to the dynamic connections between psychoanalysis and anthropology—as well as between the United States and Mexico.

Before concluding our introduction, a word about the case studies selected for our collection is in order. Although the limited space of this volume does not allow for a comprehensive inclusion of all countries within the Latin American and Caribbean region, we purposely reached out to collaborators who could offer perspectives from contexts as wide-ranging as possible. The volume thus includes essays from or on the continent's leading psychoanalytic traditions—Argentina and Brazil—as well as examples from latitudes such as Haiti, Peru, Chile, Uruguay, and Colombia that rarely factor in scholarly discussions about psychoanalysis. Editors and contributors work in clinical practices and universities in these countries as well as in Canada and the United States. Furthermore, since our primary goal is to offer an *interdisciplinary* perspective of psychoanalysis as social and political discourse in Latin America and the Caribbean, our contributions bring together licensed psychoanalysts and scholars from fields of study as diverse as health sciences, philosophy, history, anthropology, psychology, and cultural studies. It is through this plural exchange that we aim to contribute to the ongoing process of regional dialogue and theoretical translation that reveals the contours of psychoanalysis's own historical specificity and its potential to account differentially for Latin American and Caribbean contextually situated realities.

Notes

1 All translations from Spanish to English are ours, unless otherwise noted.
2 Argentines have always taken pride in being the most psychoanalyzed population in the world. According to a 2012 study by Modesto Alonso, there are 155 analysts per 100,000 people in Argentina and Buenos Aires ranks as number one for patients undergoing treatment, surpassing Vienna, the discipline's city of birth (6). The popularity of psychoanalysis goes beyond the therapist couch. At least since the 1940s, the discipline has deeply influenced artistic, political, social, and academic discourses. Scholars have explained this popularity in multiple ways. Some of the most common explanations include the early epistolary exchanges between Sigmund Freud and Argentine intellectuals, the continuous presence, since the late nineteenth century, of a large Jewish population trained in the discipline, Argentine intellectuals' admiration for all things European and, in this line, the public influence of a group of intellectuals who in the 1960s based

their thought on Lacanian psychoanalysis, and the widespread reach of associations, such as the Argentine Psychoanalytic Association, and their journals and magazines' popular circulation. For further details on the history and influence of psychoanalysis on Argentine culture, see Alonso; Balán; Bosteels; Lisman-Pieczanski and Pieczanski; Plotkin, *Freud en las pampas*; Plotkin, "Psychoanalysis, Transnationalism, and National Habitus"; Plotkin and Ruperthuz Honorato; Vezzetti.

Works Cited

Agrest Wainer, Beatriz, and Eva Rotenberg, eds. *Homoparentalidades: nuevas familias.* Lugar/APA, 2007.

Alonso, Modesto. "Los psicólogos en Argentina." *Psicología, cultura y sociedad*, 2012, pp. 1–10.

Balán, Jorge. *Cuéntame tu vida: una biografía colectiva del psicoanálisis argentino.* Planeta, 1991.

Bosteels, Bruno. *Marx and Freud in Latin America.* Verso, 2014.

Bravo, Jorge. *Versión taquigráfica de la catorceava reunión, novena sesión ordinaria de la Cámara de Senadores de La Nación.* Senado de la Nación, 2010.

Caruth, Cathy, ed. *Trauma: Explorations in Memory.* Johns Hopkins UP, 1995.

———. *Unclaimed Experience: Trauma, Narrative, and History.* Johns Hopkins UP, 1996.

Ceballos, Neolid, ed. "Contingencia." *Los acontecimientos de nuestro tiempo*, vol. 3, no. 7, 2010.

Demos, T. J. *Return to the Postcolony: Specters of Colonialism in Contemporary Art.* Sternberg, 2013.

Druet, Anne-Cécile. "The Transatlantic Element: Psychoanalysis, Exile, Circulation of Ideas and Institutionalization Between Spain and Argentina." *Psychoanalysis and History*, vol. 14, no. 2, July 2012, pp. 237–251.

Felman, Shoshana. *The Juridical Unconscious: Trials and Traumas in the Twentieth Century.* Harvard UP, 2002.

Felman, Shoshana, and Dori Laub. *Testimony: Crises of Witnessing in Literature, Psychoanalysis and History.* Routledge, 1992.

Gallo, Rubén. "A Wild Freudian in Mexico: Raúl Carrancá y Trujillo." *Psychoanalysis and History*, vol. 14, no. 2, July 2012, pp. 253–268.

Gellner, Ernest. *The Psychoanalytic Movement: The Cunning of Unreason.* Wiley Interscience, 2008.

Gherovici, Patricia, and Christopher Christian, eds. *Psychoanalysis in the Barrios: Race, Class, and the Unconscious.* Routledge, 2019.

Jameson, Fredric. *The Political Unconscious. Narrative as a Socially Symbolic Act.* Cornell UP, 2014.

LaCapra, Dominick. *History in Transit: Experience, Identity, Critical Theory.* Cornell UP, 2004.

———. *Writing History, Writing Trauma.* Johns Hopkins UP, 2001.

Legrás, Horacio. "Psychoanalysis in Latin America." *The Encyclopedia of Postcolonial Studies*, edited by Ray Sangeeta, Henry Schwarz, José Luis Villacañas Berlanga, Alberto Moreiras, and April Shemak. Blackwell, 2016, n.p.

Lemlij, Moisés, and Dana Cáceres, eds. *Psychoanalysis in Latin America.* FEPAL, 1993.

Lewcowicz, Sergio, and Silvia Flechner, eds. *Truth, Reality, and the Psychoanalyst: Latin American Contributions to Psychoanalysis.* Routledge, 2018.

Lisman-Pieczanski, Nydia, and Alberto Pieczanski, eds. *The Pioneers of Psychoanalysis in South America*. Routledge, 2015.

May, Vivian M. *Pursuing Intersectionality, Unsettling Dominant Imaginaries*. Routledge, 2015.

Plotkin, Mariano Ben. *Freud en las pampas: orígenes y desarrollo de una cultura psicoanalítica en la Argentina (1910–1983)*. Sudamericana, 2003.

———. "Introduction." *Psychoanalysis and History*, vol. 14, no. 2, July 2012, pp. 227–235.

———. "Psychoanalysis, Transnationalism and National Habitus: A Comparative Approach to the Reception of Psychoanalysis in Argentina and Brazil (1910s–1940s)." *Transnational Unconscious: Essays in the History of Psychoanalysis and Translationalism*, edited by Joy Damousi and Mariano Ben Plotkin. Palgrave Macmillan, 2009, pp. 145–176.

Plotkin, Mariano Ben, and Joy Damousi, eds. *Psychoanalysis and Politics: Histories of Psychoanalysis Under Conditions of Restricted Political Freedom*. Oxford UP, 2012.

Plotkin, Mariano Ben, and Mariano Ruperthuz Honorato. *Estimado Dr. Freud: Una historia cultural del psicoanálisis en América Latina*. Edhasa, 2017.

Pratt, Mary Louise. *Imperial Eyes: Travel Writing and Transculturation*. Routledge, 2007.

Ruperthuz Honorato, Mariano. "The 'Return of the Repressed': The Role of Sexuality in the Reception of Psychoanalysis in Chilean Medical Circles (1910s–1940s)." *Psychoanalysis and History*, vol. 14, no. 2, July 2012, pp. 285–296.

Russo, Jane A. "Brazilian Psychiatrists and Psychoanalysis at the Beginning of the Twentieth Century: A Quest for National Identity." *Psychoanalysis and History*, vol. 14, no. 2, July 2012, pp. 297–312.

Santer, Eric. *Stranded Objects: Mourning, Memory and Film in Postwar Germany*. Cornell UP, 1990.

Traverso, Antonio, and Mick Broderick. "Interrogating Trauma: Towards a Critical Trauma Studies." *Continuum: Journal of Media and Cultural Studies*, vol. 24, no. 1, Feb. 2010, pp. 3–15.

Vezzetti, Hugo. *Aventuras de Freud en el país de los argentinos: de José Ingenieros a Enrique Pichon-Rivière*. Paidós, 1996.

Zelcer, Beatriz, ed. *Diversidad Sexual*. Lugar/APA, 2010.

Section I

Reading Latin America and the Caribbean

Sociopolitical Perspectives

Chapter 1

Feminicides, Psychoanalysis, and the Status of Social Desire in Our Time

Horacio Legrás

In a conference delivered in Belgium in 1960, Jacques Lacan wonders: "can psychoanalysis be constitutive of the kind of ethics necessitated by our times?" ("Can Psychoanalysis" 34).[1] The question seems to presuppose that psychoanalysis was once an appropriate ethical answer to the requirements of the time, but that this may no longer be the case. Some of Lacan's listeners may have been taken aback by this assumption. Was not the question of the pertinence of psychoanalysis to its time settled by the Freudian intervention, when the Viennese doctor cancelled the purchase of the previous, Victorian "time," by proclaiming that the recognition of desire was the keystone of modern culture as a whole? Experience has taught us that this is not the case—that even if the unconscious designates an a-historical eternal realm, some of its actualizations are ineluctably historical. Besides, it is easy to see that the dialectic between desire and its *Zeitgeist* has suffered dramatic changes between now and the time of Freud's discoveries. In Freud's time, culture and social norms operated largely on the basis of prohibitions. Today's culture operates mainly on the basis of a productivist call to freedom and an intense questioning not just of the arbitrary nature of normative ideals, but of their mere necessity. In contrast, can we say that our time is the same as Lacan's when 60 years separate us from his words? My answer is an emphatic *yes*. From the point of view of a timely ethics of psychoanalysis, we are more contemporary with the times described in Lacan's theory than he himself ever was. The same thing is said to have happened to Freud. He may have anticipated the rise of fascism in his writings of the 1920s (especially in texts like *Group Psychology and the Analysis of the Ego*), reading in his own time the contours of a time to come for which his theory was already providing some key interpretive clues.

The question of an ethical dimension of psychoanalysis is not a Lacanian invention. It was already present in Freud under a myriad of forms, for instance, when the Viennese doctor discussed the issue of the dreamer's responsibility for his/her dreams. However, while for Freud, the question was how the subject's desire stands concerning those others implicated in that desire (what happens if I dream with the death of my brother?), for Lacan the problem is not so much the libertine defense of a complete disregard that jouissance has for the well-being of the other,

DOI: 10.4324/9781003266211-3

but rather the responsibility a subject has for that desire that constitutes him/her even if it is socially inadmissible.

The metapsychological root of the problem lies in the fact that desire escapes the regulatory framework of the pleasure principle. Although the unconscious is organized as a language, Lacan is led to talk about something that never ceases not to write itself in *The Ethics of Psychoanalysis*. This remainder incapable of signification inhabits that region that Freud located in "a beyond" from which the relentless pressure of the drives takes the form of a pathological compulsion to repeat. For Lacan, the fact that these contents remain beyond symbolization (they are repeated, not remembered) indicates that they fall under the purview of the Real. Freud already underlined a fact that will be at the center of Lacan's treatment of this Real: the repetition that the Id commands is pleasurable, even if such pleasure should repulse the conscious side of the subject. Freud refused to give a name to this pleasure. Lacan called it "jouissance" and made it one of the keystones of his clinic. The discovery of a Real to which the subject is attached in virtue of his/her jouissance opens up the properly ethical question of psychoanalysis. It is in this light that we should understand Lacan's proposition that ethics is "always the actualization of the Real" (*The Ethics of Psychoanalysis* 56). The relationship of psychoanalysis to its time is necessarily its relationship to the shape of the Real in that particular time.

Lacan made of the relationship to the Real the focal point of the ethics of psychoanalysis. Freud, who by nature and upbringing was a far more conservative thinker, mustered enough intellectual honesty to call that region beyond being the *Kern unseres Wesens*.[2] I do not want to stress too much this parallelism between Freud and Lacan to the point of robbing the French analyst of the privilege of having invented the word, the concept, and the question of jouissance. What is jouissance? If we are so far from having settled on an answer, this is due undoubtedly to its paradoxical nature: a pleasure in pain? Yes. A form of primary masochism? Indeed. A path to death? Certainly, but still a modality of happiness.[3]

Lacan spoke of a pleasure in evil. The formula stuck. The problem with this definition is that it substantivizes evil. Jouissance is not the desire for evil, it is simply the desire to go beyond the limit, the limit drawn by the law on the basis of a conception of the good. The limit can recede endlessly without affecting the economy of frustration that governs the relationship of desire to its object. This is why no amount of satisfaction, enlightenment, or liberalization suffices to squelch the dynamic to which jouissance owes the monotonous law of its behavior.[4]

There is in Lourdes Portillo's sober documentary about the feminicides of Ciudad Juárez, *Señorita extraviada*, a scene in which a woman recounts the rape and murder suffered by young girls at the hands of criminal gangs. Her narration is organized in a crescendo of horror that only ends at sunrise with the bodies of the victims burning in the desert. While this testimony may be ruled fictitious (she is not a first-hand witness), there are hundreds of forensic documents that retell a similar story. The scene has all the elements that make up the contemporary drama of an unmitigated jouissance and which make themselves present not only in the barbarism of crimes as those of Juárez but also in the psychopathology of our everyday life.

It is a hypothesis of this essay that the feminicides of Ciudad Juárez maintain a structural similarity with a generalized and sanctioned form of inscribing subjectivity in our contemporary world. This subjectivity is correlative to a world of objects organized by market mechanisms which constructs these objects as already insufficient, transient, and disposable. The subjects of consumerism do not assert themselves against the limits of their desire (as in the past) but instead are invited to entertain the fantasy of the abolition of the notion of limit itself.

Countries of Jouissance and Countries of Homeostasis

Colette Soler believes that one of the starkest features of our time is the division between "countries of homeostasis" and "countries of jouissance." Her conviction is that "We" [but who is this "we"?] "live in countries of homeostasis," that is, in countries that are not characterized by "the constant unleashing of the most extreme forms of jouissance" (10–11).

In contrast to Soler's straightforward geopolitics of jouissance, Charles Bowden gave the title *Juárez. Laboratory of our Future* to his famous journalistic and photographic exploration of the feminicides that plagued (and still plague) Mexico's northern frontier. The "ours" of the title is an unmistakable reference to the American readership of the book, since it was published in English and never translated into Spanish. For Bowden, something is at stake in Juárez that foreshadows "our" time: a time that is already ours and yet to come. Juárez would be this type of wormhole that we often see in sci-fi shows, that allows a passage between two dimensions and two universes. It is only a matter of time, Bowden seems to say, before the techniques, the anxieties, the world-forming conditions active in Juárez colonize the other side of its almost unimaginable everydayness.[5]

Academic treatment of the feminicides follows two fundamental explanatory models. The first one points toward the historical exacerbation of an entrenched misogyny characteristic not only of the figure of the perpetrator but also of those in charge of investigating the crimes and helping the families of the victims overcome the crushing effects of this murderous absurdity (Lagarde y de los Rios v). The second modality points to the socio-economic conditions brought about by the establishment of the maquila industry and the unchecked reign of neoliberalism in the northern frontier (González Rodríguez 13). These two perspectives are not without points of contact. Gender-based explanations of the feminicides do not ignore the many ways in which economic deregulation, a structural deficit in social investments, the rise of drug-trafficking, or the vulnerability of working women who often are also internal migrants or in transit toward the United States have created conditions that favored the perpetuation of the crimes. Conversely, sociological analysis underlines the effect of the destabilization of traditional social roles and the masculine resentment before a feminine figure that asserts itself as independent and sexed.

Then there is a tone, a murmur, a play of adjectives that traverses all the bibliography without developing into an extended or cohesive argumentation. It emerges in the pervasive use of words such as "pathologies," "psychosis," "sociopathy," or "unlimited psychopathy," to explain the aberrant nature of the crimes. Moreover, since it is part of our proof, we cannot forget that in Roberto Bolaño's novel *2666*, the person more obsessed with the possibility of solving the crimes goes by the name of Lalo Cura (Mad Ness). A thug-turned-police apprentice, Lalo is intrigued by the feminicides. He reads some police manuals in hopes of gaining a technical advantage that he can harness to the resolution of the crimes. In the end, however, no crime is solved, no identity restored, and no trace vivified. One murder after another is closed without consequences in the archives of the law.

The fact that the killings range from criminal activities of highly organized armed groups to more spontaneous eruptions of violence in the domestic sphere where the perpetrators are fathers, boyfriends, or husbands, makes it impossible to understand these references to the psychopathological as a personal indictment pointing to a deranged individual or group of individuals—a working hypothesis of the police in *2666*. Instead, we may be confronted with psychological traits that define not a maladapted subject but rather a predicament of adaptation itself. Rita Laura Segato makes the connection explicit in *La guerra contra las mujeres*:

> Today the psychopathic personality would seem to be the personality structure best equipped to operate functionally in the order of the apocalyptic phase of capitalism. The psychopathic profile, with its ineptitude for transforming hormonal excess into affect and emotion; its need to constantly intensify stimuli to achieve their effect; its definitive non-linking structure; its indifference toward its own pain and – consequently, and even more so – that of others; its alienation, its encapsulation, and its unrootedness from both its own landscapes and collective ties; its instrumental and objectified relation to others . . . seem indispensable for operating in an economy organized to the extreme by dehumanization and the absence of limits.
>
> (101–102)

Despite this emphasis on the subjective element of the crimes, psychoanalysis is not part of the theoretical toolbox of writings about Juárez. One wonders if a paradigm like the one Freud bequeathed to us can add anything to what we know about the nature of Juárez's violence, and of its connections with contemporary ways of relating desires to social norms in which Segato sees a distinctive trait of contemporary violence.

Now, if the feminicides themselves have not drawn enough psychoanalytic attention, the same cannot be said of the social and cultural universe that Segato sees as presiding over them. In 2013, a collective volume titled *Freud: A cien años de Tótem y Tabú* appeared in Mexico co-edited by Néstor Braunstein, Carina

Basualdo, and Betty Fuks. There is no mention of the feminicides in its pages. This is not strange in itself since most of the contributors are not Mexicans. And yet, the dramatic kernel of the book—which it has—revolves around the enormous weight that the "pathologies of the act" carry in the contemporary world, and on the role of the techno-bio-political components of neoliberalism in the causation of these pathologies.[6] In 2016, a sister book was published in Buenos Aires with the title *Mutaciones del sujeto contemporáneo* by the EOL (School of Lacanian Orientation). The themes developed in the *Mutaciones* fall squarely into what Charles Melman called "the pathologies of the twenty-first century" in a book published in Brazil in 2003 following a series of conferences in Curitiba the year before.

As in the case of *Freud: A cien años*, there is no mention of Juárez in *Mutaciones*. While psychoanalysts are averse to commenting beyond their clinical experience, something of the libidinal complexity involved in the feminicides of Juárez emerges in several of the essays. Marcelo Barros characterizes "our time" as one in which "femininity is glorified, and the violence against women takes on pandemic proportions" (90). Meanwhile, Miquel Bassols points to an unmistakable connection between violence against women and jouissance: "This new epidemics of violence against women is nothing but the impossibility of negotiating that jouissance of the Other, that inherent alterity of jouissance that the feminine jouissance makes patent" ("Trauma" 51).

The three books I have referenced earlier (*Novas Formas*, *Freud: A cien años*, and *Mutaciones*) share a common diagnosis about an unnegotiated jouissance that works as the point of origin of the violent, unmediated reactions so characteristic of the pathologies of the twenty-first century. In this diagnosis, it is possible to distinguish *an original imprint* whose disruption has consequential effects on the nature of the social link, *an element of causation* that actualizes the so-called mutations in contemporary subjectivity, and, finally, the psychic effects of the emergence of a new register in the discontent in civilization. Let's give them their proper names: the decline of authority, the paternal function, and the world of ideals is the imprint, the neoliberal and technological domination of market-driven capitalism operates at the level of causation, and the disconnection from the symbolic chain whose most radical form is a violent passage to the act represents the specific, historical form of our discontent.

In the opening essay of *A cien años*, Anne Dufourmantelle conjectures that if Freud could witness our historical moment, he would have confronted a reality where totems (identity formations) proliferate, except that the inaugural prohibition that these totems should represent is either absent or inaccessible. Dufourmantelle repeats the old analytic wisdom according to which desire receives its guide from the law. By claiming that some women are prohibited, the totemic father taught his children not only to desire according to a heterosexual logic but also to desire according to the logic of the not-all. In contrast, the social contract of the present favors an attitude of "yes, to all" with the concomitant attenuation of any figure of authority—including the increasingly irrelevant figure of paternal authority. Not much can be done to reconstruct this authority since, as Néstor

Braunstein points out, in the normative subjectivity of the twenty-first century: "the government of bodies and the sphere of the drives are defined outside the structure of the family" ("El padre" 80). One wonders if this is really a novel development. In her insightful autobiographical sketch, Marie Langer writes: "I experienced an imperial Oedipus complex. . . . Behind my father was the old Emperor of Austria, Franz Josef" (33). As the reading of Langer's memoir shows, Franz Josef stands not only for a political liberalism from which affluent Jewish families, including Langer's, were able to profit from but also for a whole set of ideals (described by Carl Schorske in *Fin-de-Siècle Vienna*) that represent a "knowing how to do" with that jouissance to which the emergence of Freud's theory itself bears historical testimony. Since not all the thrust of the drives can be negotiated in the sphere of the family, cultural ideals provide further means to bind the overflow of life set free by the limited efficacy of the pleasure principle. This does not mean that social norms always work in the sense of a taming of enjoyment. Langer's memoirs show very clearly that the rise of liberalism and increasing democratization in all aspects of life introduced a crisis in the social management of jouissance in that world. Nevertheless, the mere fact that Dora could ask herself what it means to be a woman bears testimony to the existence of an ideal of womanhood to which Dora felt somewhat responsive. It is plain that Dora's question cannot be rehearsed in our present, not because it would be politically incorrect to raise the heterosexual norm to the level of a social standard but rather because what is shameful is the idea of a standard itself. It is necessary, then, to supplement Braunstein's observation: The point is not simply that "the government of the bodies and the sphere of the drives are defined outside the structure of the family" but that, to a large extent, they are defined in terms that are antinomic to the ones through which the traditional structure of the family made sense of the neuroses of which the family itself was the origin. It would be challenging for a youngster of our time to displace his/her Oedipus onto a figure that carries certain social reverence or popularity, as Langer did with Franz Josef. The reason for that is simple—what is socially celebrated today is not the normative but the anti-normative, which in a perverse twist becomes a norm of its own.

With just one telling exception, in our world the sphere of satisfaction is beyond censorship.[7] Contemporary subjectivity is constituted fundamentally as desiring subjectivity. This cannot be bad. In fact, it has been an essential element of some of the democratic innovations of our time. However, this renewed liberation of desire is rapidly colonized by an economic system (consumer capitalism) that is only interested in desirability insofar as the former can correspond to the pre-programmed commodities that the market lines up to satiate.

There is nothing even remotely ideological in capital's dislike of ideals. It is just that ideals represent an alternate form of orientation for the subject. Ideals present the subject with a regulative rather than legislative mechanism. Counterintuitively, the fact that the ideal was practically unachievable tempered the identification of the subject with the most inflexible aspects of the law. In neo-liberal societies, where the question of happiness becomes a matter of personal responsibility, there is nothing to mitigate the guilt that subjects feel for their failure to achieve satisfaction. By decrying ideals, consumer capitalism creates a feeling of orphanhood that is functional to its logic of supplemental satisfaction. However, the idea that each conceivable desire corresponds to an already imagined object reduces the sphere of desire to that of needs, which results in the foreclosure of both desire and its temporality. Waiting time becomes an incomprehensible delay in satisfaction. This obturation of desire does not translate into any negotiation of jouissance. It represents rather its uncontrolled liberation with the hope that the tension so created will fuel new cycles of consumption and accumulation. Instead, it creates an antipoetic landscape of subjective desolation in which "the chaos of the drives threatens with invading it all" (Dufourmantelle 36). From there, the subject may find a path of discharge in the pathologies of the act, but also in consumerism which, well thought, is an acting out in itself.

The project that seeks to obturate the existential longing of the subject by offering an overabundance of answers to which no question corresponds is destined to fail. The result of this failure is the piling up of garbage that testifies to the democratic nature of consumption in our times. Every object of satisfaction is stamped with the seal of its intrinsic—and not just temporal—obsolescence. And as it is with the object, it is with the subject. It too has the destiny of a left-over, of that trash that is the residue—and the secret—of a whole way of living. In *Heterografías de la violencia*, Sergio Villalobos-Ruminott connects the sexually marked crimes of Juárez to the ubiquitous presence of the garbage dump and the landfill in Bolaño's novel (212–213). This grotesque meeting of the uncontrolled residual logic of capitalist consumerism (which in the case of Latin America takes on a special twist since it is also a place of labor for myriad informal workers) and the barbaric impunity with which the bodies of the victims are disposed of in spaces defined by anomic exceptionality distinctly overlaps with the two destinies of jouissance: either naming an unrecognizable form of satisfaction or constituting a path to death.

Strategic Options

Say we establish—along with the discourse of the master—that everything going on in society is just so much herding in which we turn left, right, or stay put in the name of a discourse of oblivious impartiality. Add to that, with certain outrage, how the discourse of consumer capitalism organizes this herding in terms of a structural preemption of lack, desire, and in the end, of the requirement of the social. Where do we go from there? An ever-growing list of psychoanalytic publications, conferences, and events tackle the pathologies of the twenty-first century, always striking a similar chord: these pathologies emerge from the market's colonization of the sphere of desire, a process made possible by the erosion of any principle of restrain to the subject's right to satisfaction.[8] The richness of the clinical archive contrasts, however, with the scarcity of concomitant theoretical propositions regarding the standing of psychoanalysis before the spreading of what Julia Kristeva calls "new maladies of the soul" (9), originating in a historical acceleration of the experience of jouissance.

The problem that confronts psychoanalytic discourse is the presupposition that only a revitalization of the law—a law that in psychoanalytic mythology is anchored in the function of the father—is able to put a limit to that un-negotiated jouissance where violence against women seems to take root. In this way, a set organized around the figures of the paternal, the patriarchal, and the law comes to figure as both the origin of the problem and its solution. This contradiction explains that, in his contribution to *Mutaciones*, Marcelo Barros denounced the reduction of the "name of the father," to the patriarchal as "a mistake that leads to the systemic misrecognition of the phenomena of violence that punctuates the iron order of late capitalism" (91). But if the system that tied paternal authority to the world of ideals has irremediably broken down, where can we find a figure of the law able to withstand the general fungibility of values characteristic of the symbolic economy of contemporary capitalism? This political problem concerns not only an analyst like Barros but also the feminist position of an anthropologist like Rita Segato, who rightly opposes the arcane of patriarchal power and its terrorizing actualizations, while simultaneously arguing for the reinforcement of boundaries and legalities. But if not through a reinforcement of the figure of the father, how should psychoanalysis react to a symptomatic acceleration of jouissance in all orders of life? It would seem that all the answers psychoanalysis has at its disposal are conservative in nature. They go, to an important extent, against the spirit of the times and more specifically, against that which in that spirit is supposed to represent progress.[9]

Let us notice that this was not at all the case with Freud. In Freud the development of psychoanalytic theory was simultaneously an answer to the question about the position of psychoanalytic discourse in the ethical economy of its time. Freud was not politically progressive. If he ended up as an icon of pop culture—with his face and cigar stamped in t-shirts, posters, and coffee mugs, not to mention the frolicking décor of Café Freud that seats a few meters from the Freud house museum in Vienna—it is because he ended up on the right side of history. Freud's construction of psychoanalysis as a liberating practice was inseparable from the idea that he was throwing light upon unknown regions of experience about which nobody wanted to know a thing—as in the case of child sexuality.

Freud himself immensely helped the creation of this narrative by describing the ethical economy of his time as firmly gripped in the stringent corset of Victorian prudishness and conservatism. Now, there are reasons—beyond Dora and her *ménage à trois*—to doubt this description. There are reasons to suspect that, even if we attribute to Freud the best of intentions, he was merely describing the moral economy of a conservative, provincial, aspirational lower middle class while the realities on the ground were a little bit more interesting. Freud didn't have his heart on the side of the licenses he advocated for his patients. In the words of one of his most enthusiastic biographers, Freud "never adjusted his old-fashioned manners to a new age, nor his equally old-fashioned ideals,. . . . [H]is adherence to an age that was becoming historical before his eyes never faltered" (Gay

507). Freud could unambiguously harness psychoanalysis to the spirit of his time because he could align his discovery with a new position enjoyed by science in the discursive economy of the age. The invocation of science gave him the courage, which he would have otherwise lacked, to break with a world of appearances and pretense, and to become, in the end, the pop-cultural hero of a sexual revolution which he would have personally opposed.

This point is worth mentioning because it is disputable that science today plays the role that it played throughout the transition between the nineteenth and twentieth centuries. With a visible nod to Heidegger's writings on "enframing," Lacan emphasizes the increasing dependence of science on the requirements of technology. In our own time, science has become an odd partner of capitalist productivism. But it is not in the instrumental dimension of the gadget—from the videogame that mesmerizes the teenager to the world of connectivity that captures the imagination of the adult—where science leaves its mark in the process of capitalist accumulation. More fundamentally, science supplies capitalism with the only function that it itself cannot perform, since its pledge to satisfaction forecloses that dimension: the managing of the Real. Science is the discourse that tells us that things are where they are supposed to be, even if we will never have the means to know what that place is or what it means for our subjective configuration. The mythology of science that populates our newspapers do not translate the Real into any form of meaning—we know that science is meaningless and athematic. Science no longer articulates the loose signifiers of existence into any narrative in which our being itself could be grounded. On the contrary, science separates the Real from any possibility of signification.

Is this not the fundamental insight that we receive from the arid forensic style used by Roberto Bolaño to recount the feminicides in *2666*? If indeed these crimes hide the secret of the world, we are never told what this secret actually is, what this secret is we are never told, and this for a structural reason: the disaffected discourse in which the crimes are narrated—unmistakably the discourse of science—is itself oblivious to questions of justice or witnessing. Bolaño's litany of scientific reports brings to mind Eyal Weizman's characterization of the forensic perspective as the now dominant gaze of the state when confronted with the unwanted residue of its biopolitical functioning:

[W]ithin the field of war-crime investigation, a methodological shift has recently led to a certain blurring. The primacy accorded to the witness and to the subjective and linguistic dimension of testimony, trauma, and memory – a primacy that has had such an enormous cultural, aesthetic, and political influence that it has reframed the end of the twentieth century as 'the era of the witness' – is gradually being supplemented (not to say bypassed) by an emergent forensic sensibility, an object-oriented juridical culture immersed in matter and materialities, in code and form, and in the presentation of scientific investigations by experts.

(4)

It seems obvious that the alignment between truth (science) and political progressivism from which Freud profited was short-lived. Science is no longer psychoanalysis's ally against obscurantism, and this is so in part because Enlightenment is no longer the point of orientation of the discourse of science.

The New Body of Jouissance

In 1972, Lacan added a fifth discourse to the topology of the four discourses developed in 1967. He called it "the discourse of the capitalist" and, with it, revised the discourse of the master. For the purpose of my exposition, it is enough to recall that the four discourses that summarize the possibilities of the social bond are all marked by a point of impossibility. The discourse of the capitalist obturates that point of impossibility. Hence the repeated references to this discourse in terms of a disavowal of castration or the injunction to ignore the restricting function of the law in reference to the mechanisms of desire. In his usually colloquial style, Lacan summarizes the situation by saying that the discourse of the capitalist is "forclusive of the things of love" ("Du discours psychanalytique" 33). This statement has been read as indicative of capitalism's animosity against the social link. However, it can also be understood in reference to the primordial function of love in analytic theory, which is no other than to force jouissance to condescend to the level of desire (*Anxiety* 179).

When Lacan asked if psychoanalysis could incarnate an ethics for our times, he had already decided that psychoanalysis should stand clinically, ethically, and politically on the side of jouissance. In Seminar XI, Lacan defends the primacy of desire above pleasure:

> Pleasure limits the scope of human possibility – the pleasure principle is a principle of homeostasis. Desire, on the other hand, finds its boundary, its strict relation, its limit, and it is in the relation to this limit that this is sustained as such, crossing the threshold imposed by the pleasure principle.
>
> (*The Four Fundamental Concepts* 33)

The word jouissance does not appear in this quote, but what lies beyond the pleasure principle if not the Real of enjoyment?

By making of jouissance—of the right to jouissance—the keystone of its discourse, psychoanalysis remains on the right side of history since few problems rank as high in the public agenda as the management of the formidable forces released by the decline of ideals.[10] However, psychoanalysis's siding with jouissance happens under the sign of a contradiction given that the liberated field of desire is the occasion of more rather than less pathological formations. (The notion of ordinary psychosis according to which everyone in contemporary culture is subjected to intermittent disenchainments from symbolic regulation is perhaps the best example of this contradiction.)

Lacan's decision of siding with jouissance is consistent with his emphasis on the Real as the point of origination of an ethical subjectivity. However, the society of enjoyment organizes its own allegiance to jouissance in a way that stands in opposition to the one favored by Lacan and his heirs. Running from a symbolic order that no longer exists, our era falls not into the freedom to which the notion of the Real is a correlate but into the immobilizing grasp of imaginary identifications. It is often said that the Lacanian father—his name and his *No*—inscribes the law of the signifier in the subject. The only thing that the name of the father inscribes, however, is the signifier of lack in the Other—the absence which, in making itself felt, makes presence possible, and along with presence, reality. The constant crisis of the social link—the decline of the notion of the social contract in times of unrestricted jouissance—seems to forebode a definitive decline of symbolic mediations. The truth is that the discourse of the market does not abandon the subject to its fate. Ideals do not disappear. They are dispersed, fragmented, and more importantly, congealed. They are turned into another commodity put at the service of obturating the lack in the Other, the lack which the ideals of yesteryear were supposed to help to negotiate. The analytic discourse has a word for this congealment: the holophrase. In the holophrase, the subject is fused to his/her words in such a way that it is difficult to keep speaking about a subject in the first place. Ideals themselves are commodified. In the words of Anne Dufourmantelle, the law that they incarnate "appears so degraded that it names only something prohibited that has been already transgressed without ever having been interiorized" (35).

In 2013, the Commission on the Status of Women of the United Nations requested a special consultation from the Lacanian AMP. Miquel Bassols signed the document in which the AMP explained widespread violence against women in terms of a deficit in the traumatic negotiation of sexual difference. Toward the end of the document, there is a passage that reads: "violence cannot be conceived in terms of social inadaptation. . . . The best pedagogical or social effort will find here a limit. It is above all a matter of operating at a personal level and finding the unconscious significations that underlie the passage to the (violent) act" ("La violencia"). There is no mention in the document of the effects of capitalism on the violence against women, which is theoretically justified because the origin of that violence lies in the impossibility of accepting castration, and in the new status of women as placeholder of the enigmatic nature of the other's jouissance. The downplay of pedagogy for the benefit of personal analytic interaction seems to ignore the fact that a person who enters into an analysis is already one step removed from the satisfaction of his drives in the dimension of the act. To say that psychoanalysis's answer to the question of aggressiveness in civilization is restricted to the interpersonal sphere of the clinic comes too close to admitting that psychoanalysis doesn't have an answer worth its status as social discourse.

A year before his conference in Belgium, Lacan directly tackled the question of psychoanalysis's silence on the social question:

> Wouldn't it be interesting to wonder about the significance of our absence from the field of what might be called a science of virtues, a practical reason,

the sphere of common sense? For in truth one cannot say that we ever intervene in the field of any virtue. We clear ways and paths, and we hope that
what is called virtue will take root there.

(*The Ethics of Psychoanalysis* 10)

According to Lacan, the psychoanalytic style of intervention is critical—in the
tradition of Kant—or even deconstructionist in the tradition of Derrida. It is
worthwhile mentioning that a posthumous text by Jacques Derrida designates
psychoanalysis as the discourse that is to lead the charge against the cruelty
of the present and the reduction of life to the parameters of the market ("Psychoanalysis Searches"). However, our time adds an element that was never as
prominent in Freud's or even Lacan's time. We live in the time of the real without
law. The science that emerged after the Renaissance found in nature its correlate—its object. The domain of technology—as Heidegger announced—eclipses
the phenomenality of the world. The domain of objectivity is increasingly har-
nessed to the question of its potential for profitability. Under these conditions,
what is real for us is the movement of a global economy whose lawlessness is not
reduced by all the money and resources poured into its study. The only constant
of our time—the thing that returns to the same place—is the symptom. Enjoyment is the compromise formation through which we encounter "the enigma of
the commodity."

In an essay that summarizes his research on contemporary forms of domination,
Néstor Braunstein claims that the ethical disjuncture of our time can be formu-
lated in terms of "the discourse of the Market or the Discourse of Psychoanalysis:
an irreconcilable option." If it is true that the ethics of psychoanalysis does not
allow it to occupy the same place occupied by the market, it is important to under-
line that this disjuncture does not apply to the object of that ethics. In other words,
at least in the tradition of thought opened up by Jacques Lacan, psychoanalysis
cannot refuse and much less condemn the sphere of jouissance as that which must
be most promptly addressed and taken into account. The dispute between psychoanalysis and the market is fundamentally, and in the last instance, a dispute
about the destiny of jouissance. This jouissance appears to us as a double-edged
sword. On the one hand, it needs to be limited, negotiated, and appeased if life and
civilization are to survive. On the other hand, jouissance is an ally in the project of
a livable subjectification of existence because it always reveals the maladaptation
of the body, its permanent insubordination in the face of disciplinary regimes, and
the fascist-like quality of the holophrase.

Notes

1 All uncredited translations are my own.
2 "The core of our being" in Strachey's translation (Freud, *An Outline of Psychoanalysis*
   37). I use the original German not only to avoid the alliteration being/being, but also
   to point out that the Lacanian being—which Lacan opposes to "existence"—is not the
   same as the Freudian being. In Lacan, being is of the order of signification. The Real,

understood as "a region beyond being" remains outside the Symbolic order. In contrast, in Freud's expression "*Kern unseres Wesens*" being is closer to substance—the dynamic origin of the energy that fuels the psychic apparatus.

3 The word happiness (from happen; the good hour—*bonheur* in French) underlines the idea that jouissance depends on an encounter with the real.

4 This is Lacan's point in his criticism of the supposedly liberatory practice of modernity: "[T]he naturalist liberation of desire has failed . . . [it] has failed historically. We do not find ourselves in the presence of a man less weighed down with laws and duties than before . . . of so-called libertine thought" (*The Ethics of Psychoanalysis* 4).

5 A systematic application of this thesis can be found in Sergio González Rodríguez's *The Femicide Machine*, whose extensive research was the starting point of Roberto Bolaño's treatment of the crimes in *2666*.

6 "Pathologies of the act" refers to the fact that as symbolic mediations become weaker, there is an increasing tendency to resolve conflicts outside the sphere of communication and through—usually violent—passages to the act. Road rage is a case in point.

7 The exception is pedophilia which, beyond its actual existence, has become a constitutive fantasy of the political present. On the social role of the suspicion of pedophilia in the construction of the contemporary common sense, see the opening pages of Zygmunt Bauman's *Consuming Life*.

8 A look at the themes of the last five international meetings of the Lacanian AMP (WPA in English) testifies to the predominance of this thematic among Lacanians. To a lesser degree, the International Psychoanalytic Association (IPA) has also been increasingly concerned with the question of the pathologies derived from the narcissistic consolidation of the hedonistic subject of consumption.

9 In a text from 2005, Jacques-Alain Miller decries what—quoting Lacan—he calls "an unexpected conjunction of philosophers and psychoanalysts to defend the name of the father" ("Introduction" 87).

10 The decline of ideals marks a mutation in the relationship of the subject to the Symbolic. A full Symbolic order that commands obedience or respect was written as A (for *Autre*). In a world in which traditional forms of marriage break down, ethnic or national allegiances compete with totemic arrangements, society is described as hybrid rather than homogeneous, and rights are no longer reserved for a modelic and restrictive form of citizen the Symbolic can no longer operate as a site of undisputed authority. Taking notice of these historical changes (but also obeying the internal consistency of psychoanalytic theory), Lacan bars the A to signal its radical *incompletude*. Identification is not today with A but with Ⱥ.

Works Cited

Barros, Marcelo. "Un nuevo paradigma del poder." *Mutaciones del sujeto contemporáneo.* EOL, 2016, pp. 85–96.

Bassols, Miquel. "La violencia contra las mujeres." *Desecrits*, 24 Nov. 2012, miquelbassols. blogspot.com/2012/11/la-violencia-contra-las-mujeres.html. Accessed 23 Apr. 2021.

———. "Trauma en los cuerpos, violencia en las ciudades." *Mutaciones del sujeto contemporáneo.* EOL, 2016, pp. 45–59.

Bauman, Zygmunt. *Consuming Life.* Polity Press, 2007.

Bolaño, Roberto. *2666.* Translated by Natasha Wimmer. Picador, 2009.

Bowden, Charles. *Juarez: The Laboratory of Our Future.* Aperture, 1998.

Braunstein, Néstor. "El discurso de los mercados, o el discurso del psicoanálisis: una opción excluyente." *Lacan, discurso, acontecimiento*, edited by Ian Parker and David Pavón-Cuellar. Plaza y Valdés, 2014, pp. 167–177.

————. "El padre primitivo y el padre digitalizado. Del *Urvater* al *Big Brother*." *Freud: A cien años de Tótem y Tabú. (1913–2013)*, edited by Néstor A. Braunstein and Betty B. Fuks. Siglo XXI, 2013, pp. 76–99.

Dufourmantelle, Anne. "*Tótem y Tabú*: Una lectura." *Freud: A cien años de Tótem y Tabú. (1913–2013)*, edited by Néstor A. Braunstein and Betty B. Fuks. Siglo XXI, 2013, pp. 33–50.

Freud, Sigmund. *Group Psychology and the Analysis of the Ego*. Translated by James Strachey. Binke, 1921.

————. *An Outline of Psychoanalysis*. Translated by James Strachey. W. W. Norton, 1969.

Gay, Peter. *Freud: A Life for Our Time*. Norton, 2006.

González Rodríguez, Sergio. *The Femicide Machine*. Translated by Michael Parker-Stainback. Semiotext(e), 2012.

Kristeva, Julia. *New Maladies of the Soul*. Translated by Ross Guberman. Columbia UP, 1995.

Lacan, Jacques. "Can Psychoanalysis Constitute the Kind of Ethics Necessitated by Our Time?" *The Triumph of Religion, Preceded by Discourse to Catholics*. Translated by Bruce Fink. Polity Press, 2013, pp. 32–54.

————. "Du discours psychanalytique." *Lacan in Italia/Lacan en Italie (1953–1978)*. La Salamandra, 1978, pp. [pages numbers].

————. *The Seminar of Jacques Lacan Book 11. The Four Fundamental Concepts of Psycho-Analysis*, edited by Jacques-Alain Miller. Translated by Alan Sheridan. Norton, 1981.

————. *The Seminars of Jacques Lacan Book VII. The Ethics of Psychoanalysis*. Translated by Dennis Porter. Norton, 1992.

————. *The Seminar of Jacques Lacan Book X. Anxiety*. Translated by A. R. Price. Polity Press, 2016.

Lagarde y de los Rios, Marcela. "Preface." *Terrorizing Women: Feminicide in the Américas*, edited by Rosa-Linda Fregoso and Cynthia Bejarano. Duke UP, 2010, pp. 1–3.

Langer Marie. *From Vienna to Managua: Journey of a Psychoanalyst*. Translated by Margaret Hooks. Free Association Books, 1989.

Maguire, Emily. *Racial Experiments in Cuban Literature and Ethnography*. UP of Florida, 2011.

Melman, Charles. *Novas formas clínicas no início do terceiro milênio*. CMC, 2003.

Miller, Jacques-Alain. "Introduction à la lecture du Séminaire L'angoise." *La cause freudienne*, vol. 59, 2005, pp. 82–90.

Schorske, Carl. *Fin-de-Siècle Vienna. Politics and Culture*. Vintage Books, 1980.

Segato, Rita Laura. *La guerra contra las mujeres*. Traficantes de Sueños, 2016.

Señorita extraviada. Directed by Lourdes Portillo, 2001.

Soler, Colette. "The Body in the Teaching of Jacques Lacan." Translated by Lindsay Watson, jcfar.org.uk/wp-content/uploads/2016/03/The-Body-in-the-Teaching-of-Jacques-Lacan-Colette-Soler.pdf. Accessed 23 Apr. 2021.

Villalobos-Ruminott, Sergio. *Heterografías de la violencia. Historia, Nihilismo, Destrucción*. La Cebra, 2016.

Weizman, Eyal. *Forensic Architecture: Violence at the Threshold of Detectability*. Zone Books, 2017.

Chapter 2

Staging Desire

The Ideological Fantasy of Argentine (Football) Culture

Andrés Rabinovich

"During the 1978 World Cup, the basement of the ESMA (Navy Mechanics School) was converted to dressing rooms and relaxation areas for the soccer players. Soldiers supplied the athletes with towels and other amenities while upstairs, out of earshot, torture went on as usual" (201). As chilling as it sounds, Marguerite Feitlowitz's account of the coexistence of the brutality of the military dictatorship (1976–1983) and the celebration of the 1978 World Cup of football (soccer) in Argentina highlights the operation of what Slavoj Žižek coined in his book *The Sublime Object of Ideology* as the "ideological fantasy." Žižek describes this notion as an "overlooked unconscious illusion" which "consists in overlooking the illusion which is structuring our real, effective relationship to reality"; in other words, people "know very well how things really are, but still they are doing it as if they did not know" (30). Why did Argentines celebrate the winning of the 1978 World Cup under the conditions in which it took place and for the purposes of portraying a national unity that served the bloodthirsty military dictatorship? A simple answer could pin this phenomenon on a strong sentiment of nationalism, but it would only scratch the surface. While it is true that nationalism may have played a part in such a fetishistic disavowal, this essay contends that there is more behind the enjoyment that is experienced by the Argentine football fandom and that "this more, this excess" structures its subjectivity in relation to a set of unconscious desires. This essay will then address the text of Argentine football culture to explore the ways in which the ideological fantasy is articulated in order to regulate people's effective relationship to reality.

Argentine Football: A Popular Culture Text

Before diving into the analysis properly, it is necessary to characterize Argentine football culture as a cultural formation worthy of study *as* popular culture. For the purposes of this essay, Popular culture will be approached through the amalgamation of two premises. First, Argentine football culture shall be considered a text of popular culture insofar as it is the culture created by and for the people, a kind of bottom-up subculture (Storey 9). This approach underscores the agency

DOI: 10.4324/9781003266211-4

of the people in shaping, interacting with, and making meaning out of a particular cultural formation. Football's horizontal disposition, as Storey states, casts aside the notion of a culture that is imposed from above and instead, places the emphasis on the practices developed for and by the people (9). Football culture's common practices create "a particular way of life" (Storey 45) marked by—as Richard Hoggart perceived in 1930's working-class culture in England—a strong sense of community (Storey 39). Argentine football culture thus serves, in this approach to popular culture, as an object of study that puts the emphasis on symbolic creation and meaning-making by the people. While it could be argued that Argentine football culture no longer fits within this definition of popular culture due to the increasing worldwide commercialization of the sport, the by-the-people-for-the-people definition allows us to examine precisely those practices that make Argentine football culture stand aside from the homogeneity that worldwide commercialization may have cast over the so-called beautiful game.

Second, I approach popular culture as an active site of negotiation and resistance of dominant cultural values. Popular culture figures itself in this approach as a battleground where certain hegemonic cultural values assert themselves as such. Raymond Williams's programmatic statement regarding the social study of popular culture sheds some light on this particular definition. For Williams, the social study of culture extends

> to an emphasis which, from studying particular meanings and values, seeks not so much to compare these, as a way of establishing a scale, but by studying their modes of change to discover certain general laws or trends, by which social and cultural development as a whole can be better understood.
>
> (quoted in Storey 45)

The hint toward the elucidation of social "laws" or "trends" in Williams's statement points precisely in the direction of an approach to popular culture that attempts to deconstruct cultural artifacts in an effort to discern the struggles that are contained in their development. While this chapter places more weight on the later approach to popular culture, when complemented with the by-the-people-for-the-people approach, it allows me to underscore the bottom-up meaning-making process that configures Argentine football culture. Having laid out my conception of Argentina football culture as a popular culture text, I turn my attention to the theoretical framework that informs my analysis.

Lacan and Žižek: Cultural Psychoanalysis

John Storey compares Lacan's theoretical enterprise with that of Freud claiming that the former "seeks to anchor psychoanalysis firmly in culture rather than biology" (103). Thus, the text of Argentine football culture will be approached primarily from an articulation of Jacques Lacan's psychoanalytic postulates with regard to the orders of the Real, the Imaginary, and the Symbolic and Slavoj

Žižek's notion of the ideological fantasy outlined at the onset of this essay. Close attention will be paid to the relationship between the Symbolic and Imaginary orders as they operate to construct the reality—which Žižek deems as a fantasy—that masks the Real of the fans' desire. For Žižek, "fantasy," "rather than fulfilling desire, is the staging of desire" (Storey 110). Thus, the focus will be placed in the process that conceals the Real of their desire, for as Žižek argues "the 'secret' to be unveiled through analysis is not the content hidden by the form . . . but, on the contrary, the secret of this form itself" (3). In such an endeavor, the Imaginary order will operate as the facilitator of the identificatory process between fans and their allegiances, whether it be a particular team or a playing style. In conjunction with the Imaginary order, the role of the Symbolic order will be useful to determine what Lacan identifies in psychoanalytic terms as "the symptom" for "it is already quite clear that symptoms can be entirely resolved in an analysis of language, because a symptom is itself structured like a language: a symptom is language from which speech must be delivered" (58). While he is, of course, referring to psychanalytic practice with an actual patient, his emphasis on the symptom being structured like language is particularly useful in trying to account for the symptom of Argentine football culture as the construction that masks its desire. The analysis and deconstruction of Argentine football culture will be focused on the rhetorical devices at play in the concealing and (re)creation of desire, for as Lacan proposes, "what is important is the version of the text . . . its rhetoric," namely, "the syntactical displacements" and "the semantic condensations" (57). The Lacanian method outlined earlier will shed light on the unconscious process of creating the fantasy of reality, for as Lacan explains in describing the subject's passage from the Real into the Symbolic, "it is the world of words that creates the world of things" (65). Therefore, the world created of things out of words, namely the Symbolic, is what structures the ideological fantasy described by Žižek. It is this relationship between the Real and the Symbolic that structures the analysis of Argentine football culture, as this essay argues that football serves this precise role in Argentine cultural life: by staging the scene of desire, it continually (re) presents the longed-for return to the Real.

Gooool!: The Return to the Real

My first focus will be on some of the practices performed by the fans in attendance at a live football game as these practices, I argue, reveal the structure of their ideological fantasy. For witnessing a live football match consists of precisely this flirting with the unconscious desire of returning to the Real, however masked under a veil of symbolic meaning. The euphoria of a goal celebration is perhaps the point at which this return to the Real appears to be achieved. This explains the anxiety that is felt before any goal is scored, that is, throughout the game. It is this anxiety that keeps the fans on edge. What all football fans in the world are longing for is precisely for their team to score, so that they can melt into an undifferentiated mass: a uniform body of euphoria. Argentine fans are no different.

Their peculiarity lies in the fashion in which goals are often celebrated in the stands. Fans will typically be pressed against the top of the stands as the flags and banners running along the bottom of the wire fence that separates them from the pitch prevent an optimal viewing of the game. When a goal is scored, the pack of fans that were bunched up at the top of the stands will avalanche down the steps of the stands in a melee of bodies where everyone becomes part of the single movement: *la avalancha*. Nicknamed after a natural disaster, this typical celebratory ritual suggests that the celebration of a goal can be read as an attempt to return to the Real, that "non-representable expression of the condition of being human" (Storey 103). Read this way, *la avalancha* is a practice that evidences the staging of desire that takes place at a soccer match: a desire that could be described in Lacanian terms as an attempt to return to the Real where all is one undifferentiated and unrepresentable mass. The issue is, however, that this unconscious attempt to return to the Real is always mediated by the Symbolic and, as such, it makes the return to the Real an impossibility. The moment the fans scream the glorious *goooooool*, the mirage of the Real is broken by the Symbolic and the mass of celebration and euphoria is evidenced in its fragmentary nature.

It is in this mediation of the Symbolic where the ground is ripe for the construction of an ideological fantasy that allows soccer fans "to mask the Real of [their] desire" (Žižek quoted in Storey 109). The cornerstone of the construction of such reality by soccer fans operates in a realm articulated by the Lacanian Imaginary and Symbolic. It is concerned with the Imaginary insofar as fans—due to the assumed image of an ideal, complete, coherent self they developed in the mirror stage—identify with a specific team. It is evident that different fans identify with different teams, but their identifying practices in the construction of their ideological fantasy remain the same regardless of their team identification. Their ego is thus bound up in their misrecognition in a particular team. The Symbolic realm comes into play because it strengthens the subject's identification with any team through language.

There are several levels to this operation of the Symbolic realm creating the coordinates for the subject's desire; I will mention only a few to illustrate this point. The main one has to do with the figure of the father understood in the Symbolic order for it is this figure that orients the subject's passage from home to the outside world. Jacques Lacan says in *Écrits* to this point that "it is in the name of the father that we must recognize the basis of the symbolic function which, since the dawn of historical time, has identified his person with the figure of the law" (66). The identification with the symbolic figure of the father is often the determinant of the team a fan supports. It is often said in Argentina, half-jokingly and half not, that one does not choose a team, that rather, one is born into it. This notion is echoed by a popular soccer chant performed by fans of many teams that says "*soy de 'x' desde que estaba en la cuna*" ("I am a fan of 'x' team all the way from the cradle").[1] Furthermore, the Symbolic order is where the identifications with teams are strengthened by the operations of language. Each team has a name and a nickname that carry several and complex associations. Take the example of Boca

Juniors. They are called the *Xeneizes*—in reference to the Genovese immigrants that founded the club in 1905—and also the *bosteros* (the horse-shitters), due to the proximity of their stadium to the Riachuelo, a highly polluted foul-smelling river. What this suggests is not necessarily that Boca Juniors fans feel a certain attachment to Genovese immigrants or to horse manure; rather, it bolsters the notion that the Symbolic order is where identifications are created between fans and their teams. It is thus this articulation of the Imaginary order—that which allows for identification—and the Symbolic order that operates in the construction of the Argentinean football fans' ideological fantasy. These attachments and meanings function, therefore, as ways to mask what appears to be their fruitless quest to return to the Real.

This schema of the soccer fans, their desire and masking thereof just presented, however, could be applied to practically any soccer culture in the world. What sets apart Argentine soccer culture is the fact that this model of identification is dialectically co-constituted with society writ large. Much like with the imaginary identification with a club team and its symbolic anchorage thereof, Argentine society presents similar procedures of masking its desire to return to the wholeness of the Real. This dialectical relationship between society writ large and football culture is clearly depicted in the case study of a heated Argentine debate: *Menottismo* vs. *Bilardismo*.

Menotismo vs. Bilardismo: **The Symbolic at Work**

César Luis Menotti and Carlos Salvador Bilardo embody what is arguably the most relevant division in football coaching philosophies in Argentina. Both World Cup winners at the helm of the national team, these two coaches have emerged as the flagbearers of two philosophically distinct playing styles that have sparked a heated debate among Argentine soccer fans. This binary, however, transcends the realm of soccer and carries within it the echoes of a rift that runs through Argentine culture since the country's independence from Spain in 1810. From the *unitarios* and *federales* in the nation's dawn, passing through the *peronistas* and *radicales*, to the most recent *kirchneristas* and *anti-kirchneristas*, Argentine culture has been plagued by binary oppositions that interpellate its population to be on a particular side of a given division.[2] It is because of the pervasiveness of such oppositions throughout Argentine culture that the *Menottismo* versus *Bilardismo* rivalry demands a close reading. This rivalry reifies what appears to be the country's primary ontological bifurcation, carefully embedded in a symbolic web of meaning. In identifying with one or the other coaching philosophies, Argentines reveal much more than their soccer style preference—they take sides in an ideological debate that gets played out on the pitch.

The fact that people gave such dichotomy its name—neither coach coined the terms associated with their playing styles—further supports the notion that the binary divide is necessary for Argentines to identify themselves with. As Lacan points out, "[T]he effect of full speech is to reorder past contingencies by conferring on them the sense of necessities to come, such as they are constituted by scant freedom through which the subject makes them present" (48). Therefore, the retroactive naming of both coaching styles allows us to posit that the *Menottismo* vs. *Bilardismo* debate expresses an unconscious necessity that the Argentine people made present by naming each coaching style. This necessity to designate the coaching style debate, I argue, is the same that underlies the ideological divide of the country. The creation of symbolic distinctions presents Argentines with an apparent choice of identification, thus allowing them to construct their ideological fantasy. If we are to follow this proposition, then the creation of the soccer-style dichotomy embodies the country's historical struggles. This notion would be validated by one of Fredric Jameson's central points in *The Political Unconscious*, since, for Jameson, "history . . . is inaccessible to us except in textual form, and that our approach to it and to the Real itself necessarily passes through its prior textualization, its narrativization in the political unconscious" (20). Stretching Jameson's "textual form" to include Argentine football culture as a text, *Menottismo* and *Bilardismo* can be situated within a much wider cultural debate that has ideological as well as philosophical implications that account for the embedded politico-philosophical struggle that is preserved within their systems of meaning.

It will be helpful, therefore, to give an account of both coaching styles to get a sense of their key differences. *Menottismo* came to be after César Luis Menotti won Argentina's first ever World Cup in 1978, showcasing a team that prioritized a visually pleasing style of football. Based on the playing style of this team, *Menottismo* bases itself upon the ideal of what Brazilians call *jogo bonito*, that is, a beautiful game. It is typically associated with letting the ball run more than the players by prioritizing short and accurate passing executed by highly technically able players. In a nutshell, the players' technique is prioritized over their tactical disposition. A team that follows this philosophy would rather win a game 4–3, prioritizing an aesthetically pleasing style of play than to win 1–0 by scoring early and defending the rest of the game. The latter is precisely what a *bilardista* team would do. What is novel about the *bilardista* philosophy then, is the categorical change in the *modus operandi*. Through this approach, the aesthetically beautiful football is replaced by the doctrine of the necessity to win. What is important in *bilardismo* is to win at all costs. If a Bilardo team was up on the scoreboard, it would gladly decide to sacrifice the one-touch, finesse-heavy style of football for a system that favored defense over anything else, to the point that it might not feature a forward if it was necessary. The ideology of the *jogo bonito*—embodied in the short accurate passing along with an unnegotiable predilection for playing the ball on the ground characteristic of *Menottismo*—is therefore replaced in *Bilardismo* by long aereal balls and man-marking. One could argue that the change from *Menottista* philosophy to the *Bilardista* can be seen as a passing from a sort of Platonic idealism to a Machiavellian pragmatism.

Much like with schema of the Argentine football fan at the club level laid out earlier, similar roles are played by the Imaginary order and the Symbolic order in the construction of this coaching dichotomy. It is evident that by supporting either one of the playing styles, fans would be identifying with what purports to be a discourse carried out on the field. Whether *Menottistas* or *Bilardistas*, fans would ally themselves with each style solidified by the Symbolic construction of what each style is saying on the pitch. It is here where the dichotomy transcends the realm of football: Its symbolization into a discourse allows its transposition to other cultural formations. It is now necessary, therefore, to situate this debate as something more than a soccer squabble.

To do so, I will follow the analytical pattern very aptly observed by Clifford Geertz in his famous 1980 article "Blurred Genres: The Refiguration of Social Thought": a synecdoche-based approach where a particular field—football— reveals aspects of society writ large. In order to render these coaching styles visible in the extra-football realm, it will be helpful to lay out their respective representative anecdotes. Here it is useful to borrow from Barry Brummett's application of Burke's representative anecdote as a critical method. Brummett sees the representative anecdote as "a method used by the critic [which] is a lens, filter, or template through which the critic studies and reconstructs the discourse. . . . The critic represents the essence of discourse by viewing it as if it follows a dramatic plot" (162). The interpretation of the two coaching styles will then allow us to see the values and ideologies they support. Starting with *Menottismo*, its representative anecdote could be summarized as follows: football is art. This representative anecdote captures the essence of the style since it highlights its expressive nature and its prioritization of aesthetic beauty. On the other hand, the representative anecdote for *Bilardismo* could be summarized as: football is work. While it is undeniable that, for all players and coaches at the elite level, football is indeed work, the representative anecdote of this coaching style highlights a utilitarian approach and its primary concern with obtaining results at all costs. By comparing both representative anecdotes, it could be posited that, while *Menottismo* goes against the grain of modern capitalist society, *Bilardismo* supports it. Menotti himself fleshed out the political implications of this dichotomy in his book *Fútbol: juego, deporte y profesión* when he claimed that "There is a *fútbol* of the right and a *fútbol* of the left: the *fútbol* of the right wants to suggest to us: that life is struggle, that it demands sacrifices, we should become ironmen and win via all the methods. Obey and function, that is what the powerful want out of their players. Thus, they go along creating more and more idiots, the useful idiots that go along with the system" (34). Deeply imbued with symbolic meaning, the apparently opposed coaching styles come to be discursive constructions whose essences are expressed in their respective representative anecdotes. The Symbolic articulation of these principles, therefore, plays a key role in constructing narratives for each coaching style that make the identification with either one possible.

Another aspect that solidifies the connection between the playing styles and their ideological implications is the system of meaning in which each one is inserted. A way to approach this task is to posit that neither *Menottismo* nor *Bilardismo* means what they say. As Lacan has argued, "in language, signs take on their value from their relations to each other in the lexical distribution of semantemes as much as in the positional, or even flectional, use of morphemes" (84). Belonging to such a relational structure, the role of words is to point to a different word in a metonymic chain that forms their systems of meaning. It is in this sliding of meaning where the two playing styles also slide off the pitch and represent values that denote a philosophical attitude in Argentine society writ large. By examining the systems of meaning that are associated with each one of the styles, we can see how the football culture goes far beyond the lines that delimit the pitch, thus expanding what Lawrence Grossberg called the "cultural formation": "[a concept that] describes the lines that distribute, place and connect cultural practices, effects and social groups. . . . Different social groups have differential access to specific clusters of practices and these relations are themselves part of the determination or articulation of the formation." (71). In this way, Argentine football culture exports its sensibility—that is, the formation's effects in people's daily lives and thus the way in which a particular formation is lived (Grossberg 72)—beyond its presupposed limits.

The most illustrative association is that of the opposition between *lírico* (lyric) and *rústico* (rustic). While the former term stems from an art form—poetry—the latter is used to denote a rural way of life. The first term is commonly associated with the kind of player that would play in a *Menottista* team, while the second term is typically associated with a player of a *Bilardista* team. The relation between *Menottismo* and a lyric kind of player is a clear one. This term refers to a player whose main attribute is an aesthetically pleasing way of playing the game. The relation between a rustic kind of player and a *Bilardista* kind of player might be rather far-fetched on the surface, but it makes sense if we take the rural way of life as a kind of primitive way of life, concerned largely with the satisfaction of basic needs for survival. It is no coincidence that the *Bilardista* style has often been referred to as a *Picapiedra* style, which is the Spanish translation of "The Flinstones." The Flinstones description as the modern Stone Age family does *Bilardismo* justice since it points simultaneously to the modern stage of the game of soccer and to the primitive quality associated with Stone Age humans whose main concern, from a modern standpoint, was to secure the necessary means of subsistence. Thus, these respective correspondences clearly separate *Menottismo* and *Bilardismo* into two clearly distinct camps: while the former exists in a system of meaning that pivots on the concept of the aesthetically valuable, the latter is situated in a context of survival.

It is in the ideological divide presented in the *Menottismo* and *Bilardismo* dichotomy that the echoes of Argentine society's constitution come to the surface. As Menotti himself aptly puts it, his style favors a rebellious stance against the modern capitalist ideology. An ideology that, as the *Bilardista* style suggests, conceives of work as strenuous effort in pursuit of an outcome. This ideology, radically opposed to *Menottismo*, advances the idea of an obedient attitude of the citizens who are to follow the rules of the system in order to prosper. *Menottismo* throws a wrench into the works of modern-day dominant capitalist ideology by questioning the goal in favor of the means. It calls for an ethical behavior that prioritizes the way in which things are done over their outcome. While the correspondence of these playing styles to the different political factions cited at the top of this chapter would entail an extremely nuanced analysis, the dispute between *Menottismo* and *Bilardismo* does reify the division between opposites that lies at the core of the country's sociopolitical unconscious. Argentines identify themselves dialectically—Just as *unitarios* acquire their meaning in relation to *federales*, so does *Menottismo* mean in relation to *Bilardismo*.

What has been outlined so far with regard to the *Bilardismo* and *Menottismo* dichotomy has been the symbolic construction of two different potential identifications with which the fans might align themselves. In other words, as the title of this section suggests, I have been concerned here with the work of the Symbolic order in creating two distinct identificatory models. My subject, the Argentine football fan, is thus thrown into a pre-established world of meaning that confronts them with two options. Thus, the ideological fantasy is constituted: it is the fans' identification with either coaching philosophy that dialectically unites *Menottismo* and *Bilardismo*, for it is in the sense of identity where the support of either playing style converges. Much like the identification that a club team provides for Argentine football fans, their identification with either coaching style is nothing other than the same staging of desire, since both coaching styles have been coined by the fans based on the World Cup victories by Menotti' and Bilardo's teams (the only two World Cup winners in Argentine history). This shared aspect speaks of a binary that, while representing different ways to achieve a goal (pun intended), they are both endorsed by the people thanks to their respective success.

Similarly, the ideological divide that is evidenced in the country's history continues to be reified in binaries that point to the same staging of desire. Namely, while both sides propose an ideological stance with regard to running the country, the common ground remains the identification with Argentina as a whole coherent unit. Transferring Lacan's tools to the realm of political analysis, it could be argued that both sides of the ideological debate express a desire to return to the Real, that is, the time when Argentina did not exist in the Symbolic order. Thus, what the *Menottismo* vs. *Bilardismo* rivalry symbolizes is the fragmentation of the self, brought about by the country's entrance in the Symbolic order. Likewise, the ideological divide is representative of the same dynamic where the Argentine population identifies with either one of the symbolically divergent factions as an identificatory practice, thus obscuring the inevitable fragmented nature of the self. It is in such a manner that the ideological fantasy is constructed to mask Argentines' desire: to return to the Real where all is one mass that cannot be represented.

Conclusion

As a concluding remark, it is important to return to Žižek's distinction. We must acknowledge that the ideological fantasy is a way to structure people's effective relationship to reality, insofar as reality is nothing but a fantasy that aids in masking the Real of people's desire. My article by no means attempts to uncover what those desires are. Rather, it sheds light on the construction of the ideological fantasy as a means to stage a symbolic return to the Real order, as contradictory as this may seem. Whether it is in the celebration of a goal or the winning of a World Cup, Argentines have invested football culture with a fantasy that mimics the fulfilment of desire embodied in this pseudo return to the Real order. This is why, to go back to Žižek, people "are doing it as if they did not know" (30): because by means of their ideological fantasy, their effective relation to reality is structured in such a way that they simultaneously stage and mask the Real of their desire. This is perhaps why, aware of the questionable victory over the best Peruvian national team to ever play, the Argentine public celebrated nonetheless.[3] This victory allowed them to continue staging their desire in the games that followed concluding in their *quasi* return to the Real: the euphoria of winning the country's first World Cup. Knowing fully well the political consequences—covering up the brutality of the dictatorship—the nation celebrated nonetheless, because their ideological fantasy was left intact.

Notes

1 The following link contains a rendition of the chant by Boca Juniors supporters: www. youtube.com/watch?v=LVfMSjiOHl8 (minute 0:20).
2 *Unitarios* was a political faction that favored a centralized government out of Buenos Aires, thus favoring the commercial power of the metropolis due to its open access to naval trade. *Federales* referred to the opposing political faction that, as the name suggests it, supported the idea of a federal government where every province had equal power to decide upon the country's interests and governance. *Peronistas* and *radicales* are the two parties that have alternated office for the better part of the twentieth and twenty-first centuries. *Kirchneristas* are those who supported the Kirchner presidents, Néstor (2003–2007) and his successor and wife, Cristina (2007–2015), while *anti-kirchneristas* are, of course, those who oppose them.
3 For a detailed account of the suspicion over the controversial Argentina vs. Perú match, see Archetti 144.

Works Cited

Archetti, Eduardo P. "Argentina 1978: Military Nationalism, Football Essentialism, and Moral Ambivalence." *National Identity and Global Sports Events: Culture, Politics, and Spectacle in the Olympics and the Football World Cup*, edited by Alan Tomlinson and Christopher Young. SUNY UP, 2006, pp. 133–147.

Brummett, Barry. "Burke's Representative Anecdote as a Method in Media Criticism." *Critical Studies in Mass Communication*, vol. 1, no. 2, 1984, pp. 161–176.

Feitlowitz, Marguerite. *A Lexicon of Terror: Argentina and the Legacies of Torture*. Oxford UP, 1998.

Geertz, Clifford. "Blurred Genres; The Refiguration of Social Thought." *American Scholar*, vol. 49, no. 2, 1980, pp. 165–179.

Grossberg, Lawrence. *We Gotta Get Out of This Place: Popular Conservatism and Postmodern Culture*. Routledge, 1992.

Jameson, Fredric. *The Political Unconscious: Narrative as a Symbolic Act.* Cornell UP, 1981.

Lacan, Jacques. "The Function and Field of Speech and Language in Psychoanalysis." *Écrits.* Translated by Bruce Fink. W. W. Norton & Co., 2004.

Menotti, César L. *Fútbol: juego, deporte y profesión.* El Gráfico, 1980.

Mundo Xeneize. "Soy de Boca desde la cuna. Boca 1 – San Martin de San Juan 0. Apertura 2011." *Youtube,* chanting by Boca Juniors fans, 11 Sept. 2011, www.youtube.com/watch?v=LVfMSjiOHl8. Accessed 12 June 2020.

Storey, John. *Cultural Theory and Popular Culture: An Introduction.* 6th ed. Routledge, 2012.

Žižek, Slavoj. *The Sublime Object of Ideology.* Verso, 1989.

Chapter 3

Titanyen and Collective Trauma in Haiti

Jana Evans Braziel

Its very name, Titanyen—"little nothing" in Kreyòl—captures the paradoxical ambiguity of the place both as a dumping field for dead bodies and as the darkest recess, a cavernous black hole, in the tortured memories and tormented imaginations of the collective Haitian psyche. What better (or worse) semiotic sign and linguistic register to denote the fact of what too many Haitians already believe to be the state authority's regard (or disregard) for their lives and their bodies? How better (or worse) to register the offensive and pervasive disposability with which Haitians are too often treated? Titanyen—little nothing—lives as if worthless, as if nothing at all. But, as Simon Critchley provocatively suggests in his book *Very Little . . . Almost Nothing*, this little nothing, or Titanyen, can also be an act of mourning (74). It can be seen as a requiem, a dirge.

Death, dying, and the dead are ever present in Haiti and in Haitian culture, particularly in Vodou rites, rituals, and iconography. The Gede *lwas*—the ancestral spirits in Vodou—are the living embodiments of death, dying, and the dead: as the ancestral spirits of the dead, the Gede *lwas* are always dwelling among the living. Writers and artists, like *mambos* (Vodou priests) and *oungans* (Vodou priestesses), and like everyday Haitians, depict the visual, artistic, and lived realities of death and dying, as well as the pervasive presence of the dead, the *morts-vivants*, the *les vivant et les morts*: and in doing so, the space/place of Titanyen figures prominently. Literary writers like Marie-Célie Agnant, Evelyne Trouillot, and Dany Laferrière have all engaged the space/place of Titanyen in the Haitian imaginary and in the collective imagination. Agnant, in her novel *Le silence comme le sang*, recounts how the protagonist Mnemosyne, her name from the Greek goddess of memory, includes a letter to her friend Claire and describes haunted memories of political violence in her Haitian homeland as an experience of being snarled between the dog and the wolf; and she asks Claire if she is aware of all the corpses devoured by dogs in Titanyen (10). Eventually, Mnemosyne travels to Titanyen to visit the mass grave that haunts her memories. Like literary writers, visual and sculptural artists, particularly those influenced by the Gede *lwas*—such as the Grand Rue sculptors, André-Eugène, Celeur, Guyodo, and others, but also painters like Édouard Duval-Carrié—also create powerful images of death and dying.

DOI: 10.4324/9781003266211-5

Literary scholars and art critics have also written poignantly about these literary and artistic engagements with death, with dying, and with the dead (Bascombe; Vignoli; N'Zengou-Tayo; Mata Barreiro; Cosentino; Smith; Braziel). Art historians and scholars, myself included, but also Donald Cosentino, Katherine Smith, Leah Gordon, Veerle Poupeye, Barbara Prézau Stéphenson, and others have all probed the iconographic and artistic representations of death and dying in Haitian Vodou and in its vibrant visual arts.

Like artists and writers, photographers and film directors have also directly engaged with the visual registers and representations of death, dying, and the dead: saliently among these are the filmic representations of Raoul Peck.[1] Cinematically, Peck visually travels to Titanyen, the black hole of Haitian history, in two different films: *Corps plongés* (1998) and *Assistance mortelle* (2013). In an earlier, short documentary *Desounen: Dialogue with Death* (1994), Peck cinematically meditates on death and dying through the Vodou postmortem burial rituals known as *Desounen*. In *Corps plongés*, the exiled protagonist Dmitri, living in New York, is haunted and traumatized by his wife's murder by the military junta who reigned terror on the country from 1991 to 1994, imagining her body dumped in the fields at Titanyen. In *Assistance mortelle*, Peck details how the traumatic site of political violence later becomes a memorial site for commemorating the people who died in the 2010 earthquake on the first (2011) and second (2012) anniversaries of the disaster. In this chapter, I analyze Raoul Peck's post-quake filmic meditations in *Assistance mortelle* on Titanyen as the space/place of collective trauma in the Haitian psyche.

In stunning, visual imagery, first-account observation, and compelling eyewitness testimony, Peck's *Assistance mortelle* gives viewers a close-up vision of death following the earthquake. In addition to the narrator's voice that inflects sorrow and sarcasm into this subjective documentary essay, the film is also punctuated by letters written by an unnamed *she* and *he*, addressed to *Chèr ami/Chère amie* (Dear Friend). In the French edition of the film (*Assistance mortelle*), the epistolary voice-overs are read by Peck himself (the *he*) and by Céline Sallette (the *she*); and in the English language edition, by the director's brother Hébert Peck and by Natalie Paul, the *he* and *she*. According to the film credits included at the end of both editions—*Assistance mortelle* and *Fatal Assistance*—the letters are based partially on Peck's diary of the disaster and its aftermath, partially on correspondence between himself and Mary Bowman, a senior aid worker based in the country during the period of post-quake reconstruction. The film, strikingly, is also multilinguistic, featuring interviews, commentary, speeches, and newscasts in Kreyòl, French, and English, as well as fragments in other languages, and it also features a spectacular soundtrack with original compositions by Alexei Agiui. Suffice it to say: sound in Peck's cinema plays as beautifully as image and ideas. Furthermore, Peck's main interlocutors in the film include government officials such as Joséus Nader, an engineer and Director of Public Works for the Government of Haiti and Jean-Max Bellerive, Haiti's Prime Minister and Co-Chair (with

Bill Clinton) of the Interim Haiti Reconstruction Commission as well as minor interlocutors such as Gabriel Verret, Executive Director of the IHRC and Philippe Mathieu, Director of Oxfam Québec and Paul Nemours, a Haitian teacher and earthquake survivor. It is precisely, in fact, the polyphony of diverse and divergent voices in Peck's film that multi-tonally, if not symphonically, contests the monolithic account and accounting of the capitalist system.

What and Where Is Titanyen?

Titanyen, located north of Port-au-Prince and south of Cabaret along the Côte d'Archaie, is the notorious place where François Duvalier, and later his son Jean-Claude Duvalier, had their brutal Tonton Macoutes torture and then kill political dissidents, outspoken activists, or simply dump dead bodies. Titanyen remained an open wound throughout the post-Duvalier era too (a period known as Duvalierism-without-Duvalier) and, periodically, during military coups and de facto regimes, opponents of the state were routinely raped, maimed, killed, or left for dead. Titanyen continued as a deadly dumping site, a macabre space of Haitian death and dying, during the military regime of Raoul Cédras (1991–94) and his paramilitary armed militia, Front for the Advancement and Progress of Haiti (FRAPH)—an ironic *nom du guerre* to say the least—and an organization backed by the CIA and the International Republic Institute (IRI). One of those discarded individuals, left for dead, was Alerte Belance, a Lavalas activist who was tortured in 1993 for her political support of Jean-Bertrand Aristide and who, remarkably, survived. Throughout the period of Président Jean-Bertrand Aristide's exile (1991–94), known as a "Reign of Terror," the fields of Titanyen bled blood red once more. Again, in late February 2004 through May 2004, in the immediate aftermath of the second military coup d'état that overturned the second democratically elected presidency of Aristide, anti-Aristide political militia, popularly known as *chimès* or ghosts, once more defiled the bloody and already horribly sullied grounds of Titanyen when political assassinations and extra-juridical murders led to 800 bodies being buried in a mass grave on March 7, 2004; and violence led to an additional 200 bodies being buried *en masse* on March 28, 2004 (Sanders). After the devastating 2010 earthquake in Haiti, a natural disaster that resulted in an estimated 240,000 to 310,000 Haitian deaths, and a disaster compounded by the failures of international aid, delayed reconstruction, and other man-made and catastrophic consequences, thousands of dead bodies were transported by trucks from the capitol and dumped *en masse* (once more) at Titanyen. As Jerry Philogene explains, "For centuries, as a neocolonized nation, Haiti has been figured as one large, unruly, racialized body marked by disease, poverty, and contamination. . . . [N]owhere was this truer than in the 2010 images of dead rotting bodies laid out for public viewing. . . . Many of the anonymous dead were buried in a sparsely populated area north of Port-au-Prince called Titanyen" (114).

The media spectacle of death and destruction, of Haitian bodies on display photographically and televisually, as Sibylle Fischer also compellingly recounts, only reinforced the horrific idea of Haitians as *titanyen*, as little nothing, of seemingly inexorable disposable life, or, as Giorgio Agamben would say, *vita nuda*. For Philogene,

> [t]heir carelessly discarded Black bodies are the inheritors of the blight of coercive neoimperialist global forces, malevolent Haitian dictators, inadequate infrastructure, and environmental destruction. These dead bodies stand in for the metaphorical death of Haiti; both are seen yet rarely mourned.

(114)

To be sure, as Philogene himself concludes, "the postearthquake images present a perplexing dilemma that speaks to the affective powers and indexical nature of images and to the visuality of dead bodies as they are bounded by historical, political, and racial circumstances" (114). But it is one line in particular that reverberates and echoes in Philogene's striking and insightful account: we are struck by the language, the phrasing, "seen yet rarely mourned" (114). Embodying the biopolitical forces of material existence, ground down and destroyed by the necropolitical forces of systemic state failures, these Haitian corpses piled up at Titanyen quintessentially and tragically define the *homo sacer*, bare life, disposable bodies, and the national and geopolitical "ungrievable."[2]

As Sam Durrant cogently argues, "trauma studies gains a more obviously political purchase in the shift from individual to collective trauma," and, as he further conceptualizes, the field is on "surer ground when it theorizes the state's role in the process of subjectification, as Butler does in *The Psychic Life of Power*" (93). And while others may do so, Durrant rejects the idea that the "recent turn to the biopolitical" effaces psychoanalytical approaches to trauma studies, asserting that Žižekian and Lacanian approaches elucidate the ways in which trauma is "both constitutive of the subject's entrance into the social ('symbolic') order" and is also "re-experienced whenever the fabric of that social order is ripped" (93). For these reasons, theorists who build upon Michel Foucault's concept of the "biopolitical" further demonstrate "the role of ideology not only in subject-formation but also in insulating the subject from the various forms of violence that simultaneously underwrite and threaten its existence" (Durrant 93). These ideas are provocative for understanding the space/place of Titanyen as one of Haitian collective trauma. My own conceptualizations of trauma, state violence, and political ideology in Haiti are informed by biopolitical and necropolitical approaches, particularly those by Giorgio Agamben, Judith Butler, and Simon Critchley, thinkers influenced by Michel Foucault but also by the philosopher Emmanuel Levinas. Titanyen is, I argue, a space/place defined by necropolitics, the vexed and vexing politics of death.

Director Raoul Peck, in an interview with Christopher McAuley, reflects on trauma as productive of "an accumulation of broken individuals who repress their wounds" and in which "the individual is lost" (128–140). This accumulation of pain, of grief, of broken individuals, of repressed woundedness, constitutes both a foundation trauma in the Haitian collective psyche and an unleashed reservoir of grief for those deemed by state and extra-state actors as "ungrievable." Truth and reconciliation commissions, and perhaps one is needed in Haiti, become cathartic expressions of collective grief, a profound overflowing of what has been historically repressed. State violence demands state redress: ungrievable lives and deaths demand collective expressions of grief and truth and forms of juridical reconciliation. In this chapter, I theorize Peck's haunted presencing, his obsessive if also oblique filming of Titanyen in *Assistance mortelle* as a ritualistic return to the site of Haiti's collective trauma: in the documentary film, Peck thus powerfully ties the political violence, torture, and state killings of the Duvalier dictatorship and its military aftermaths to the mass deaths that occurred as a result of the earthquake; by doing so, Peck cinematically and painfully captures the myriad collisions of natural and unnatural (or man-made) disasters that have plagued the country and traumatized its citizens over the past half century.

Filming Titanyen

Peck's *Assistance mortelle* features, indelibly, videotaped footage taken from "a surveillance camera inside the collapsing National Palace" (Vitiello, "Disrupting Conventional Film Structure" 48) in both its opening and closing sequences—underscoring the devastation wrought by the quake and its aftermath (a point to which I will return). Whereas the aid accounting system tallies up its donations, accomplishments, buildings repaired, houses constructed, pounds of rice donated, and bottles of water delivered, Peck's reverse angle shot casts this account (and accounting) into a different light. In the opening scenes, Peck foregrounds a native voice, a Haitian voice, and someone who witnessed and survived the devastating earthquake and has dedicated all his time, energy, effort, and expertise to the rescue, recovery, and rebuilding process: in Peck's reverse angle shot, we hear and see the events and its aftermath through the words and eyes of Joséus Nader, the Director of Public Works for the Haitian Government, an engineer, and a civil servant. The shattering and cataclysmic violence of this moment, recounted by Nader, is underscored visually through incorporated live footage of the earthquake. Only after this opening scene does Peck incorporate video footage from the earthquake itself: we see a dust cloud suffusing a courtyard; shelves tumbling; walls falling; a woman running, then falling to the ground as the plume of dust envelops her and the courtyard. Immediately after the video footage of the *bagay*, the "thing," as some Haitians refer to the earthquake in Kreyòl, the camera returns to Nader who is driving along Route 1 north of the capitol toward Titanyen, the site of mass burials post-quake.

Nader continues his account and offers another accounting: that of the victims who died during and after the earthquake. Nader also reminds viewers that the rescue teams were overwhelmed by the sheer numbers of bodies, their removal from debris, their transportation to Titanyen, their mass burial, and the incapacity—of the drivers, at the morgue, in the streets—to properly care for the dead. We are in Titanyen, the sacred yet defiled space/place of death, dying, and dwelling among the dead.

Titanyen visibly, palpably comes into refracted view in *Assistance mortelle*. In what follows, I analyze the cinematic (and oneiric) filming of Titanyen—as "present(ing)" or "presencing"—in *Assistance mortelle*, in Haitian history, and in the Haitian psyche as the space/place of collective trauma. My analysis is organized around four distinct, yet interrelated plots (as in historical, narrative threads and as in land or ground—that of possibility or of impossibility). "Plot," as a noun, denotes location, setting, and narratological line of development. "Emplot," as a verb, enacts a narrative structuring of disparate threads and seemingly disconnected historical events into a coherent, narrative whole. For Paul Ricoeur, *mise en intrigue* (emplotment) is the narrativization of time (or the imbrications of *temps et récits*, time and narrative), and as such, *intrigue* (plot) is the active and temporal mediation and synthesis of heterogeneous elements.[3] Or as Pellauer and Dauenhauer explain: "plot" is the "synthesis of heterogeneous concepts into a kind of discordant concordance" (n.p.)

The first plot (or *intrigue*) defines and unsettles all of the others; and it is located in two distinct yet entangled and structurally constituted sites—the Champs de Mars and Titanyen, the Palais national and the dictator's killing fields. The first plot stages what we could call "amnesiac memorials": willed and willful acts of state administrative ceremonies created to silence. After the earthquake in Haiti and on the screen in Peck's film, we see state ceremonies honoring the dead and the victims of the earthquake and state memorials at two specific sites: the site of the collapsed Palais national with the fallen bright white dome shrouded in Caribbean sunlight, flags flying overhead, behind the kelly green wrought iron gates and fencing; the second site is the barren landscape of Titanyen, wooden crosses planted into the defiled ground, a stage set up at the wasteland, rows-upon-rows of linen-upholstered chairs, oddly out of place, yet neatly assembled in an elevated, covered seating area in the open field. These two sites—as ones of collective trauma—are intimately connected in Haiti: both are marked by state power, state violence, and ultimately, also by state failure; and yet, they are willed and willful acts of state administrative amnesia, memorial and ceremonies created to cover over, silence, forget; not to uncover, express, and remember. Without truth, no reconciliation. Without grief, the dead remain ungrievable. The second plot meditates upon amnesiac and willed acts of constructing camps on killing fields and rechristening Titanyen as Corail; the third plot reflects upon the intractable terrain of dwelling with death; and the fourth plot intimates the residual parameters of *lespwa* (*l'espoir*), or hope, and resilience in envisioning imaginary houses. These four plots are historical, material, conceptual, and cinematic archives held and stored at Titanyen.

Plot 1. Amnesiac Memorials

As mentioned earlier, Titanyen becomes the site of amnesiac memorials in *Assistance mortelle*. As Laënnec Hurbon explains

> This should be the meaning of the earthquake memorial project, the inauguration of which on January 12, 2012, two years later, still leaves any observer in the greatest perplexity. Can we see, for example, in Titanyen, the space chosen by power for the memorial, as an appropriate place, worthy, and able to lead to mourning and restorative oblivion?
>
> (translation mine; 10–11)

In the first days and weeks following the earthquake, Titanyen, already stained with blood and ossified with bone, became a newly inflamed, raw, and open wound, a mass grave for those who died in the quake. Four months after the earthquake, Titanyen was transformed by political will and administrative resolve into Camp Corail as first thousands and then hundreds of thousands were resettled there. On January 12, 2011, the first anniversary of the earthquake, Titanyen became the official memorial site for the Haitian Government and the international community. Titanyen: odd and unsettling space/place for remembering the dead. Six days after the first anniversary of the earthquake, Jean-Claude Duvalier—exiled in Paris since 1986; frail, ill, near death himself—returned to Haiti, to his homeland and his country that had violently uprooted all traces of the dictator, of his father before him, father and son, all vestiges of his henchman, the notorious Tonton macoutes. Misery after misery, as Haitians say.

Open wounds; unfinished business; social promises unfulfilled; sovereignty not yet (perhaps never fully) restored. These are traumatic returns: traumatic returns of the same; a perpetual and unending cycle of violence, coup d'états, never-ending transitions toward democracy, that ever elusive beast. Peck's filmic framing of the 2012 memorial poignantly underscores the collisions of state violence and natural disaster. The stills of once-ousted now returned Duvalier at the 2012 memorial on the second anniversary of the earthquake; his presence at the memorial service; his stunning appearance at Titanyen; his presidential handshake with Michel Martelly—all affronts to historical memory; all visceral reiterations of palpable, corporeal violence; all killings once more of the dead, of the living-dead. Peck does not orchestrate the moment: he cinematically captures and frames the coincidence of historical savagery, its brutal returns of the same. Historical time periods physically bridged: from Cold War "development" to neoliberal, international aid and post-disaster reconstruction in the post-quake wake, two men (Duvalier:: Martelly)—we are truly on the profane yet sacred, defiled yet hallowed ground of dead aid, of fatal assistance. We are in Titanyen.

Plot 2. Camps on Killing Fields

In the immediate aftermath of the natural disaster, especially after the cholera out-break in October 2010, internally displaced person (IDP) camps, notably Camp Corail and individual camps with biblically named settlements, Canaan and Jeru-salem, were set up around Titanyen, a barren landscape with no social services and no access to potable water. Peck's camera captures, as Cyclone Tomas was approaching in late October 2010, the transporting of busloads of Haitian IDPs from Port-au-Prince and Portail-Léogâne to Camp Corail by Sean Penn and J/P Haitian Relief Organization (J/P HRO), the actor's nongovernmental organiza-tion. Interspliced with interviews by Gérard-Émile "Aby" Brun, CEO of Nabatec, SA, the lead construction corporation in Haiti that built the transitional shelters at Camp Corail; Daniel Wordsworth, President and CEO of American Refugee Committee, now Alight, an NGO that managed the camps, water, and sanitation; and Prime Minister Jean-Max Bellerive, who served as Co-Chair of the Interim Haiti Recovery Commission (IHRC) with former U.S. President Bill Clinton, we hear from Jean-Michelle Dorville, Représentant (secteur 4) du camp Corail, who decried the unhygienic conditions of the IDP camps and also call out to the Hai-tian Government, INGOs, and the international community for opportunities for work, secure housing, food, potable water, health care, and education, all of the things that improve life and well-being.[4]

Like the body counts that define the documenting of disaster, disposable bod-ies are also a recurrent cinematic motif in the film. From the privileging of house and school construction over debris removal, which negatively impedes human movement (through streets and alleys)—and well-being, to the subhuman living conditions in IDP tent camps, particularly in Corail, the policies and decisions set and made by the IHRC for Haitians and the Haitian Government reinforced the regrettable idea that Haitian lives did not matter—or, at least, did not fully mat-ter. The dumping of dead Haitian bodies and the mass burial of them at Titanyen is mirrored in the *en masse* relocation—without forethought; without long-term planning; without considering the social and familial ramifications—of thousands of homeless Haitians in October 2010 to Corail, a site 11 miles north of Port-au-Prince, the capitol city where commerce occurs, buying and selling happen, and what limited resources are available are doled out. This happened, of course, just as the cholera outbreak erupted in the country: brought in by Nepalese UN soldiers who dumped raw sewage into the river near Mirebalais. Almost 10,000 Haitians eventually died from the outbreak, the first cholera outbreak in Haiti in over a 100 years.

Interviews with Prime Minister Max Bellerive and Joël Boutroue, former UN Resident and Humanitarian Coordinator and adviser to the Prime Minister, affirm that the international community (or core group: a Special Representative of the United Nations Secretary-General, a Special Representative of the Organization of American States, and the Ambassadors of Brazil, Canada, France, Germany, Spain, the European Union, and the United States) systematically, strategically, and deliberately funneled the overwhelming majority of international donations through international nongovernmental organizations (IGOs), based and effectively controlled by foreign states and foreign investors, rather than allocating funds and the control of funds to the Haitian Government. As Prime Minister Bellerive decries, the international community prefers to donate to organizations such as UNICEF, rather than to the Department of Public Health. Endlessly trapped, or so it seems, in historical cycles and past accusations of corruption, Haiti stands indicted of the future crime (or offense) before it can even possibly be committed. As structural adjustment and international assistance increase, sovereignty diminishes.

Corail became a camp built on defiled ground, the dumping fields of Titanyen. Laënnec Hurbon, Alice Corbet, Laura R. Wagner, and Mark Schuller, as anthropologists working with internally displaced persons (IDP), all meditate on the bizarre, violent, and violating construction of IDP camps at Titanyen; and also on the jarring and amnesiac rechristening of the large swath of dusty, arid, desert-like, and mostly unsettled land, once known as Titanyen into Corail Cesselesse, or Camp Corail, itself further divided into smaller settlements and sections, Canaan, Jerusalem, Corail secteur 3, Coral secteur 4, and Onaville by international nongovernmental organizations (INGOs). "Titanyen," as Wagner explains in *Haiti is a Sliding Land*, are "the treeless hills to the north of Port-au-Prince, past Cité Soleil. It is also . . . one of the largest post-earthquake settlements—and one of the most critiqued and reviled" (xxiv).

Evoking the collective trauma embodied in the space/place of Titanyen, Corbet writes: "In the collective imaginary, Titanyen is therefore bound to a place of abandonment for waste and bodies, treated as carnal envelopes that have become unusual or uncanny" (n.p.). Agamben's ideas are certainly provocative ones for thinking through the post-earthquake tent camps in Haiti following the 2010 natural disaster—as Valerie Kaussen has already demonstrated. Agamben's ideas also provide, and presciently so, language and conceptual tools for understanding the ways in which entire countries, perhaps even continents exist *as if* camps for internally displaced persons. Of course, after a while, temporary shelters and camps give way to more permanent settlements, and INGOs are rapidly working on water sanitation and waste management,[5] amidst the ossified remains of dead bodies and unsettled, restless spirits.

Plot 3. Dwelling With Death

"O Lord, How Long Shall I Cry For Help, And You Will Not Hear? Or Cry To You 'Violence!' And You Will Not Save?" (Habakkuk 1:2). Mass graves, open wounds, murdered but not buried bodies; these are those denied burial rituals, whether evangelical, Catholic, or Vodou, and to a smaller scale, Jewish or Muslim or even atheist. No last rites; no final prayers; no *Desounen* rites for Vodouissants; no farewells; no preparations; no goodbye. For those rounded up as internally displaced persons, transported to Titanyen—renamed Corail—and resettled in IDP camps; for those on dirt floors under make-shift tents or donated tarps, crowded into small, insecure huddles, these IDPs are death dwellers, those dwelling with death, those dwelling with and among the dead, those who were tortured, killed, dumped by Duvalier's henchmen; those later murdered by post-Duvalier military regimes; or simply (though just as brutally) by opposition gangs and mercenary guns-for-hire; and also, overwhelmingly, those killed and dumped *en masse* during and after natural disasters. Dwelling with Death. Death dwellers. Does the body remember the pain of others? Does the earth palpably embody the excruciating and corporeal memories of those innumerable and uncounted dead? Does it remember? Do we?

In Vodou, the concept of the self (in Kreyòl: *pwòp tèt ou*; in French: *soi*) is fourfold and includes the body, the *gwo bon anj* (big good angel, or great spirit), the *Mèt tèt* (the *lwa* that one serves, that rules one's head, and that most often possesses the serviteur), and the *ti bon anj* (little good angel). In the Vodou funeral rites known as *Desounen*, the Kreyòl word for "disunion" or "disaggregation," the *oungan*, Vodou priest, or *mambo*, Vodou priestess, prepares the deceased for burial: *Desounen* separates the *gwo bon anj* and the *mèt-tèt lwa*, or *lwa mèt-tèt*, from the body, which decomposes and returns to earth (as dust), and also from the *ti bon anj*, or soul, which goes to heaven. The *gwo bon anj* and the *mèt-tèt lwa*, unless they pass into the body of another serviteur present at the *Desounen*, both return to *Ginen*. When the *gwo-bon-anj* (big good angel) returns to Ginen following the *Desounen* rites, it remains there for one year and a day, at which time another Vodou rite, the *ouete mò nan ba dlo*, allows the *gwo-bon-anj* to move from Ginen to the realm of the living above.[6] Leslie G. Desmangles describes the *ouete mò nan ba dlo* ritual, which occurs exactly one year and a day after the desounen ritual, as one that reunites the ancestral spirit's gwo bon anj with the community of serviteurs (81–83).

If the *Desounen* rites are not held for the deceased, the spirit, or *gwo bon anj*, will roam the world restlessly and without peace, and the body may haunt the earth as a *zonbi*. Philogene similarly laments: "The images that inundated the global mainstream news media were of individuals haphazardly buried in massive shallow, makeshift, communal graves, individuals unable to obtain the appropriate rituals of burial normally granted to citizens due to the destruction caused by the earthquake and the mayhem that followed" (114). Peck's fantastically fictionalized (or spiritually ritualistic) documentary account of Haitian refugees (*Desounen: Dialogue with Death*), then, is not only a "dialogue with death," as Christians may understand and as its subtitle reveals, but also a dialogue or supplication to *Gédé* or the *Gédé lwas*, asking Bawon Samdi, lord of the dead, to allow those who died at sea to enter Ginen and not wander the ocean floors eternally; it is Desounen for those who died crossing the Atlantic. In *Assistance mortelle*, Peck both decries burial without rites; and the documentary also enacts a lugubrious mourning for the dead and a filmic postmortem rite for those dumped *en masse* at Titanyen.

Plot 4. Imaginary Houses

Peck's camera zeroes in on one Corail dweller in particular: the director visits with him, so to speak, in his salon, listens as he spins yarn for a spell. In an extended scene, the viewer receives an intimate and up-close glance into Wikens's world, his life, his post-quake imagination. Wikens, habitant de Canaan camp, places branch stakes in the dusty ground, marking off each room in his imagined and imaginary house: pointing to a far corner, he tells the cinematographer and his viewers, over there will be the bedrooms; here, pointing closer to where he stands on the dirt, the dining room and the salon or living room. Beyond the walls-yet-to-be-built, Wikens speaks of his garden, filled with root vegetables, leafy plants, and flowering shrubs and trees, perennial and annual blooms. Others have a tarp, a t-shelter, a plyboard, and corrugated tin dwelling: Wikens imagines more—three bedrooms, a foyer, a dining room, indoor kitchen, salon, porch, garden outside his door; and for now, the wooden stakes driven into dusty earth are all he needs to envision it. As Gaston Bachelard reminds us, "When it comes to excavated ground, dreams have no limit" (18). Wikens is, as Bachelard suggests, imagining and building "the house from cellar to garret" (3).

Wikens's determined will-to-see marks a resolute will-to-survive and will-to-endure beyond the earthquake, beyond temporary houselessness, beyond Titanyen. Dare we utter? Wikens seems to define that *je ne sais quoi* of Haitian resilience, even though the critiques of this ideal and the ways that it naturalizes suffering, survival, persistence in the face of trauma, and resolve despite misery after misery are real.[7] As Celeste recounts,

> Reports of economic and sexual exploitation carried out by nonprofit organizations, the UN, and missionaries have emerged. Haiti's continual identification as one of the poorest nations – but also as a nation capable of enduring the direst conditions – shape narratives of Haiti as exceptional. Thus, much public perception of Haitians is limited to the simplistic binary of poverty and resilience that denies ongoing histories of colonization and exploitation.
> (183–184)

Arguing for a paradigmatic shift "from resilience to humanity," Celeste concludes with a single line in Kreyòl: "Se sèlman moun nou ye" (We are only human) (187). In other words, we are neither criminals nor abject, dehumanized beasts; nor are we superhumans capable of enduring extraordinary pain and suffering.

Titanyen's Traumatic Returns

We begin and we end in the same place: Titanyen. One witness—Nader—disrupts the coherent plotting of the film, its emplotted cinematic narrative; and he serves as the truth-teller, the witness-nearer in the film. Filming from Titanyen, Nader testifies to the ways in which national (or state) violence collides with international aid in violating ways, as they both profit from people's death. Small countries remain in the same state. The conceptualizations of trauma and traumatic returns by Emmanuel Levinas are salient here. For Levinas, the ethical subject is constituted in relation to an "original traumatisme" ("Substitution" 79) that places one in relation to alterity, an other who violates and threatens to kill and destroy. And in traumatic neurosis, the subject returns to this "original scene of the trauma, its deafening shock, [and] is compulsively and unconsciously repeated in nightmares, insomnia or obsessive reflection" (Critchley 238). Peck, as director and filmmaker, returns to Titanyen as the space/place of original traumatisme in the collective Haitian psyche. As Critchley elaborates

> under the effect of the traumatism of persecution, the deafening shock or the violence of trauma, the subject becomes an internally divided or split self, an interiority that is radically non-self-coincidental, a gaping wound that will not heal, a subject that wants to repeat compulsively the origin of the trauma, a subject that becomes what Levinas calls a recurrence of the self without identification, a recurrence of trauma that is open to death, or – better – open to the passive movement of dying itself, dying as the first opening towards alterity, the impossibility of possibility as the very possibility of the ethical subject.
>
> (194)

I end where I began, full circle, I end where Peck ends: reflecting on Titanyen as the space/place of collective trauma in the Haitian psyche. State formations and state failures are structurally bound to the dynamics of state violence as traumatic returns. Perverse state logic operates at Titanyen: IDP camps constructed on the ossified remains and ruinous relics of dead bodies; memorial services held at the very site where the most heinous acts of Duvalier violence and murder transpired and at the very site of mass graves of individuals whose bodies were crushed, maimed, killed, and dumped in Haiti's single most destructive natural disaster: the earth's trembling and the concrete buildings crumbling on January 12, 2010. Monument to death and disaster, Titanyen becomes then a willful forgetting and willed rewriting of narrative trauma in the collective Haitian psyche: site of remembering; site of forgetting; amnesiac moments that compound death and dying, both from political violence, state murder, and torture and from natural disaster. Peck's film renders this willful forgetting and willed rewriting as legible, visible, discernible, yet palpably horrible too.

Notes

1 For film analyses and critical interventions into death and dying in Raoul Peck's oeuvre, see specifically the contributions by both Toni Pressley-Sanon and Joëlle Vitiello.
2 See Judith Butler's theorizations of the "ungrievable" and its relations to war, violence, and colonial subjection in *Precarious Life* and *Frames of War*.

3 As Ricoeur writes in *Temps et Récits*, "Plot is mediating in a third way, that of its unique temporal characteristics. These permit us to call, by way of generalization, plot a synthesis of the heterogeneous" (103).
4 For an extremely critical assessment of camp management at Corail, see Baram; Katz.
5 According to the *National Plan for the Elimination of Cholera in Haiti, 2013–2022*, it is only recently that efforts have been undertaken to alleviate this situation through the construction and start-up in 2011 of two excreta treatment stations in Morne à Cabri and Titanyen, not far from the capital, for the disposal and treatment of wastewater from latrines and septic tanks. Each treatment station is designed to receive a volume of 500m^3 of excreta from latrines and septic tanks (17).
6 On *boule zen*, see Métraux; Desmangles.
7 See especially Celeste (183–187).

Works Cited

Agamben, Giorgio. *Homo Sacer: Sovereign Power and Bare Life*. Translated by Daniel Heller-Roazen. Stanford UP, 1998.
Agnant, Marie-Célie. *Le silence comme le sang*. Editions du Remue-ménage, 1997.
Assistance mortelle. Directed by Raoul Peck, 2013.
Bachelard, Gaston. *The Poetics of Space*. Penguin, 2014.
Baram, Marcus. "Camp Corail: Haiti's Development King Defends Role in Site Location of Huge Refugee Camp." *Huffington Post*, 2011, www.huffpost.com/entry/camp-corail-haitis-develo_n_810038. Accessed 15 June 2021.
Bascombe, Carla. "Around Us, History Never Stops: Interrogating Post-quake Haiti in Évelyne Trouillot's Absences Sans Frontières." *Karib – Nordic Journal for Caribbean Studies*, vol. 4, no. 1, 2018, pp. 1–9.
Braziel, Jana Evans. "« *Atis Rezistans* » (Resistance Artists): Vodou Street Sculpture at the Grand Rue, Port-au-Prince." *Callaloo*, vol. 39, no. 2, Spring 2016, pp. 419–437.
———. *"Riding with Death": Vodou Art and Urban Ecology in the Streets of Port-au-Prince*. UP of Mississippi, 2017.
Butler, Judith. *The Force of Non-Violence*. Verso, 2020.
———. *Precarious Life*. Verso, 2004.
———. *The Psychic Life of Power*. Stanford UP, 1997.
Celeste, Manoucheka. "Beyond Resilience in Haiti." *NACLA Report on the Americas*, vol. 50, no. 2, 2018, pp. 183–187.
Corbet, Alice. "Community After All? An Inside Perspective on Encampment in Haiti." *Journal of Refugee Studies*, vol. 29, no. 2, doi:10.1093/jrs/fev022. Accessed 10 June 2021.
Corps plongés. Directed by Raoul Peck, 1998.
Cosentino, Donald. "Baby on the Blender: A Visual History of Catastrophe in Haiti." *Small Axe* vol. 36, Nov. 2011, http://read.dukeupress.edu/small-axe/article-pdf/15/3 (36)/134/472366/SMX36_13Cosentino_Fpp.pdf. Accessed June 11 2021.
Critchley, Simon. *Very Little . . . Almost Nothing: Death, Philosophy, Literature*. Routledge, 1997.
———. "The Original Traumatism: Levinas and Psychoanalysis." *Questioning Ethics: Contemporary Debates in Philosophy*, edited by Richard Kearney and Mark Dooley. Routledge, 1999, pp. 230–242.
Desmangles, Leslie G. *The Faces of the Gods: Vodou and Roman Catholicism in Haiti*. U of North Carolina P, 1992.

Desounen: Dialogue With Death. Directed by Raoul Peck, 1994.

Durrant, Sam. "'Undoing Sovereignty': Towards a Theory of Critical Mourning." *The Future of Trauma Theory: Contemporary Literary and Cultural Criticism*, edited by Gert Buelens, Sam Durrant, and Robert Eaglestone. Routledge, 2014, pp. 91–110.

Fischer, Sibylle. "Haiti: Fantasies of Bare Life." *Small Axe*, vol. 23, June 2007, pp. 1–15.

Foucault, Michel. *The Birth of Biopolitics: Lectures at the Collège de France, 1978–79*, edited by Michel Senellar, translated by Graham Burchell. Palgrave Macmillan, 2008.

———. *La Volonté de Savoir*. Éditions Gallimard, 1976.

———. *Naissance de la Biopolitique: Cours au Collège de France, 1978–1979*, edited by Michel Senellart. Éditions de Seuil / Gallimard, 2004.

Gordon, Leah. *Kanaval! Vodou, Politics, and Revolution in the Streets of Haiti: Photography and Oral Histories*. Soul Jazz Books, 2010.

———. *Pòtoprens: The Urban Artists of Port-au-Prince*. Pioneer Works Press, 2021.

Hurbon, Laënnec. "La culture ou le pilier absent de la reconstruction." *Observatoire de la reconstruction*, no. 1, May 2012, pp. 10–11.

Katz, Jonathan. "Fights over Land Stall Haiti Earthquake Recovery." *Associated Press*, 11 July 2010.

Kaussen, Valerie. "States of Exception – Haiti's IDP Camps." *Monthly Review*, 1 Feb. 2011, https://monthlyreview.org/2011/02/01/states-of-exception-haitis-idp-camps/. Accessed 15 May 2021.

Laferrière, Dany. *Tout bouge autour de moi*. Grasset, 2010.

Levinas, Emmanuel. *Entre nous: Essais sur le penser-à-l'autre*. Grasset, 1991.

———. *God, Death, and Time*. Translated by Bettina G. Bergo. Stanford UP, 2000.

———. *La psychanalyse est-elle une histoire juive?* Seuil, 1981.

———. *La mort et le temps*, edited by Jacques Rolland. Éditions de l'Herne, 1991.

———. *Le temps et l'autre*. B. Arthaud, 1947.

———. *Otherwise Than Being or Beyond Essence*. Translated by Alfonso Lingis. Nijhoff, 1981.

———. "Substitution." *Emmanuel Levinas: Basic Philosophical Writings*, edited by Peter Atterton, Simon Critchley, and Robert Bernasconi. Indiana UP, 1996, pp. 79–96.

———. *Time and the Other*. Translated by Richard A. Cohen. Duquesne UP, 1987.

———. *Totality and Infinity*. Translated by Alfonso Lingis. Duquesne UP, 1969.

Mata Barreiro, Carmen. "Le moi femme – le nous histoire: voix et vies dans l'oeuvre de Marie-Célie Agnant." *Revue des lettres et de traduction*, no. 7, 2001, pp. 361–374.

McAuley, Christopher. "Filmer sans compromis: Interview avec le cineaste Raoul Peck." Translation by Claudine Michel, *Journal of Haitian Studies*, vol. 9, no. 2, Fall 2003, pp. 128–140.

Métraux, Alfréd. *Voodoo in Haiti*. Translated by Hugo Charteris; critical introduction by Sidney W. Mintz. Schocken Books, 1972.

N'Zengou-Tayo, Marie-José. "Unwelcome Neighbors: The Haitian Popular Migration in the Writings of Some Caribbean Writers." *Journal of Caribbean Literatures*, vol. 3, no. 1, Summer 2001, pp. 129–142.

Philogene, Jerry. "'Dead Citizen' and the Abject Nation: Social Death, Haiti, and the Strategic Power of the Image." *Journal of Haitian Studies*, vol. 21, no. 1, Spring 2015, pp. 100–126.

Poupeye, Veerle. *Caribbean Art*. Thames & Hudson Ltd., 1998.

Prézau Stéphenson, Barbara. *15 ans d'art contemporain en Haïti*. Livres en Folie, 2015.

————. *La Richesse culturelle d'Haïti – Mythe ou Réalité?* Livres en Folie, 2010.

————. *Le cercle Atlantique*. Paris, 2020.

Prézeau-Stephenson, Barbara, and Veerle Poupeye. *Tessa Mars: Ile modèle, Manman zile, Island Template*. NAIMA, 2020.

Ricoeur, Paul. *Temps et Récit*. Éditions du Seuil, 1983.

Sanders, Richard. "The Canadian-backed Coup Regime's Reign of Terror: How CIDA's NCHR-Haiti Cleverly Promoted and then Covered up Atrocities." *Magazine of the Coalition to Oppose the Arms Trade (COAT)*, no. 61, 2007, http://coat.ncf.ca/ourmagazine/links/61/3-19.pdf. Accessed 15 June 2021.

Smith, Katherine M. "Atis Rezistans: Gede and the Art of Vagabondaj." *Obeah and Other Powers: The Politics of Caribbean Religion and Healing*, edited by Diana Powers and Maarit Forde. Duke UP, 2012, pp. 121–145.

————. "Dialoguing With the Urban Dead in Haiti." *Southern Quarterly*, 2010, pp. 61–90.

————. *Gede Rising:* Haiti in the Age of *Vagabondaj*. Dissertation submitted to University of California-Los Angeles (UCLA), 2010.

————. "Genealogies of Gede." *Extremis: Death and Life in Twenty-First Century Haitian Art*. Fowler Museum of Art, 2012, pp. 85–99.

————. "Lansètkòd: Memory, Mimicry, Masculinity." *Kanaval! Vodou, Politics, and Revolution in the Streets of Haiti: Photography and Oral Histories*, edited by Leah Gordon. Soul Jazz Books, 2010.

Trouillot, Evelyne. *Absences sans Frontières*. Editions Chèvre Feuille Etoilé, 2013.

Vignoli, Alessia. "L'universalisation de la catastrophe haïtienne dans Tout bouge autour de moi de Dany Laferrière." *Dalhousie French Studies*, no. 116, 2020, pp. 161–169.

Vitiello, Joëlle. "Disrupting Conventional Film Structure: Letters, Voice-Over, and Traumatic Irruption in Raoul Peck's Films." *Raoul Peck: Power, Politics, and the Cinematic Imagination*, edited by Toni Pressley-Sanon and Sophie Saint-Just. Lexington Books, 2015, pp. 37–59.

————. "Lucid Cameras: Imaging Haiti After the Earthquake of 2010." *Journal of Haitian Studies*, vol. 17, no. 2, Fall 2011, pp. 6–32.

————. "Up Through the Cracks: Raoul Peck's *Moloch Tropical* and the Ghosts of Haitian History." *Cultural Dynamics*, vol. 27, no. 3, 2015, pp. 313–339.

Wagner, Laura Rose. *Haiti is A Sliding Land: Displacement, Community, and Humanitarianism in Post-Earthquake Port-Au-Prince*. Dissertation: Anthropology Department, University of North Carolina at Chapel Hill, 2014.

Chapter 4

A Phantom in the Andes

An Anasemic Reading of *La hora azul* and *La distancia que nos separa*

Pablo G. Celis-Castillo

Albeit provocative, seeing the armed conflict between the terrorist organization known as the Shining Path and the Peruvian government in the 1980s and 1990s through a psychoanalytic lens has been seldomly done.[1] Examining the cultural production associated with this internal war through psychoanalysis has been an even less common enterprise.[2] Although the motivations for this lack of psycho-analytic cultural readings are many and valid (including, of course, the Euro-centricity usually attributed to the practice), I believe that examining Peruvian cultural products thematically associated with the period of political violence experienced in the country during the last two decades of the twentieth century through a psychoanalytic prism allows us to articulate a more nuanced picture of the conflict as well as of its political and social causes and consequences. To illustrate psychoanalysis's critical potential in the context of the Peruvian armed conflict, I provide here detailed readings of two of the most popular novels related to the war: *La hora azul* (2005) by Alonso Cueto and Renato Cisneros's *La distancia que nos separa* (2015).

Despite having been published a decade apart, these two literary works share several narrative characteristics that make them particularly apt for psychoana-lytic readings. First, there is the devotion that both protagonists, *La hora azul*'s Adrián Ormache and the unnamed protagonist/narrator of *La distancia que nos separa*, have toward their mothers. There is also the affective distance that exists between the characters and their fathers, both military men in charge of the Peru-vian government's counterinsurgency campaign and, thus, connected to the sys-tematic human rights abuses committed during the years of political violence by both armed actors of the conflict. Additionally, both characters seek emotional and therapeutic support from healthcare providers: Adrián from his friend Platón Acha, a dentist (Cueto 93–94), and the protagonist/narrator from Elías Colmenares, specifically described in the novel as a psychoanalyst (Cisneros 15).[3] Freudian readings of the characters' maternal devotion could yield an interesting discus-sion about the protagonists' Oedipal tendencies. A Lacanian problematization of the distance that exists between the characters and their fathers would produce a stimulating illustration of how the dynamics of the "Letter/law of the Father" are

DOI: 10.4324/9781003266211-6

perceived in the narrative structure of the novels. A discussion about the analysts' role in both works could also be the basis of critical analyses. Yet, despite the intriguing critical postures that could be extracted from these approaches, I prefer to endorse a different type of psychoanalytic approach. One that does not separate completely from Freud or Lacan but that is able to establish a more nuanced affective relationships between the characters' behavior and the contextual particularities with which the two novels dialogue. I am referring here to the concept of the transgenerational "phantom" first proposed by Nicholas Abraham and later expanded in his works alongside Maria Torok. Initially defined by Abraham as "a formation of the unconscious that has never been conscious [that] . . . passes . . . from the parent's unconscious into the child's" (173), the presence of a phantom "indicates the effects, on the descendants, of something that had inflicted narcissistic injury or even catastrophe on the parents" (174). In other words, a phantom is formed by the traumatic consequences caused by a parent's drama. This drama is strong and usually terrifyingly shameful. It is, in fact, so unbearable that it becomes a secret. This secret, in turn, is unconsciously transmitted to the parents' offspring who, unaware of this transmission, display psychic symptoms that do not seem to have a clear origin but that, through a retrospective analytical practice, Abraham and Torok called "anasemia" (from the Greek words *ana* [back] and s*emia* [signification]), can be traced back to the parents' dramatic experience (Rashkin, *Family Secrets* 43).

Somewhat less well-known than Freudian or Lacanian psychoanalytic frameworks, the phantom allows us to elucidate with greater clarity the complex social realities of the Peruvian armed conflict within the narrative parameters of the novels by Cueto and Cisneros. Through anasemic readings of both protagonists, we are able to discern the systematic and long-standing nature of the racial discrimination that chronically affects Peruvian society in the present and that fanned the flames of the war in the recent past. Thus, by examining a range of rather obsessive behaviors in the novels' protagonists, behaviors that are considered here symptoms that point to the presence of a phantom, I propose that the main characters of *La hora azul* and *La distancia que nos separa*, through their actions and thoughts, confirm that the shameful secret their parents transmitted to them is nothing else but the racism, indifference, and contempt that the Peruvian elites feel toward the indigenous and mestizo majorities of the country. These emotions, I argue, have been transmitted effectively yet inadvertently in the mostly white and *criollo* Peruvian elites since colonial times and have thwarted the social and political empowerment of the subaltern populations of the country; those who unsurprisingly suffered the most during the conflict and who are still deeply marginalized today.

The existence and prevalence of racism in Peru cannot be considered a secret. Yet the fact that racism is still overtly and overwhelmingly present in the country puts Peruvian society's behavior at odds with the explicit and official discourse of racial equality and diversity historically advanced by the state and the elites who control it. Although this discourse has been widely promoted since the beginning of the Republic, it became particularly poignant since the Truth and Reconciliation Commission (henceforth referred as TRC)—the ad-hoc governmental organization tasked with investigating the many instances of human rights abuses committed during the conflict—released its findings in 2003. One of the most bewildering conclusions included in the TRC's *Informe final* was that three quarters of the almost 70,000 victims of the conflict were indigenous Quechua-speaking peasants and that this disproportion was a direct result of the general historical contempt that exists in the country toward this populational segment (Lerner 13). In other words, the shameful secret at work in Peru, as it will be shown in my analysis of the two novels, is not the existence of racist attitudes among Peruvian elites. It is, instead, the fact that the country's social and political classes are not willing to admit that their behavior starkly contradicts their discourse. As I analyze in the pages that follow, the protagonists of *La hora azul* and *La distancia que nos separa*, metonymic representatives of the Peruvian elites, explicitly state their desire to learn the truth about the conflict but are ultimately unmoved to action when they uncover it. Furthermore, through this dismissive behavior, they are, in theory, extending the social conditions that make racism prevalent in the country into the future.

Both novels also allude to the prevalence of the phantom in the social spheres Cisneros and Cueto represent. *La distancia que nos separa* is marketed and promoted as a fictional biography of Cisneros's real father, a military leader who was indeed involved in the conflict. Its protagonist's passivity, therefore, corroborates the existence of this racism and indifference among the newer generations of the Peruvian elites who, despite showing an interest in learning about the conflict, are unable and unwilling to jeopardize their social status to address the moral shortcomings highlighted by the violence.[4] The aloofness of the protagonist of *La hora azul* verifies too the existence of the phantom among the *limeño* social and literary elites of which Cueto is an undisputed member. The presence of this phantom in Cueto's novel is particularly poignant, in fact, because it registers its presence even among those well-intentioned segments of the Peruvian elites who, in the early 2000s, embraced the findings of the TRC, denounced the human rights committed during the conflict, but ultimately did little or nothing to pursue the type of social reconciliation promoted by the Commission.[5]

Profession, Ventriloquism, and Silence

The phantom of racism and indifference in both novels manifests itself through a variety of psychic symptoms in their protagonists' behaviors. These can be traced anasemically through the identification of specific elements within the text. The choice of profession of the unnamed protagonist/narrator of *La distancia que nos separa* is one of these elements. At a certain point in the novel, the character states that he chose to be a journalist "not because of journalism but to cover an unconscious emergency: the arrival of the day in which [he] had to declassify his father's archives" (349).[6] This assertion is significant for two reasons. First, because it connects the novel to the armed conflict by presenting itself as a work of *autoficción* (self-fiction) entirely focused on the character's father (and thus the author's), Luis Federico "el Gaucho" Cisneros Vizquerra, one of the most controversial Peruvian military leaders in the 1970s and 1980s who was accused of several instances of human rights abuses during the early part of the conflict (7),[7] and, second, because it confirms the existence of a "secret" in the father's "archives" that needs to be "declassified" by the protagonist/narrator. As Lorena de la Paz Amaro notes, however, "the secret that the Cisneros son hopes to reveal does not seem to be the same as the one expected by the informed reader about the participation of the Cisneros father in the Peruvian government during the years of the war" (103). The secret that the protagonist/narrator ultimately finds is connected, instead, to the fact that "el Gaucho" was not able to get married to the girlfriend he left in Argentina when he moved to Lima to join the Peruvian Army due to a military regulation that did not allow any officer to change his marital status during the first five years of service. Albeit dramatic, this secret is far too benign to serve as the basis of a phantom. Nonetheless, its presence alludes to the fact that the protagonist/narrator's motivations to become a journalist went beyond vocation or intellectual interest and that these motivations are, in fact, psychically connected with declassifying a secret transmitted to him by his father.

To begin the anasemic analysis of this symptom and, thus, trace it back to the phantom of racism and indifference I referenced earlier, I resort to Esther Rashkin's fascinating work bridging Abraham and Torok's psychoanalytic paradigms and cultural studies. She states, for instance, that

> The symptoms displayed by an individual haunted by a phantom lie beyond the scope of any hermeneutic theory or tool previously offered by psychoanalysis. This is because the processes of symptom-formation associated with the phantom differ from the mechanism known as the return of the repressed. What returns to haunt is the "unsaid" and "unsayable" of *an other*. The silence, gap or secret in the speech of someone else "speaks," in the manner of a ventriloquist, through the words and acts (readable as words) of the subject.
>
> (*Family Secrets* 28)

Using this explanation as an analytical prism, I conclude that the protagonist/narrator's intimate interest in declassifying and disclosing the contents of official archives, an integral part of his journalistic career, is an illustration of his role as a ventriloquist for "el Gaucho" who, as the novel indicates, was ostensibly interested in declassifying, denouncing, and outright defying the political elites' inefficiency to consolidate and guarantee the well-being of the country (144, 224).

This notion is further confirmed when the protagonist/narrator symbolically addresses his late father directly and tells him the following:

> Have you transferred to me your incomplete endeavors? My inheritance is something that I did not claim but that fell on my shoulders; something that was implanted in me. Since I realized that, I do not trust certain goals or purposes: many of those are your old objectives, only hidden.
>
> (347)

The character's interest in disclosing secrets (his "words and acts" to use Rashkin's terminology) is, then, a continuation of "el Gaucho's" unrelenting and unfinished search for the shameful secret that lies at the center of Peru's unstable and problematic social and political reality. In other words, the emphasis that the protagonist/narrator puts in declassifying his father's archives is akin to searching for the shameful secret that gave birth to the chronic social fragmentation experienced in the country that was particularly highlighted during the years of the conflict.

Neither the protagonist/narrator nor "el Gaucho" is able to identify this shameful secret. The theory of the phantom, however, provides us, anasemic readers of the novel, with an additional set of tools to identify this foundational drama. As discussed earlier, Rashkin indicates that those who receive the phantom become ventriloquists for "*[t]he silence*, gap or secret in the speech of someone else" (*Family Secrets* 28, my emphasis). In order to find the shameful secret that causes the social fragmentation in Peru, therefore, we need to focus not only on what is said in the text. Instead, we should also seek this secret in the silence or, more specifically, in what is left unsaid or is unsayable about the country's multiple social chasms throughout the text of the novel.

In a culturally heterogenous country such as Peru and especially in the context of the armed conflict, the massive influence that the racist attitudes inherited from colonial times has in the social fragmentation of the country cannot be ignored. Yet, despite the fact that racial differences are present in most social dynamics among Peruvians, the text of *La distancia que nos separa* contains only two racialized terms in its almost 400 pages: "cholo" and "zambo."[8] The former appears twice in the novel, in the same paragraph, and in both instances the word is used as a nickname (and not as a slur) to refer to two inconsequential characters who were friends of "el Gaucho" and also officers with the highest ranks in the Peruvian military: "El Cholo Balta" and "El Cholo Noriega" (175). The latter term is repeated a total of nine times in the novel and it is also used as an endearing nickname to refer to Garcés, an enlisted soldier of mixed race who served as a domestic worker in the Cisneros household for several years and who, for being "a hard worker . . . earned the family's unanimous trust" (144).

The limited use of racialized terminology and the endearing context in which "cholo" and "zambo" are used in the novel does not mean that race is an unimportant element in the text's narrative structure. Far from it. The apparent silence about race in *La distancia que nos separa* does, in fact, suggest that Peruvians from the social and political elites, like the protagonist/narrator and his father, approach racism as a natural part of the experience of living in the country. Jean Franco points out that, in Peru, "the language and discourse of discrimination" is not seen as an "obvious form of degrading insult but also as *'common sense'* and political philosophy" (2, my emphasis). The fact that the protagonist/narrator does not feel the need to use additional racialized terms in the novel, not even to illustrate the manner of speaking of his characters, indicates, thus, that he is no longer able to see the insulting potency of these terms. This becomes clear when one considers that, although the character mentions that "el Zambo" Garcés was eventually virtually adopted by him as an "older brother and accomplice" (144), he never mentions his first name. Although Garcés plays an important role in the protagonist/narrator's life, the main characteristic for which he is remembered is not his devotion to the family or his strong work ethic but, instead, that he was of mixed race.

Since the phantom of racism and indifference is transmitted generationally, the seemingly natural omission of racialized terminology that does, in fact, animate the sentiments of racism among the Peruvian elites is also a characteristic in "el Gaucho's" behavior. Making the contemporary relevance of the outdated national project of the early Peruvian republic evident, for instance, the character vehemently teaches the protagonist/narrator about the greatness of the ancient Mochica, Chavín, and Tiahuanaco indigenous civilizations but fails to mention anything about the precariousness experienced by contemporary indigenous communities (315). Furthermore, when discussing his views about how to deal with the Shining Path, el Gaucho explicitly shows his racism by explaining that all those involved in the conflict "have the same features of the men from the mountains" using, once again, a euphemistic phrase that galvanizes the silence present in the text in terms of race or racism (204).

This silence, moreover, is also paradoxically telling when one considers that the protagonist/narrator does not seem to recognize the complicit role he plays in the extensively discriminatory Peruvian society. As a matter of fact, he sees himself on the other side of the political spectrum. Without any reservations, the character shares with the readers the details of the political awakening he experienced while attending college in the late 1990s when, according to his narration, he was able to feel "the rage of those who have spent years suffering and complaining in 'a shitty country,' backward, unequal, where thousands treated each other with contempt and disputed few opportunities to improve their lives" (270). He neglects to explain, however, what is behind the suffering, contempt, and inequality that afflicts those who are not able to access the few available opportunities to improve, namely, the racial and cultural discrimination that places the indigenous and mestizo majorities at the bottom of the country's social structure and the white elites, of which he is part, on its apex.

Silence is also an important aspect of *La hora azul* albeit in a different manner than in *La distancia que nos separa*. Instead of being a symptom of a phantom, silence is what triggers other symptoms in Adrián Ormache, the novel's protagonist. In his efforts to gather information about his father's involvement in the war, Adrián befriends and eventually has an affair with Miriam, a young indigenous woman who, as a teenager, was kidnapped and raped by his father while he served in Ayacucho, the Andean region of Peru where the conflict had its epicenter. Miriam has a son named Miguel and, although it is never explicitly said in the novel, the text suggests that this child is, in fact, Adrián's half-brother. In his analysis of the novel, Víctor Vich notes that Miriam and Miguel "do not speak or speak little and are represented to the readers with a margin of silence" (240). For Vich, "their silence is their answer to, or their testimony about everything that has happened" (240). In other words, silence is how they deal with the unhealed wounds left by the conflict. This silence, however, infuriates Adrián whose need for information is incompatible with Miriam's decision to remain silent. This becomes clear when, after she refuses to answer his questions in a restaurant, he tells her that "next time [he] will [get] a girl that would at least speak [to him], not a mute like [her]" (248). The issue is that, unbeknownst to Adrián, Miriam's silence is telling him everything he needs to know about her experiences during the war: that it is her prerogative whether to speak or not about her trauma. In other words, Adrián is not really listening to Miriam and, as Vich indicates, he is only trying to fit her experiences within his "'knowledge' about the Peruvian reality that is never questioned and where there are no destabilizing elements" (236).

It is important to mention here that there is an intimate relationship between the silence that appears in the novels and the social realities in Peru. In a poignant criticism of the TRC's *Informe final*, Anne Lambright notes that the document "claims that the conflict cannot be labeled an ethnic conflict because the parties involved (the insurgents and the state) did not define themselves ethnically but politically" (16). Furthermore, she indicates that "[t]he *Informe* . . . avoids terms that point to an ethnically or racially inflected conflict (such as indigenous, Quechua, Ashaninka), preferring terms like 'peasant,' 'humble,' 'poor,' or 'disenfranchised'" (16). These word choices, then, purposely marginalize the shameful truth that the conflict's violence was able to reach such brutal levels only because the majority of its victims were indigenous and, thus, insignificant in the eyes of the white *Limeño* elites. Saying it in another way, the use of euphemisms to refer to the indigenous population that endured most of the conflict's violence due to the inaction and indifference of those in power is how the *Informe final* buries Peruvian society's most shameful secret: the fact that it would have been able to intervene to prevent or ameliorate the suffering of the indigenous population that were disproportionately victimized during the conflict but that it chose not to do anything due to the structural racism and contempt that has been inherited from colonial times.

The Obsession With "Truth"

The psychic symptom featured in these two novels that most clearly connects the moral shortcomings highlighted during the conflict and the phantom of racism and indifference inherited by the Peruvian elites is the overwhelming desire that their protagonists feel to uncover the "truth" about their father's past, especially their participation in the war, and particularly their involvement in instances of human rights abuses committed during the conflict. Adrián in *La hora azul* and the unnamed protagonist/narrator of *La distancia que nos separa*—a powerful lawyer and a popular media personality, respectively, who are unquestionable members of the white *Limeño* elites—are obsessed with gaining as much information as possible about their late fathers, both of them high-ranking officers in the Peruvian armed forces. The term "obsession" is not used here lightly since their behavior proves that they are willing to do anything and everything to uncover the truth about their fathers, even if this implies resorting to physical violence or jeopardizing their family and professional lives. Adrián, for instance, gets into a fight with one of his father's men when he finds out that his mother had been blackmailed by the former military man with scandalous pictures depicting his father and Miriam (123). The protagonist/narrator of *La distancia que nos separa*, conversely, wants to dedicate all his time to his investigation so he resigns to his job as a radio presenter using as an excuse the fact that "he needed the four hours a day that [his job at the radio station] demanded to write" about his father's life (70–71).

This significant level of obsession is certainly not unusual in a psychic situation where a phantom is involved. Rashkin points out, for instance, that "[t]he language and behavior of the child who has unknowingly received this silent communication or 'phantom' may be diagnosed as *obsessive*, compulsive, phobic . . . even epileptic" (*Unspeakable Secrets* 94, my emphasis). What makes these characters' obsessions particularly compelling in the Peruvian contemporary context, nonetheless, is that they are reflective of the truth-seeking processes executed by the TRC while investigating the human rights abuses committed during the two decades of internal conflict. As the Commission did during its three years of existence, Adrián and the protagonist/narrator of *La distancia que nos separa* feel they have a mandate to learn as much as they can about their fathers and about the pain they may have inflicted on others during the years of political violence. They also speak with witnesses and do extensive archival work. Furthermore, they feel the same sense of guilt (or perhaps we can call it shame) that the government-organized Commission felt when it concluded that, in Peru, there was "a general guilt, a guilt of omission, that involves all of those who *let things happen* without raising any questions during the years of violence" (Lerner 14).

Although most academic discussions about the TRC refrain from questioning its good intentions, some scholars have been critical of certain aspects of its work, especially of the emphasis the Commission placed on finding the truth about the conflict. Lambright, for instance, comments that, in the discourse adopted by the TRC, the truth-seeking process brings a sort of moral purification to the country and that it functions as a redeeming process that could yield "both justice and reconciliation" and thus would be able to "set a renewed Peru free" (13). Lambright finds this fascination with the truth troublesome. Echoing Elizabeth Jelin's ruminations on how memory creates social conflict and political struggle, Lambright points out that the TRC never asks itself "whose truth is the true truth?" (13). Furthermore, she indicates that the Commission also neglects to question "its adequacy to address social justice issues in Peru" (13). At the heart of her concern lies the fact that, in her view,

> the Peruvian Truth Commission (despite its best intentions) locates the atrocities of the times within a juridical and therapeutic discourse that marginalizes indigenous and rural Andean experiences and eschews potential acts of reconciliation and national reconstruction based on Andean cultural values and social practices.
>
> (2)

In other words, and once again explicitly refraining from questioning its laudable intentions, Lambright considers the TRC's fascination with its own truth-seeking process as an inherently flawed approach to addressing the moral shortcomings highlighted by the conflict, namely the racism and marginalization endured by the indigenous populations of the country. According to Lambright, this inadequacy is primarily underscored by the fact that "even though the Commission was extra-official, composed by the government but independent, in the end it was a Lima-based bureaucratic organization that would determine the whats, whys, and hows of truth gathering and reconciliation in Peru" (10). That is to say, the TRC efforts were aimed at enforcing the social integration of the marginalized segments of the country, not at co-determining with them the terms of this integration. Lambright extends this point further by astutely pointing out that although "[t]here is a call to integrate indigenous peoples" in the Commission's discourse, they are to be integrated "as citizens of a national project very much rooted in neoliberal aspirations of modernization and economic prosperity," a prescription that has proved to be not only ineffective but indeed harmful for marginalized and socially vulnerable population segments (12).

Lambright's poignant criticism of the TRC is relevant when reading the obsessive behavior of Adrián and of the protagonist/narrator of *La distancia* as a psychic symptom of the shameful phantom they have inherited from previous generations. The extreme importance the Commission gives to truth-seeking is eerily akin to the rather destructive obsession the protagonists of the two novels display in their gathering of information about their fathers' involvement in the war. They are both moved by sentiments of guilt about not having known their late fathers and, thus, not having known the truth about the conflict and the many injustices committed therein. Yet, just as the Commission, they are not able (and perhaps not willing) to recognize and assume responsibility for their role or complicity in the deeply unequal Peruvian society.

This inability (or unwillingness) to conduct an exercise of moral self-assessment has been amply analyzed in the context of *La hora azul*. For instance, while discussing the final scene of the novel, in which Miriam's son—and quite possibly

Adrián's half-brother, Miguel—thanks the lawyer for providing him with the financial support he needs to pursue a college education, Vich notes that

> the fact that the victim "thanks" someone who is a representative of power reinforces the vertical communication between one social section and another, and it could be said that it promotes complacency towards the inherited guilt. [Because,] after all, after listening to [Miguel's] thanks, Ormache will begin to feel good about everything he is doing and will go back home a bit happier.
>
> (242)

Keeping in mind that this is the last scene of the novel and that it takes place after Adrián has met Miriam, listened to her story, established a sexual relationship with her, and witnessed her death, Miguel's gratefulness is quite significant when discussing Cueto's novel as part of the cultural corpus of the armed conflict.[9] The fact that financing Miguel's studies, without integrating him fully into his family or social circle as the novel indicates (300–301), is enough for Adrián to consider as redressed his father's heinous kidnapping and raping of 17-year-old Miriam indicates that discovering the truth is insufficient to instate social reconciliation in Peru. The fact that Adrián is satisfied with his father's decision to finance Miguel's studies—without offering to integrate him into his family or social circle (300–301)—as sufficient moral redress for the father's heinous crimes against 17-year-old Miriam indicates that discovering the truth is insufficient to instate social reconciliation in Peru. It is, in fact, a perhaps unintentional but nonetheless accurate snapshot of how widespread the phantom of racism continues to be among the Peruvian elites. To this point, Vich concludes that

> the narrative universe of La hora azul suspends politics, and all of it is a cruel testimony of how power has started to function in contemporary Peru. It is, of course, a power that is now "more solidary," "more human," but that ultimately maintains a strong paternalistic structure.
>
> (244)

The still paternalistic yet slightly more humane character that Vich attributes to the contemporary Peruvian elites through his reading of La hora azul appears in a different but similarly powerful manner in La distancia que nos separa. In Cisneros's novel, the unnamed protagonist/narrator's quest for the truth about his father, once again, a fictionalized version of the author's actual father, the controversial Peruvian Army General Luis "el Gaucho" Cisneros, is presented as an uncomfortable yet necessary subjective enterprise for the character. He states, for instance, that his inquiry into his father's past has as its main motivation the desperation he feels for "not knowing [,] [not] being sure, [and] suspecting so much about 'el Gaucho's' life" (61). He also explicitly indicates that what brings this desperation is that he has stopped believing the stories that others have told him about his father as well as those his father told about himself (61). Furthermore, he states that he is specifically looking for "the authentic stories and photographs of those disheartening and abhorrent passages that are not part of the authorized history of [his] father," namely the "veiled, shameful, or infamous facts that also took place but that nobody is bothered to describe" (62).

The importance the protagonist/narrator places in exploring his father's most questionable actions appears, a priori, as a positive model for the Peruvian elites to consciously and retrospectively assess their responsibility in the suffering inflicted on so many indigenous individuals during the armed conflict (and before). Although the character does, in fact, uncover several unflattering facts about his father's life (such as his friendship with and admiration toward the leaders of the military junta that ruled Argentina in the 1970s and 1980s, and the abandonment of his first wife and three older children to start a new family with a younger woman), he is unable to take a sufficiently critical posture toward "el Gaucho," assuming instead a more emotionally nuanced perspective of his father that, ultimately, redeems him.[10] For instance, after discussing how his father had decided to take a job as the military attaché in the Peruvian embassy in Paris, a position that according to the protagonist/narrator was considerably below his rank, the character explicitly states that he "cannot judge him, that [he is] nobody to judge him" (151). This redeeming tone is consolidated toward the end of the novel where the protagonist/narrator provides the following conclusion:

> Although it may not seem so, the villains are also made of wounds. My father was a uniformed villain. His uniform was a scab. Open sores that nobody saw were under, he never showed them. If I expose these open sores is to heal my father. Because my father is not a scab, not a wound. Not anymore.
>
> (354)

By giving discursive predominance to "el Gaucho's" emotional wounds (or scabs), this conclusion effectively tells the reader that the questionable behavior of the protagonist/narrator's father should only be marginally considered in the retrospective analysis of his life. In other words, the novel insinuates that "el Gaucho's" emotional disappointments (such as taking a job that was beneath him or not being able to marry his adolescent girlfriend due to military regulations) somehow erases the suffering he may have inflicted on others (his older children, his first wife, the victims of his authoritarian tendencies and of the counterinsurgency efforts he led in Ayacucho while serving as minister of war, etc.). The fact that he also experienced emotional anguish, this conclusion suggests, is enough to redress the wrongs he committed or may have committed when alive.

Conclusion: Limited Reconciliation

The allegorical connection that exists between the TRC's truth-finding objective and the protagonists' task in both novels underlines the insufficiency and inadequacy of the TRC's model of "reconciliation." Defined in its 2003 *Informe final* as "the implementation of a process to reestablish and refound the fundamental links among Peruvians, links that were intentionally destroyed or deteriorated by the explosion of the conflict" (IX: 13), Peru is still far from reconciliation; at least from the type proposed by the TRC. Kimberly Theidon sustains that "locally based processes of administering both retributive and restorative justice have been remarkably successful" in some indigenous communities in Ayacucho aimed at reincorporating members who were exiled or shunned for their participation in the conflict (107). The success of this micropolitics of reconciliation has not been recreated at the national level, however. Even when the TRC was still active, "members of the *criollo* political elite [in Peru] lined up to distance themselves from the very idea of reconciliation" (Theidon 107). This discursive rejection of the process of reconciliation, beyond its political and legal motivations, drives Theidon to reflect upon how the conflict's mainly indigenous victims remain distant for "middle-and upper-class residents of Lima," a social reality that reminds us "that when members of the criollo political elite imagine the community that constitutes '*El Perú,*' no Quechua-speaking campesino appears in the portrait" (108).

Theidon's disheartening but accurate appraisal of the fragmented and unequal social situation in post-conflict Peru also applies to the social conditions represented in *La hora azul* and *La distancia que nos separa* and, even further, to the social attitudes of those segments of the Peruvian elites who initially endorsed the TRC's model of reconciliation. These segments, of which both Cisneros and Cueto are members, were perhaps appalled by the findings of the Commission but did little or nothing to substantially address their role in the extremely unequal social circumstances of the country, a situation that has remained unchanged during the last 500 years. The most bewildering characteristic of this situation, thus, is that the racism and indifference that yields this fragmentation, as Franco points out, is a "pervasive and stealthy common sense that is not perceived" by the elites but only by those at the lowest levels of the social hierarchy (3). The racism, indifference, and contempt toward the indigenous populations in Peru that catalyzed the brutality of the conflict have become an unconscious response in the country's social dynamics. It has become a phantom.

Notes

1 Juan Carlos Ubilluz's *Nuevos súbditos: cinismo y perversión en la sociedad contemporánea* (2006), an astute critical assessment of globalization, is perhaps the best-known scholarly volume dedicated to seeing Peruvian society through psychoanalysis.
2 Ubilluz is also of the few scholars who have used a psychoanalytic prism to analyze Peruvian cultural production thematically connected to the conflict. *Contra el sueño de los justos: la literatura peruana ante la violencia política* (2009), a volume he co-wrote with Alexandra Hibbett and Víctor Vich contains chapters where he analyses works by Mario Vargas Llosa and Luis Nieto Degregori with the aid of psychoanalytic (mostly Lacanian) notions.

3 The protagonist/narrator only visits Colmenares once at the beginning of the novel. This fleeting interest in psychoanalysis, according to de la Paz Amaro, reduces its role in the text's plot to a simple rhetorical strategy that "allows the narrator to legitimately open the gates of memory" (101).

4 I have addressed the problematic model of reconciliation proposed by *La distancia que nos separa* elsewhere. Please see Celis-Castillo ("The First Steps").

5 For discussions about the role of the limeño literary elites in the representation of the conflict, please see Castro; Cox.

6 Unless otherwise noted, all translations are mine.

7 The origin of the nickname given to the real Cisneros Vizquerra is not discussed in the novel, but it could perhaps be attributed to the fact that he was born in Argentina, the homeland of the iconic South American figures known as "gauchos" or perhaps a reference to the colloquial use of the term in Argentina to refer to someone who is particularly brave and resilient. The novel endorses the latter possibility as the origin of the fictitious Cisneros Vizquerra's name. It was, in fact, given to him as a child by a doctor in Buenos Aires who, while stitching a cut he had inflicted in his own hand to impress other children, commented on his stoic behavior by telling his mother "Madam, your son is a true gaucho" (37).

8 Both terms are linguistic remains of the practices of racial taxonomy established during colonial times. They were originally used to refer to individuals of mixed races found at the bottom of the social hierarchy (mostly Indians and Blacks). They are used often in contemporary Peru and although they can be used as endearing nicknames to imply camaraderie, they are mostly uttered as racial slurs.

9 The Oedipal implications of Adrián's sexual relationship with Miriam, the woman his father also desired, are clear. This analysis, nonetheless, goes beyond the scope of this chapter.

10 For a more in-depth exploration of the narrator/protagonist's model of reconciliation, please see Celis-Castillo ("The First Steps").

Works Cited

Abraham, Nicolas, and Maria Torok. *The Shell and the Kernel*, edited, translated, and with an Introduction by Nicholas T. Rand. Vol. 1. U of Chicago P, 1994.

Castro, Dante. "¿Narrativa de la violencia o disparate absoluto?" *Sasachakuy tiempo: memoria y pervivencia*, edited by Mark R. Cox. Editorial Pasacalle, 2010, pp. 25–30.

Celis-Castillo, Pablo G. "The First Steps Towards Reconciliation: Memory Work, Critical Consciousness, and Emancipation in Renato Cisneros's *La distancia que nos separa*." *A Contracorriente: Una revista de estudios latinoamericanos*, vol. 18, no. 1, Fall 2020, pp. 57–78.

Cisneros, Renato. *La distancia que nos separa*. Seix Barral, 2015.

Cox, Mark R. "Describiendo lo ajeno: narrativa criolla sobre la guerra interna en Ayacucho." *Conflicto armado y políticas culturales de la memoria en el Perú*, número especial de *Hispanic Issues On Line (HIOL)*, vol. 17, 2016, pp. 33–46, conservancy.umn.edu/handle/11299/184553. Accessed 9 May 2021.

Cueto, Alonso. *La hora azul*. Ediciones Anagrama, 2005.

De la Paz Amaro, Lorena. "El discurso autobiográfico y la responsabilidad de los 'hijos' en un contrapunto escritural: en torno a *Los rendidos*, de José Carlos Agüero, y *La distancia que nos separa*, de Renato Cisneros." *Cuadernos del CILHA*, vol. 18, no. 2, 2017, pp. 95–119.

Franco, Jean. "Alien to Modernity: The Rationalization of Discrimination." *A Contracorriente: una revista de estudios latinoamericanos*, vol. 3, no. 3, Spring 2006, pp. 1–16.

Lambright, Anne. *Andean Truths: Transitional Justice, Ethnicity, and Cultural Production in Post-Shining Path Peru*. Liverpool UP, 2015.

Lerner Febres, Salomón. "Prefacio." *Informe final* by Comisión de la Verdad y Reconciliación del Perú. Vol. 1. CVR, 2003, pp. 13–17.

Perú, Comisión de la Verdad y Reconciliación. *Informe Final*. 9 vols. CVR, 2003.

Rashkin, Esther. *Family Secrets and the Psychoanalysis of Narrative*. Princeton UP, 1992.

———. *Unspeakable Secrets and the Psychoanalysis of Culture*. SUNY P, 2008.

Theidon, Kimberly. "Histories of Innocence: Postwar Stories in Peru." *Localizing Transitional Justice: Interventions and Priorities After Mass Violence*, edited by Rosalind Shaw et al. Stanford UP, 2010, pp. 92–110.

Ubilluz, Juan Carlos. *Nuevos súbditos: cinismo y perversión en la sociedad contemporánea*. IEP Instituto de Estudios Peruanos, 2006.

Ubilluz, Juan Carlos, Alexandra Hibbett, and Víctor Vich, eds. *Contra el sueño de los justos: la literatura peruana ante la violencia política*. IEP Instituto de Estudios Peruanos, 2009.

Vich, Víctor. "Violencia, culpa y repetición: *La hora azul* de Alonso Cueto." *Contra el sueño de los justos: la literatura peruana ante la violencia política*, edited by Juan Carlos Ubilluz, Alexandra Hibbett, and Víctor Vich. IEP Instituto de Estudios Peruanos, 2009.

Chapter 5

From "Work of Mourning" to "Spectral Figurations"

Contributions of Psychoanalysis to the Listening of the Emotional Management of Absence in Cases of Political Violence in Latin America

Translation: Veronika Brejkaln

Juan Pablo Aranguren-Romero and Juan Nicolás Cardona-Santofimio

The figure of the disappeared and the impunity that often surrounds this individual has produced an alteration of habitual cartographies regarding our understanding of the emotional management of absence. By situating the lost object as a non-living-undead or an absent-present, the disappeared designates a state of affairs in which the categories of life and death cease to be fully applicable. As such, forced disappearance not only *disappears* but also produces the *appearance* of other entities, which have tended to be situated in the field of the morbid, the pathological, or the deficient by the sciences of the "psy." Here, we refer to the emergence of what we call "spectral figurations": figures that not only run through the absence-presence dimension of the disappeared in the daily lives of those who search for this individual but also connote particular modes of emotional management and question the most classic ideas about what has been called "the work of mourning."

The modes of emotional management in the face of these forms of political violence challenge several of the epistemic frameworks that psychoanalysis and psychology have opened on mourning, since they trouble notions such as reality testing and demand a critical look at the assumption of some psychic elaboration processes, as derived from some interpretations of Sigmund Freud's essay, "Mourning and Melancholia." For the most part, these new developments have produced a kind of condemnation of the spectral ontology of the disappeared, coupled with attempts to make the experience of family members fit in the field of mourning under figures that announce grief's freezing or ambiguity.

However, it is also from Latin America that the use of a language of ghosts and specters has gained relevance within research on the contexts of political violence

DOI: 10.4324/9781003266211-7

and the emotional management of the relatives of the disappeared, pointing out the need to explore alternative meanings that recognize the ways in which the relationship with absence builds worlds and leads to an environment of habitability. This article proposes, first, a critical discussion of the more traditional notions of grief which are partly inherited from the psychoanalytic perspective grounded in the notion of the work of mourning to then show the emergence of other concepts that, also from psychoanalysis, have made possible the understanding of spectral presences in the contexts of political violence in Latin America. Thus, the article also questions the categorical distinctions between mourning and melancholia, proposing the need to explore more mobile and fluctuating categories between both affective phenomena. It also critically reflects on the libidinal psychodynamics of mourning, which indicates that the lost object is always an irreplaceable object without any necessary correspondence. The article shows how, in the Latin American context, spectral figures essentially emerge in resistance to impunity.

Mourning and Melancholia: The Epistemological Problem of Forced Disappearance

Undoubtedly, from its beginnings, psychoanalysis has been interested with almost the same zeal in the work of mourning as in the spectral. In fact, ghosts appear and manifest themselves in different ways in "Mourning and Melancholia," where Freud articulates various hypotheses about the relationship between the human and the spectral, also developed in *Totem and Taboo*. However, these Freudian analyses have been poorly integrated into the conceptualization of grief.

In "Mourning and Melancholia," Freud seeks to distinguish the phenomena of melancholia from the normal process of mourning. The comparison begins with an exhaustive description of grief as a psychic phenomenon caused by the loss of a loved object, be it a person or an abstraction. Here the subject faces an examination of reality that shows them that the loved object no longer exists. As a result, a process of decathexis becomes imperative, whereby the libido is detached from the lost object, demanding the renouncement of its investment in it. This will be slow and arduous work, as the first reaction to loss is an understandable reluctance to leave the libidinal position: "normally, respect for reality gains the day. Nevertheless, its orders cannot be obeyed at once. They are carried out bit by bit, at great expense of time and cathectic energy, and in the meantime the existence of the lost object is psychically prolonged" (Freud, "Mourning" 245).

Grief requires active psychic work that is processed piece by piece on the libidinal links and ties with the object (Díaz 19), in such a way that, when faced with the initial mechanism of denial that resists the reality of loss, the latter obtains its triumph and the subject finds themselves able to redistribute their psychic energy to other substitute objects that begin to appear: "each single one of the memories and situations of expectancy which demonstrate the libido's attachment to the lost object *is met by the verdict of reality that the object no longer exists*" (Freud, "Mourning" 255; our emphasis).

However, in the face of events that go hand in hand with repression and political violence, wars, and armed conflicts, what is the reality that must be respected? What is the verdict that reality pronounces? Are these perhaps not the contexts of a field of production of the living dead, souls in pain, bodies without mourning, and dead without relatives that highlight the uncertain, the open, and the abject as their proof of reality? Are they not, then, about scenarios in which the verdict only accounts for the unacceptability of the injustices and horrors of war?

In the contexts of political violence and war, then, reality tests that entail a representational catastrophe emerge: bodies without names and names without a body—as in the case of forced disappearance—but also fragmented bodies, subjects that become mere suffering bodies, bodies that are constituted as simple war machines. This split between body and subject alludes to an impossibility that, nevertheless, emerges with a certain strange recurrence in all the scenarios of war and political violence. Taylor characterizes these scenarios in light of what he calls "percepticide," insofar as they are alterations of the referents with which one can make sense of the world (123–124), but before which signifiers also emerge that seek to conjure this catastrophe of meaning.

In the figure of the disappeared, for example, the absurdity of the split between body and subject and the attempt to make sense of what makes no sense pass as the signifier. The figure of the disappeared runs on the side of uncertainty and ambivalence: "A living-dead, neither absent nor present, an empty space or the void itself" (Gatti, *El detenido-desaparecido* 29). The event of disappearance destroys the basic coordinates that on a day-to-day basis allow us to make sense of events: presence and absence, here and there, life and death. However, "by virtue of a prolonged uncertainty, the absence of information, the search repertoires that unfold everyday, and the anguished and perennial wait" (Agudelo and Aranguren 3), disappearance also constitutes a scenario where family members demand the deployment of repertoires of meaning to manage the catastrophe.

As such, the repertoires of meaning that are deployed attempt not only to refit what was split between body and subject—for example, the search processes aimed at restoring the body of the disappeared person that would be on the side of the reality test—but also to highlight that bordering place that was engendered in the figure of the disappeared (precisely that of an absence-presence), which would be on the side of what we have called spectral figurations (Aranguren et al. 9).

Evidently, these figures of the spectral are not easily understandable under the concepts on which the "work of mourning" is built within the Freudian approach: proof, examination, and mandate of reality. This is because forced disappearance constitutes a great epistemological challenge in the apprehension of these absences-presences insofar as they allude to an attempt to break a condition proper to the subject: the link between identity, social bond, and body. If this fracture is installed as a representational catastrophe or a catastrophe of meaning (Richard 10; Gatti, *El detenido-desaparecido* 28), an emergency field of the undead (Diéguez 170) or even a specter-producing biopolitic (Mahlke 76; Schindel 59), the primacy of the reality test would collide with the complex liminal ontological status of the disappeared and with the human possibility of establishing links with the spectral presences of these absent-present emergences.

For Jean Allouch, the Freudian approach to grief has been slow to digest the savagery of the World Wars, which has left no mourning ritual. Likewise, María Elmiger highlights that the context in which Freud wrote "Mourning and Melancholia" was marked by the fact that the war-caused deaths ended up banishing mourning from the public to the intimate, without rituals that delimited the anguish or the emptiness of death.

The added complexity produced in contexts of war is articulated by Allouch in her structural critique of the Freudian model of mourning, which, in turn, is pertinent to understand the epistemological problem that forced disappearance entails. For this author, the problem of "Mourning and Melancholia" lies in the logical impossibility of making assertions about the inexistence of the other:

> From the point of view of reality, . . . the dead person is, as he is also called, a disappeared person. . . . But a missing person, by definition, is someone that can reappear, and reappear anywhere, at any time, at the next corner. . . . In spite of this, the mourner will certainly have the experience that the lost object is not there. And in another place? To speak of a reality test, it would be necessary to also be conclusive about that other place, as this is the only way to subvert the status of disappeared person. But that does not happen.
> (Allouch 71–73)

The problem of the spectrality of the disappeared person is situated in a field where neither direct nor indirect ostension is sufficient to prove the existence or nonexistence of a ghost (Cardona 47). Allouch concludes that if there is a reality that dictates a mandate on mourning, this would be, in the case of the disappeared, that of an area in which it is not possible to prove the death of the lost loved object.

Part of the problem that surrounds the figure of the disappeared person is that it has tended to be analyzed from a kind of denial of its impossible character. Precisely, the experience of those looking for the disappeared has been characterized by uncertainty and ambivalence, which is why, in the field of psy sciences, the catastrophic dimension, the impossibility, and the nonsense that surround the disappearance are collected under categories such as frozen mourning (Rando 46), complex grief, or ambiguous loss (Boss 60–65). In these categories, it is common to resort to the analytical frameworks derived from a duty to mourn which, given the exceptional conditions caused by the disappearance, faces its incompleteness. That is to say, the relationship with the disappeared person is presented as a missing ritual in which it would somehow suffice—although it is no small thing—to have a body to close.

In this way, some of the aforementioned perspectives have contributed to overdetermining the role of forensic sciences in the grieving process, since the expectation of closure centered on the reality test of the loss depend on the discovery of the body (Garibian et al. 18). This same type of approach has ended up highlighting the search for a corpse when, in many cases, the experience of the relatives is also situated in the expectation of finding the missing person alive (Pérez-Sales and Navarro 330). However, impunity in the face of enforced disappearance has ended up showing that the elaboration of grief does not culminate with rites after the exhumation process, but is usually confronted with the sociopolitical conditions of the context and in the struggle of the relatives for justice and truth (Aranguren et al. 7).

An Impossible Zone Where Ghosts Reside

We have raised the idea, following Jean Allouch, that the figure of the disappeared usually travels through an area where it is not possible to prove the death or life of the lost loved object. This area is a kind of liminal space where spectral figures live quite comfortably. Thus, the emergence of ghosts in contexts of political violence in general, and enforced disappearance in particular, is linked not only to the absence of a body or a ritual, but also to the paradoxical condition of disappearance and the sociopolitical contexts in which this practice occurs. Although the ghost may assume the role of representation of absence-presence of the disappeared, and although it seems to fit well within the process of libidinal disinvestment associated with the work of mourning, it does not emerge as a substitution of the beloved lost object. On the contrary, it constitutes a presence that simultaneously covers the absurd dimension of being a disappeared person and marks the resistance to narratives of closure typical of the teleology of the elaboration of mourning and of the reconciling pretensions of the "post scenarios" (Aranguren et al.). Thus, spectral figurations are reluctantly accepted socially, not only due to the fact that their representational dimension militates on the opposite side or contrary to the epistemic frameworks of modernity but also because they highlight the fissures of the ideals of the models of transitional justice that invite to heal the wounds of a violent past.

This impossible area has been the subject of psychoanalytic exploration by suggesting new interpretive paths on the psychodynamics of losses. Several authors have questioned the categorical distinctions between grief and melancholia, thus generating more mobile, fluctuating, and porous conceptualizations between both affective phenomena that allow us to better apprehend the problem of forced disappearance and its emotional management. However, we must recognize that, even in their initial Freudian conceptualization, these categories have tended to overlap one another. Like mourning, melancholia is conceptualized by Freud as a reaction to a lost object, but in this case the object may not really be lost. It could be said that the fundamental problem of the melancholic consists of a failure both in the discernment of the object and in the type of loss that this implies. Thus, even if there is an identifiable lost object, it is not known what was really lost with it: ambivalence—of the affects—and ambiguity—of the status of the lost object—are predominant in the melancholic phenomenon. Moreover, the work of the libidinal processing of mourning, which is given piece by piece on the links with the object, is identical, according to Freud, to that of melancholia, but "in melancholia the relation to the object is no simple one; it is complicated by the conflict due to ambivalence, . . . in which hate and love contend with each other; the one seeks to detach the libido from the object, the other to maintain this position of the libido against the assault" ("Mourning" 256). The limits between the two phenomena are therefore porous in their initial definitions, thus avoiding an easily identifiable synthesis such as melancholia or expressions such as sorrowful mourning that easily overlap with it. As María Elmiger states, melancholia appears as a paradoxical mourning in Freudian thought (60).

Exploiting these paradoxes, Esther Peeren suggests that the spectral status of the disappeared makes the emotional reaction of the bereaved closer to what could be conceptualized as a "melancholic mourning" (146). That is, a non-pathological, persistent, painful, and endless reaction that welcomes the ambiguity of the relationship with an object that is not known to be irretrievably lost. Peeren, like Allouch, suggests that the reality test category loses explanatory weight in understanding the grief of ambiguous loss, which should also lead us to abandon the idea that the relationship with spectrality is based on a pathological denial of reality. Furthermore, a socially broad relational perspective is accentuated, which highlights grief as a space for interaction with emptiness: "the void left by their unexplained removal can be conjured only by other, on their terms, which must, moreover, make sense in the wider social realm" (Peeren 146). Peeren agrees with Elmiger in that in order to elaborate on this subjective void, generated by trauma and sustained in melancholic mourning, it must be situated in a plane of social listening that passes "through systems of a language that includes its equivalents: legal system, political system, linguistic systems, and even the various semiological systems, in order to be translated and tied to private practices and the intimacies of the unconscious" (Elmiger 58). The need to advance in the listening of the spectral which considers these sociopolitical dimensions and representations is, as we will see, the central axis of the emergence of these figures in Latin America.

The Emergence of Spectral Figures in Latin America

Since the mid-1980s, various therapeutic experiences in Latin America have challenged normalizing and transitional perspectives on enforced disappearance. Most of them, arising in the Southern Cone and Central America and influenced by psychoanalysis as well as liberation psychology, were conceived as accompanying practices aimed at listening differently to the uncertainty, ambivalence, and psychosocial impacts of impunity. This would constitute a perspective that linked the defense of human rights with mental health, materialized in projects such as the Psychological Assistance Team of the Mothers of Plaza de Mayo that emerged in the late seventies and later consolidated in the Argentine Work Team and Psychosocial Research (EATIP) in the early nineties; the Psychiatric Medical

Program of the Foundation for Social Aid of the Christian Churches (FASIC), the Latin American Institute of Mental Health and Human Rights (ILAS), and the Centre for Mental Health and Human Rights (CINTRA) in Chile; the Community Studies and Psychosocial Action Team of Guatemala; or in the important contributions of the psychoanalyst Marcelo Viñar in Uruguay.

People involved in these therapeutic experiences agree on the impossibility of basing the therapeutic accompaniment of cases of disappearance on traditional conceptions of the work of mourning (Edelman 73). They also highlight the need to place the experience of trauma into the social fabric as a social catastrophe (Kordon and Edelman 42) and the importance of recognizing the significance of disappearance both in the intimate sphere and in the social sphere (Viñar 60). At the same time, these mental health practitioners and activists underscore the relevance of questioning standardized psychodiagnostic settings insofar as these replicate the limitations of the category of post-traumatic stress disorder. This questioning of PTSD was referring to, among other things, the inability to think in contexts of current political violence in the region that was witnessed in the *post* stage of the traumatic event and the need to recognize the uniqueness and particularity of the event in each subject (Lira and Weinstein 6). At the same time, these reflections were intertwined with the need to establish, on the part of the therapist, a non-neutral ethical stance in the face of events of political violence. This has been pointed out by Ignacio Martin-Baró in regard to the role of psychology in contexts of war and inequality (302), which therefore assumes a compromised bond with the suffering of the other (Lira 19). All this imply the willingness to accept experiences that are traversed by the silencing and silences of official memories and by singular forms of memory as well as by absences that were present in particular ways (Sluzki 121).

Thus, the therapeutic experience in Latin American contexts has shown that disappearance constitutes, without a doubt, a significant event for the family member and that it possesses a high de-structuring potential because it dislocates the relationship between body and identity as it disrupts the spatiotemporal dimensions that determine the daily life of the subject. In any case, family members are faced with making daily life habitable through practices that affect the places to which they travel, the times in which they are situated, and the relationships they build with others. Far from being a way of filling the void of the absent person, overcoming the absence, or attaining closure, this "making habitable" refers instead to the ways and practices that the subject undertakes to emotionally manage the relationship with the disappeared. Thus, forced disappearance implies that family members, as well as the therapist, find themselves in an imprecise territory, between life and death, a "really swampy territory: words and things sink; their union is devastated" (Gatti, *The Language of Victims* 99). As expressed by Mahlke (77), fantasy cannot be distinguished from reality. Therefore, the expression of what happened is difficult and appeals to narratives that do not fit section by section with logos and rationality, but rather comfortably run through the absence of meaning (Gatti, *El detenido-desaparecido* 115).

However, a large part of research on the memories of relatives of the disappeared in Latin America has shown the relevance of the use of images and objects as a materialization of loss (Catela 129–130). Photographs, together with the objects belonging to the disappeared, have been shown as essential and significant pieces in the relatives' memories, particularly because they provide material support to the memory and because this materiality tends to express itself as an imperative of collective memory. Photographs and objects, at the same time as they are shown as banners of the memory of the disappeared, also reveal an immaterial dimension of memory that is expressed beyond the image or the objects themselves: they are sensitive and affective experiences. Although they derive from the social uses of objects, they are at the same time an attempt to ward off emptiness, absence, and the catastrophe of meaning caused by disappearance. Thus, family members caress the photographs, speak to them, ask them for advice or help, and preserve the items of daily use and clothing as if they kept something of the body of the absent person.

In these experiences, the relatives of the disappeared express non-tangible forms of memory that make up a form of habitability of the disappearance; that is, daily practices which are established with the ghost of the disappeared, not to ward off absence or fill the void, but to build a possible world on the ground of impossibility. In other words, in the face of the attempts by disappearing practices to fracture the body-subject link and in the face of the pretense of splitting the body of identity, family members' forms of memory make images and objects incarnate something of the absent body or distill some of its trace. A remnant of the body of the disappeared survives, exudes; the objects left by the disappeared incorporate—make a body—of the absent (Agudelo and Aranguren). It is for this reason that, in many cases, artistic initiatives tend to better represent the emotional experience of family members because "from their spectral and fragile materiality, and due to their ability to perform, execute, and occur in time as a symptomatic appearance" (Diéguez 222), they can invoke the missing person in their phantasmatic mode of production.

Creativities and Intangible Inheritances

The place that art occupies in the representation of the spectral status of the disappeared person bears a certain correlation with the figure of the acetic man who runs between ghosts, as portrayed by Giorgio Agamben. In *Stanzas*, Agamben traces a genealogy of melancholia that has its roots in the medieval conceptualization of acedia: an affective constellation that transits between *malitia, rancor, pusillanimitas, desperatio, torpor*, and *evagatio mentis*. The latter is the most defining characteristic of acedia, being an imaginative disturbance that leads the subject to run between internal and external phantasms. Acedia is also presented as a form of mourning that creates joy insofar as it motivates the search for what one is deprived of: "the slothful testifies to the obscure wisdom according to which hope has been given only for the hopeless, goals only for those who will always be unable to reach them" (Agamben 7).

The sad search for the unattainable was the characteristic that melancholia would have inherited from acedia. In the melancholic, the libido behaves as if it has lost its object, although it has not really lost anything. Such simulation opens an experiential field conducive to entering into a relationship with ghosts as an attempt of appropriation of a situation in which a loss which is not a loss occurs. Thus, in the intermediate zone between reality and unreality typical of melancholia, Agamben recognizes a radical creative strategy in which one can enter into a relationship with a lost object, a spectral possibility that is less fixed and more open than Freud could have conceptualized (Eng 13).

It is significant that Agamben considers melancholic mourning as an artistic practice that attempts to grasp the ungraspable and narrate the unspeakable. This aspect is also highlighted by Julia Kristeva in *Black Sun*, where she takes up the Greek notion of melancholia as a balanced diversity that produces reflexivity and creativity in a dance between black bile and foam: "Aristotle breaks new ground by removing melancholia from pathology and locating it in nature but also mainly by having it ensue from heat, considered to be the regulating principle of the organism, and mesotes, the controlled interaction of opposite energies" (7).

For Kristeva, melancholia is also presented as the experience of inexorable pain due to the loss of an object where the signifier fails to express its lost referent. Indeed, the melancholic mourns not for an object but for some "thing"; that is, for something rebellious to meaning: the indeterminate, the ungraspable. The melancholic thing is evoked—hence its relationship with the aesthetic and the corporeal: melody, rhythm, and semantic versatility—but it cannot be signified. And, although no erotic object can replace the irreplaceable—there is no substitute object to catechize or to de-detect the lost thing—the subject does not renounce attempts to represent their loss. In this way, for David Eng, the inadequacy of the signifier to the hole of loss can be read as the extension of the representative flexibility of melancholia that facilitates the work of mourning where it seems impossible. As Aranguren et al. argue, representative flexibility creates disparate bodies and (im)possible living spaces, and, according to Agudelo et al., unpredictable political practices and unexpected spectral relationships.

In considering the logic of melancholia, we could argue that this emergence of spectral figures would not be exclusive to the relationship with the disappeared. Instead, it would allude to a possible relationship with the dead in contexts different from those of political violence and war. We find a clue to this idea in Freudian thought itself. Years before publishing "Mourning and Melancholia," Freud wrote his famous work, *Totem and Taboo*, and in the chapter titled "Taboo and Emotional Ambivalence," he makes spectrality a central theme. The author begins the text by pointing out that the notion of taboo has two opposite meanings: that of the sacred and that of the impure. Of particular significance is the idea of reserve that expresses the prohibitions and restrictions of particular cultures, with one of the most important and universal taboos being the taboo of the dead.

Thus, in the analysis of the most common customs among peoples to safeguard themselves from the wrath of the dead, there are nominal taboos. These consist of the general prohibition of pronouncing the name of the deceased. Freud finds in this an essential association between name and person, which would turn out to be the fundamental link with which he could come into contact with the dead: "they feel that to utter his name is equivalent to invoking him and will quickly be followed by his presence" (Freud, *Taboo* 57). Even more interesting is the double possibility of a relationship with the spectral that arises from this reflection:

> Mourning has a quite specific psychical task to perform: its function is to detach the survivors' memories and hopes from the dead. When this has been achieved, the pain grows less and with it the remorse and self-reproaches and consequently the fear of the demon as well. And the same spirits who to begin with were feared as demons may now expect to meet with friendlier treatment; they are revered as ancestors and appeals are made to them for help.
>
> (Freud, *Taboo* 66)

To a certain extent, the work of mourning that is proposed in the analysis of the taboo of the dead outlines a different conception from that of "Mourning and Melancholia." Thus, rather than a libidinal disinvestment and substitution of the lost object, what occurs in this relationship with the dead is a transformation of the subjective position with respect to the lost object. From this emerges the possibility of establishing a spectral link with the deceased which allows a transition from demonic hostility to veneration and friendly invocation.

In this sense, we can affirm that the spectrum can emerge not only due to the absence of a body (that is, due to the absence of a reality test) but also due to the need of the sufferer to process, administer, or master a relationship with the absent. In this way, the emergence of spectral figures is not only a representational attempt to capture the catastrophe of meaning that forced disappearance entails but also a way of establishing a link, in another way, with the absent, including the deceased.

This relationship is particularly significant in the Latin American context. Research in the region has shown that the relationship with the dead and the disappeared is constantly integrated into spectral figures. In contexts of political violence and war, these figures and the porous boundaries between waking life and dream content, life and death, as well as souls and bodies are condensed. Cecconi, for example, has shown that in the context of political violence in Peru, dreams are a scenario for the spectral emergence of the disappeared who appear loaded with requests for the search for their bodies, even inspiring trips and specific practices aimed at finding them (Cecconi 155). Likewise, Woodrick has indicated that, in cases of violent deaths among the Yucatecan Mayans, the work of mourning does not necessarily imply an acceptance of the loss or a libidinal disinvestment of the object, since the deceased person in the strict sense does not abandon the living. In this way, deep relationships and communications are woven between the living and the dead, and even souls appear in dreams on a recurring basis (Woodrick 410). This point has also been reviewed in regard to the place of the dead and the disappeared among the Emberá in Colombia (Losonczy 70). Similarly, Garrard-Burnett argues that, in the Guatemalan context, the lack of justice has implied that people feel disappointed and frustrated, which is why they are more likely to seek remedies in the spectral relationship with the deceased and the disappeared (185); a point equally evidenced by Delacroix (64) in the context marked by the existence of clandestine graves in Peru.

Thus, faced with the difficulty of developing mourning processes or funeral rituals, and with the advent of exhumation practices, dreams are shown as the scene of emergence for these spectral figures. Thereby, dreams function as carriers of distressing or hopeful content or as revealers of commands of the dead or disappeared regarding justice, the search for their bodies or even as clues about the occurrence of their death (Mahlke 78; Mandolessi 60; Robben 137; Tello 36; Schindel 255).

The Absence of Justice as a Field of Emergence of the Spectrum

It is possible that the emergence of spectral figures in contexts of political violence in Latin America responds to ancestral and pre-Columbian forms of emotional loss management and to the particular relevance that the relationship with ancestors entails for different cultures. It is even possible that this relationship with the spectral is also an extension of the baroque-colonial forms of relationships with the dead in the region. However, it is evident that spectral figures emerge, above all, as a response to the sociopolitical conditions of impunity. Hence, it is possible to argue that the spectral dimension refers to an emotional management of absence much more than it refers to the exceptional.

Along these lines, Nicolas Abraham and María Török propose that inexpressible traumas generate such emotional upheavals that they lead mourners to bury the lost loved object in an intrapsychic crypt. This phenomenon is especially prevalent in griefs for abnormal losses; those in which mourning rites have been denied or those that are the product of great injustices. From this perspective, melancholic grief is not the result of the loss of an object but rather emerges from the loss of an object traversed by an irreparable, abrupt crime. This situation has the characteristic of not being able to communicate effectively and it is common that the loss cannot be recognized as such neither by the subject nor by their social context. In this case, the spectral phenomenon arises from the cryptic incorporation of the other inside the mourning subject:

> Inexpressible mourning erects a secret tomb inside the subject. Reconstituted from the memories of words, scenes, and affects the objectal correlative of the loss is buried alive in the crypt as a full-fledged person, complete with its own topography. . . . A whole world of unconscious fantasy is created, one that leads its own separate and concealed existence. Sometimes in the dead of the night, when libidinal fulfillments have their way, the ghost of

the crypt comes back to haunt the cemetery guard, giving him strange and incomprehensible signals, making him perform bizarre acts, or subjecting him to unexpected sensations.

(Abraham and Török 130)

The violent context in which the disappearance occurs and the impossibility of enunciating impunity itself make the disappeared a privileged object for its intra-psychic encryption in the suffering person. Put in this way, forced disappearance is shown, on the one hand, as an attempt to break the social bond, a disintegration of the libidinal ties that sustain the subject in the incommunicability of his loss, and, on the other, as an impossibility of libidinally disinvesting the absent loved object. As Piera Aulagnier maintains, some objects are not substitutable and under certain conditions the subject needs to maintain certain endowments to contain the functioning of his psychic structure (Aulagnier 70). The times, places, and objects of the disappeared person not only resist being decathected but even their spectral figuration shows it as an absence that demands its own libidinal investment or, as Winnicott says, an absence that claims for itself that "the negative is the only positive" (43).

These reservoirs of loss (Laplanche 249) imply a psychoanalytic challenge of renewed polyphonic listening. The mourner lends their own skin to the ghostly lost object, assumes their voice, and aligns themselves with it: they share the anger and pain that they jointly externalize. The melancholic mournings that involve a crypt confront analytical listening to dual-channel attention, where the bereaved is listened to, but also where the ghost and its afterlife mandates resist impunity and silence:

The phantom object haunts the process of countertransference as well and this fact represents a real danger in psychoanalytic therapy. Analysts may unwittingly target the phantom object, not realizing that for the melancholic the phantom (the incorporated object) is the only partner. Assigning aggression to the love object, the analyst actually speaks out the melancholic's most precious and most carefully concealed against treasure. And yet, we analysts are meant to recognize the love object behind all the disguises of hate and aggression. The realization that the one is pleased by the other's grief over him; the recognition not of the hate but of the love felt by the object for the subject; the acceptance ultimately of the narcissistic bliss at having received the object's love despite dangerous transgressions – this is what melancholics expect from psychoanalysis.

(Abraham and Török 136)

Works Cited

Abraham, Nicolas, and Mária Török. *The Shell and the Kernel: Renewals of Psychoanalysis*. U of Chicago P, 1994.

Agamben, Giorgio. *Stanzas: Words and Phantasm in Western Culture*. U of Minnesota P, 1993.

Agudelo, Juan Ángel, and Juan Pablo Aranguren. "Habitar la desaparición: Memorias sonoras de familiares de personas desaparecidas en Colombia." *Psicoperspectivas*, vol. 19, no. 3, 2020, pp. 1–11.

Agudelo, Juan Ángel, et al. "Materialidades espectrales: Resistencias sensibles a la desaparición forzada en Colombia." *Razón Crítica*, no. 9, 2020, pp. 103–130.

Allouch, Jean. *Erótica del duelo en tiempos de la muerte seca.* El cuenco de plata, 2006.

Aranguren, Juan Pablo. et al. "Inhabiting Mourning: Spectral Figures in Cases of Extrajudicial Executions (False Positives) in Colombia." *Bulletin of Latin American Research*, vol. 40, no. 1, 2021, pp. 6–20.

Aulagnier, Piera. *Un intérprete en busca de sentido.* Siglo XXI, 1994.

Boss, Pauline. *La pérdida ambigua. Cómo aprender a vivir con un duelo no terminado.* Gedisa, 2001.

Cardona, Juan Nicolás. *Fantasmagorías: un mosaico filosófico sobrenatural.* Fallidos editores, 2020.

Catela, Ludmila da Silva. *No habrá flores en la tumba del pasado: La experiencia de reconstrucción del mundo de los familiares de desaparecidos.* Ediciones Al Margen, 2009.

Cecconi, Arianna. "Cuando las almas cuentan la guerra: sueños, apariciones y visitas de los desaparecidos en la región de Ayacucho." *Las formas del recuerdo: Etnografías de la violencia política en el Perú.* Instituto de Estudios Peruanos, 2013, pp. 153–192.

Delacroix, Dorothée. "La presencia de la ausencia. Hacia una antropología de la vida póstuma de los desaparecidos en el Perú." *Íconos. Revista de Ciencias Sociales*, vol. 24, no. 67, 2020, pp. 61–74.

Díaz, Victoria. *La escritura del duelo.* Universidad de los Andes-Universidad EAFIT, 2019.

Diéguez, Ileana. *Cuerpos sin duelo. Iconografías y teatralidades del dolor.* Ediciones Documenta/Escénica, 2013.

Edelman, Lucila. "Ética y Derechos Humanos." *Psyberia*, vol. 2, no. 4, 2010.

Elmiger, María. "Variaciones actuales de los duelos en Freud." *Desde el Jardín de Freud*, vol. 11, no. 11, 2011, pp. 31–50.

Eng, David. "Introduction: Mourning Remains." *Loss: The Politics of Mourning.* U of California P, 2003, pp. 1–28.

Freud, Sigmund. "Mourning and Melancholia." *On the History of the Psycho-Analytic Movement, Papers on Metapsychology and Other Works (1914–1916).* The Hogarth Press, 1957, pp. 237–258.

———. *Totem and Taboo and Other Works (1913–1914).* The Hogarth Press, 1955, pp. ix–164.

Garibian, Sévane, et al. "¿Por qué exhumar', ¿Por qué identificar?" *Restos humanos e identificación: Violencia de masa, genocidio y el "giro forense".* Miño y Dávila, 2017, pp. 9–20.

Garrard-Burnett, Virginia. "Living with Ghosts: Death, Exhumation, and Reburial among the Maya in Guatemala." *Latin American Perspectives*, vol. 42, no. 3, 2015, pp. 180–192.

Gatti, Gabriel. *El detenido-desaparecido: Narrativas posibles para una catástrofe de la identidad.* Trilce, 2008.

———. "El lenguaje de las víctimas: silencios (ruidosos) y parodias (serias) para hablar (sin hacerlo) de la desaparición forzada de personas." *Universitas Humanística*, no. 72, 2011, pp. 89–109.

Kordon, Diana, and Lucila Edelman. "Algunas consideraciones sobre la articulación entre psiquismo y sociedad." *La impunidad: Una perspectiva psicosocial y clínica.* Sudamericana, 1995, pp. 42–57.

Kristeva, Julia. *Black Sun: Depression and Melancholia.* Columbia UP, 1992.

Laplanche, Jean. *Essays on Otherness.* Routledge, 1999.

Lira, Elizabeth. "Desaparición Forzada, Trauma y Duelo: Chile 1973–2014." *Recursos psicosociales para el post-conflicto,* 2016, p. 131.

———. "Trauma, duelo, reparación y memoria." *Revista de Estudios Sociales,* no. 36, 2010, pp. 14–28.

Lira, Elizabeth, and Eugenia Weinstein. *Psicoterapia y represión política.* Siglo XXI, 1984.

Losonczy, Anne-Marie. "Murderous Returns: Armed Violence, Suicide and Exhumation in the Emberá Katío Economy of Death (Chocó and Antioquia, Colombia)." *Human Remains and Violence: An Interdisciplinary Journal,* vol. 2, no. 2, 2016, pp. 67–83.

Mahlke, Kirsten. "Figuraciones fantásticas de la desaparición forzada." *Desapariciones: Usos locales, circulaciones globales,* Siglo del Hombre Editores. Universidad de los Andes, 2017, pp. 75–97.

Mandolessi, Silvana. "El tiempo de los espectros." *El pasado inasequible: desaparecidos, hijos y combatientes en el arte y la literatura del nuevo mileno.* Eudeba, 2017, pp. 49–69.

Martín-Baró, Ignacio. *Psicología de la liberación.* Trotta, 1983.

Peeren, Esther. *The Spectral Metaphor: Living Ghosts and the Agency of Invisibility.* Palgrave Macmillan, 2014.

Pérez-Sales, Pau, and Susana Navarro García. "Balance global. Exhumaciones en América Latina: estado actual y retos pendientes." *Resistencias contra el olvido: Trabajo psicosocial en procesos de exhumaciones en América Latina.* Gedisa, 2007, pp. 327–362.

Rando, Therese. "The Increasing Prevalence of Complicated Mourning: The Onslaught is Just Beginning." *Omega. Journal of Death and Dying,* vol. 26, no. 1, 1993, pp. 43–59.

Richard, Nely. *La insubornidación de los signos: Cambio político, transformaciones culturales y poéticas de la crisis.* Cuarto Propio, 2000.

Robben, Antonius. "State Terror in the Netherworld: Disappearance and Reburial in Argentina." *Death, Mourning and Burial: A Cross-Cultural Reader.* Blackwell, 2004, pp. 134–148.

Schindel, Estela. *La desaparición a diario: sociedad, prensa y dictadura: 1975–1978.* Eduvim, 2012.

Sluzki, Carlos. *La presencia de la ausencia. Terapia con familias y fantasmas.* Gedisa, 2014.

Taylor, Diana. *Disappearing Acts: Spectacles of Gender and Nationalism in Argentina's Dirty War.* Duke UP, 1997.

Tello, Maria. "Historias de (des)aparecidos. Un abordaje antropológico sobre los fantasmas en torno a los lugares donde se ejerció la represión política." *Estudios en Antropología Social,* vol. 1, no. 1, 2016, pp. 33–49.

Viñar, Marcelo. Violence sociale et realité dans l'analyse. *Violence d'Etat et psychanalyse.* Dunod, 1989, pp. 41–66.

Winnicott, Donald. *Realidad y Juego.* Gedisa, 1971.

Woodrick, Anne. "A Lifetime of Mourning: Grief Work Among Yucatec Maya Women." *Ethos,* vol. 23, no. 4, 1995, pp. 401–423.

Race, Class, Gender, and Sexuality

Intersectional Perspectives

Section II

Race, Class, Gender, and
Sexuality

Intersectional Perspectives

Chapter 6

In Defense of Psychoanalysis

How Afro-Brazilian Histories Subvert and Get Subverted by the Psychoanalytic Experience

Claudia dos Reis Motta and Antonio Luciano de Andrade Tosta

The emergence of postcolonial theory in the 1970s and the critical discussions that the field has generated about the characteristics and consequences of European colonialism throughout the world have led to a steadier suspicion of elements and practices of European origin in other cultures and societies. In Brazil, before scholars such as Edward Said, Bill Ashcroft, Frantz Fanon, Leela Gandhi, Homi Bhabha, and Walter Mignolo gained prominence worldwide due to their intellectual contributions, similar ideas expressing concern with the relations between Brazil and Portugal and other (neo)colonial powers had appeared in the country. There are elements in, for example, Oswald de Andrade's 1928 *Anthropophagic Manifesto*, Alberto Guerreiro Ramos's 1958 *A Redução Sociológica*, as well as in later texts by Silviano Santiago and Roberto Schwarz that could easily be understood in terms of postcolonial thinking (Tosta 217–226; Filgueiras 347–363). Postcolonial scholars in Brazil quickly targeted the Catholic and Protestant religions, understandably, given the oppressive role that religion played during the Portuguese colonization. The country's educational system, which started formally with the Jesuits, and remains based on European models, was under scholarly attack as well (Silva and Carvalho 156; Jesus, n.p.; De Paula 71–84).

Not surprisingly, psychoanalysis has also made the list of suspects, especially for Afro-Brazilians. At the core of Afro-Brazilians' complaint is their experience of racism, which, some claim, psychoanalysis is unable to understand. The way psychoanalysis first arrived and how its ideas were initially diffused in Brazil also help explain such mistrust. As we shall see, psychoanalysis was connected to the mental hygiene movement and to the spread of eugenic ideas, which targeted Afro-Brazilian and indigenous populations as inadequate. Other more current reasons to discredit the field as a treatment option for Afro-descendants are the scarcity of Afro-Brazilian psychoanalysts, the discipline's indifference toward Afro-Brazilian history and experiences, and the lack of psychoanalysis-based research on racism or the enslavement of Africans during the colonial period (Sperry n.p.; Console n.p.).

DOI: 10.4324/9781003266211-9

Our chapter first outlines the discourse against psychoanalysis, as well as its origins in Brazil, to understand why the discipline has become a target for non-believers. Second, the essay draws from Fanon's ideas and from Freudian and Lacanian thought to discuss the relevance of psychoanalysis for Afro-Brazilians. Finally, the chapter examines fragments of clinical listening between three Afro-Brazilian analysands and Claudia dos Reis Motta, one of the authors of this chapter, and excerpts of written narratives by two of them in order to illustrate the aforementioned theoretical discussions and to argue for the value of psychoanalysis for Afro-Brazilians.[1]

Psychoanalysis and Racism in Brazil

The criticism against psychoanalysis's relevance for Afro-Brazilians is quite real and must be taken seriously. A recent example of such disapproval came from Brazilian psychiatrist Luiz Sperry. In the title of one of the entries in his blog, Sperry asks his readers "where to find Blacks" in psychiatry and psychoanalysis and comments that medicine is a field practically dominated by White people in Brazil, a country where most of the population is Black.[2] Due to a scarcity of Black psychiatrists, he claims, there are no psychoanalytic studies on racism in Brazil—an ironic outcome given that one of the pioneers of psychoanalysis was Virgínia Bicudo, a Black psychologist and sociologist from São Paulo, who was also the first woman in Latin America to undergo analysis and the first nonphysician to be recognized as psychoanalyst (Pereira n.p.).[3] Along these lines, Milene Amaral Pereira stresses that Bicudo's work is "invisible" in psychology programs in Brazil and neither cited nor valued in academic bibliographies (Pereira n.p.). The fact that Bicudo's work has only recently begun to receive more attention (see, for example, Müller da Silva; Teperman and Knopf; Moretzsohn) reflects the country's deep-rooted history of prejudice and discrimination against Afro-descendants.

Psychoanalysis is indeed often perceived as part of this deep-rooted history of racism. The context of the arrival and development of the discipline is relevant to understanding this postcolonial mistrust. Psychoanalytic ideas had a close connection to the movement of mental hygiene, which also had European origins (Bortoloti and Cunha 63; Garcia 958–959). Arthur Ramos, for instance, a psychiatrist, social psychologist, ethnologist, folklorist, and anthropologist who, according to some scholars, "institutionalized Black Cultural Studies" in Brazil (Guimarães 53) and corresponded with Freud (Garcia 957), headed the Ortho-phrenia and Mental Hygiene Section of the Instituto de Pesquisas Educacionais in Rio de Janeiro in 1934 (Perestrello 205). Bicudo worked for the School Mental Hygiene Section of the School Health Service of the Department of Education in São Paulo in 1933 and later taught psychoanalysis and mental hygiene at the São Paulo's Escola Livre de Sociologia e Política. There, she met Durval Marcondes, a sociology student who was already a Psychoanalysis and Mental Hygiene Professor (Moretzsohn 213–214). Marcondes was hired as a psychiatrist for the

Inspectorate of School Hygiene and Sanitary Education of São Paulo's Secretary of Education in 1924, the same year he received his medical degree (Garcia 957). The hygienist movement wanted more than to cure illness. It was part of a "civilizing-educational" project, targeting the "undisciplined, uneducated, those who had bad habits" (Torquato 52). Psychiatry was in a position of prominence, considered a valuable tool to carry out such a project, and psychoanalysis was a complementary method to organicist and classificatory psychiatry (Torquato 55). Hygienists viewed Brazil's miscegenation as a huge obstacle to civilize the country. The nation's African and indigenous heritage was regarded as "instinctive" and synonymous with "excessive passions" (Torquato 52). Hygienists had an "intense dialogue" with the eugenic ideas, which ended up shaping hygienist policies (Bortoloti and Cunha 63). Eugenics advocated for improving the quality of the human species, aiming at the reproduction of desirable genetic characteristics while rejecting undesirable ones. It believed in racial hierarchy and argued for selective mating and sterilization. As Costa explains, "Psychiatrists began to ask for sexual sterilization of sick individuals, to preach for the disappearance of racial miscegenation among Brazilians, to demand a ban on the immigration of non-White individuals, to call for eugenics courts and eugenic paternity pay" (89). The members of the *Liga Brasileira de Higiene Mental* (LBHM) claimed the existence of "degenerate, less evolved, abnormal or inferior" people in the country who were predisposed to have mental problems. Their goal was to change that, as they saw these individuals as harmful. The groups "to be improved" included Afro-descendants and indigenous peoples. In fact, "Blacks, in particular, were considered natural candidates for a place in the asylum, since, according to psychiatric discourse, they had degenerative traits typical of their racial condition" (Mansanera and Da Silva 134).

Eugenics significantly influenced many of the precursors of the early psychoanalytic movement in Brazil. As a result, psychoanalytic discourse became part of the eugenic movement that spread throughout Brazil (Torquato and Rocha 428). Durval Marcondes was one who mixed "Freudian discipline and hygienist formulations attributing to psychoanalysis a pedagogical and moralizing status radically different from that indicated by Freud" (Torquato and Rocha 430). Another strong defender of eugenic ideas was Porto-Carrero, who coordinated the novel Brazilian League of Mental Hygiene in 1926 (Abrão 126). Elisabete Mokrejs states that Porto-Carrero drew his interests from "the themes of 'eugenics' as well as from totalitarian ideas that, although not clearly specified, emphasized the action of the elite and of the state in guiding the interests of individuals" (156–157). Luciana Cavalcante Torquato is even more emphatic. She argues that he "vigorously defended eugenics and mental hygiene as battles to be fought for the regeneration of the race and the Brazilian people" (58). Torquato claims that Porto-Carrero, paradoxically, used psychoanalytic propositions "to imprint traces of eugenics" (66). According to her, he often cited Freud to justify his authoritarian thinking (67).

Citing Cristiana Facchinetti, Torquato mentions that the concern that the Blacks "had become the primary factor of degeneration of the Brazilian people" was central to the hygienist politics in Brazil (72). Eugenicists proposed an increase in the immigration of certain European groups, which would help them to achieve their goal of purifying the country by "whitening" the Brazilian people. As Mansanera and Da Silva put it, "If immigration were massively White, the whitening process would sooner or later take place (134)." There are, therefore, more than enough reasons for Afro-Brazilians to be at least suspicious of psychoanalysis. The improper and selective manipulation of Freud's ideas at the time not only disregarded Afro-descendants' history of enslavement and oppression, but it also dehumanized them, judging the group as unfit for reproduction and the creation of families.

Confronting Freud: Fanon, Racism, and Psychoanalysis's Merit

Yet, despite the complex and paradoxical history outlined in the previous section, psychoanalysis provides a rich conceptual framework for understanding and thinking through racism. In her chapter in *O Racismo e o negro no Brasil*, Da Silva alerts to the fact that psychoanalysts and psychologists should consider the issue of racism and its role in the construction of "identity and identification processes" that produce psychic suffering to Blacks and non-Whites. She stresses that these identity and identification processes are defined by "negative attributes created to legitimize the racist ideology . . . of the Brazilian people" (75). In the same book, Fúlvia Rosemberg states that Brazilian racism acts on two planes: the material and the symbolic. On the material plane, Blacks and indigenous people do not have the same access to public resources as Whites, "which is due to the history of colonization and slavery and the current conditions of distribution of public goods" (131). On the symbolic plane, we are in a society in which there is an ideological hegemony of "the superiority of Whites over others, including Blacks," making them inferior; this symbolic plane is "devastating," complains the author (130).

By the same token, Tânia Corghi Veríssimo argues about the incidence of "disavowal" (*Verleungnung*) in racist discourses in Brazil. Understood as the refusal or renegation of reality, the concept of disavowal is characterized by an ambiguous relation to perception where the subject simultaneously acknowledges and refuses to accept a threatening realization, seeking an alternative perception. The author indicates traps of language that naturalize racism and hide something unspoken in the subtext, such as "Fulano is Black, but he is honest" or "Despite his color, he works well" (236). Veríssimo questions whether the mechanism of disavowal would not also be present in the way Brazilians deal with our violent slave history (238–239). In relation to racism, she writes that this belief can "constitute itself in a transcendent and floating field of truth and lie in which no one believes, and, at the same time, everyone believes," pointing to a lack of elaboration about the painful and traumatic reality that colonization imposed (239). The author exemplifies the presence of disavowal with the existence of a restaurant called "Senzala," a signifier that goes back to the holocaust experienced by the Black race, but that was reinserted in Brazilian culture, supported by the "myth of social democracy" (239). For her, that case makes it clear that "disavowal is a mechanism of social bonding" (239). This becomes a way to avoid facing the pain of racism and its history, as this would cause a "narcissistic jolt" (240).

Da Silva and Veríssimo provide good examples of how psychoanalytic concepts can help us better grasp contexts of racism. We could, indeed, continue their line of thought to propose that the transformation of the issues that Afro-Brazilians face cannot happen through the disavowal of castration[4]—understood as the lack that structures the subject—since refusal leads to imaginary gateways such as Manichaean dichotomies of good versus bad, victimization, and/or identification with the White oppressor. Other consequences are the placement of the Black body as a fetish for the White to enjoy, and Whiteness as a fetish for the Black. Fanon noted, in fact, that the young anti-Black Antillean identifies with the White exploiter who, as a "civilizer," "brings the truth to the savages, an all-White truth" (132). He also highlighted how Black persons can be phallic symbols for Whites, an "ideal of virility," while being at the same time a target for torture (139).

The gateway for Afro-Brazilians, and all those who so desire, to achieve transformation, however, is not through the Imaginary but, as Rosemberg implied, via the Symbolic (131). In order to re-signify trauma and reposition themselves before their marks, Black people must speak about racism during analysis. Black clients bear in their discourses the signs of non-placement, invisibility, and the feeling of inferiority imposed by the colonization process. Signifiers such as "sulky," "whip me," "I have to suffer," "escape route," "heavy," "*banzo*,"[5] and "laziness" are common occurrences for Motta's Afro-descendant clients. All these signifiers allude to the enslavement of Africans in Brazil as well as to stereotypes that were created by the ruling classes in relation to Afro-Brazilians to depreciate their value.

In the preface to the Brazilian edition of Fanon's *Black Skin White Masks*, Lewis R. Gordon draws attention to the "neurotic and melancholic situation of Black people in the modern world" (17). According to Fanon, Gordon observes, one of the main causes of melancholy is the "loss by which they cannot be what or who they are" (17). Fanon claims that Black people find themselves in "a zone of nonbeing, an extraordinary sterile and arid region, an utterly naked declivity where an authentic upheaval can be born" (8). He believes that it is crucial for Blacks to face their own underworld so they can free themselves from the desire to be White, as well as from the hatred against Whites. This ambivalence, after all, alienates the Black person. Yet, Fanon warns us, this is not an easy task: "In most cases, the Black man lacks the advantage of being able to accomplish this descent into a real hell" (8). Nevertheless, the "liberation of the man of color from himself" is an urgent task, he says (8; 33).

The aforementioned concepts allow us to pose three questions that are of utmost importance for elucidating the links between racism and psychoanalysis: What is the experience of analysis like for a Black Brazilian person? What kind of discourse are Blacks reproducing and producing? How can the analyst facilitate sessions to help Black people break with their historical, generational, and, thus, psychic imprisonments? In what follows, we illustrate the possible changes that the analytic experience can bring to Afro-descendants by examining fragments of clinical listening between three Afro-descendant analysands and Motta as well as excerpts from two written narratives by two of these analysands. These three clients, while talking about their transference, admitted to Motta that at some point in their analyses they had questioned her legitimacy as their psychoanalyst. Although Motta identifies as Afro-descendant, she is a light-skinned Black person, and it would not be unusual for *mestizos* like her to not identify as Black in Brazil. Moreover, darker-skinned Black people are certainly more often victims of prejudice and discrimination. Colorism is a fact in Brazil (Devulsky.) Their mistrust confirms Da Silva's remarks about Afro-Brazilians' preference for Black psychoanalysts. Nevertheless, their experience of analysis, as expressed in the two narratives and in the fragments of clinical listening discussed, is evidence that, despite any justified skepticism some Afro-Brazilians might hold toward psychoanalysis, psychoanalytic treatment could indeed be valuable for them and for their analysts, if appropriately conducted. Reflecting upon her work with Afro-Brazilians, for instance, Motta points out that listening to Black clients, as well as going through her own process of analysis, has helped her to reflect upon, as well as recognize, her Black and indigenous roots. It has helped her to drop identifications with the bourgeoisie and the Catholic religion, for example, which are inheritances of Brazil's colonized history.

We can indeed find echoes of Fanon's words in the discourse of one of Motta's Black clients during analysis: "There is no way to talk about how I am without talking about it first"; "I'm *banzado*"; "as if I could not find a place"; "oblivion"; "loneliness that crosses the Black woman"; "crossing of racism, of machismo"; "without a place in the world"; "out of place." The client states strongly her need to speak about her condition before she can talk about other events in her life. She mentions her poor state of mind and cites experiences such as loneliness, displacement, racism, and machismo, which are barriers that she faces daily and are connected to her identity as an Afro-Brazilian woman.

This is how another Afro-Brazilian analysand explains the importance of his personal analysis:

> It's a very intense process . . . that potentiates our capacity of being human. We were taught to keep ourselves quiet, to overthrow our pain. . . . [I still have] the memory of my mother telling me to stop crying, or hearing, 'Are you a man or a sack of potatoes?' . . . For being Black, big and from the slums, I had to bear the pain and be strong, because the history of our people required strength to bear the lashings and survive them. . . . [We were expected to] keep quiet, because to expose the pain is to show weakness. . . . And the turning point is to be able to talk about this pain, exposing ourselves, exposing these wounds, understanding that beyond the color of our skin we are human

beings who carry a history of power and potentialities, that just like the other feels pain, I also feel it and that I can talk about it, about this pain, because healing comes through speaking and listening. . . . This potentiates us. . . . By listening to our pain, we start listening to the pain of the other. . . . As we build respect for ourselves, we start to respect the other as well, as we can only give to the other what we are able to give to ourselves. . . . Psychoanalysis helps in this development. [It allows] a daily dialogue of exposure with ourselves, all the time.

The narrative of this analysand expresses how the colonizing discourse, to which his mother has also been submitted, has imposed a position of subjection to him since childhood: He must bear the lashings, hold back his tears, and shut up. The fact that the analysand's mother had the same experience shows the historical and generational reproduction of the Master–Slave relationship as expressed in Afro-Brazilian families. This is where the experience of analysis comes in. It provides not only an awareness of this paralyzing plot but also the opportunity for one to turn toward healing through speaking and listening, as this analysand points out. It is through a cut in the pre-established and impregnated discourse of the analysand that a new subjective position emerges extracted from inside himself, as he listens to himself, and recognizes that he also brings a history of potency and potentialities.

Fanon's treatment of psychoanalysis in *Black Skin, White Masks* is critical to reflect on the experience of analysis and to delve into our three questions. Although Fanon structures his text with Freud's theory, he also challenges Freudian thought. For example, Fanon highlights psychoanalysis's important contribution to Blacks: "I believe that only a psychoanalytical interpretation of the Black problem can lay bare the anomalies of affect that are responsible for the structure of the complex" (10). Yet, the author stresses that neither Freud nor Alfred Adler nor Carl Jung considers Black people in their investigations (151). He argues that they did not necessarily have to, as "it is too often forgotten that neurosis is not a basic element of human reality" (151). Furthermore, he remarks, "Like it or not, the Oedipus complex is far from coming into being among Black people" (152). Fanon also calls attention to the importance of the family for psychoanalytic theory, which "represents in effect a certain fashion in which the world presents itself to the child" (141). Moreover, the family, which projects itself onto the social environment and on the very state, resembles the nation (141–3). He proposes, however, that, although that is true for the "White family" (149), it will not be for the Black child in "contact with the White world" (143), since "the young Black person subjectively adopts a White man's attitude" (147). Last, Fanon criticizes Freud's emphasis on the "individual factor," remarking that "the Black man's alienation is not an individual question. Beside phylogeny and ontogeny stands sociogeny" (11).

On the one hand, Fanon is right in his claim about how important it is for Blacks to become aware of the process of socio-economic depreciation they face and that real changes in this sphere need to materialize nowadays in the form of public policies, for example. On the other hand, there are some crucial points in Fanon's assertions that need to be revisited. First, it is a misinterpretation to think that psychoanalysis does not deal with the collective, since psychoanalysis claims that the subject is constituted in a relationship with the other, and that the alienation process permeates the social, cultural, and economic arenas through unconscious discourse. This alienation needs to be recognized and read for subversion to happen. The Black person may have an opportunity in the social sphere, for example, but if they are imprisoned in the Slave's discourse, they may become paralyzed when faced with the possibility of growing. The opposite is also true. For example, when enslaved Blacks were "freed" in Brazil, slavery remained a reality for them, since they had no real opportunities to emancipate themselves socio-economically. Even though analysis is particular to each subject, it is also crossed by the collective and deals with the collective. Our narratives carry the generational history of our family and our people. Thus, when the analysand speaks on the couch, they are not alone. Social ties and ancestry follow them. In *Group Psychology and Analysis of the Ego*, Freud argues that "the contrast between individual psychology and social or group psychology . . . loses much of its sharpness when examined more closely" (91). According to him, a person's relations with their family, the analyst, and/or their physician (the central theme of psychoanalytic research) can be considered as "social phenomena" (91). Furthermore, by dealing with the analysands' narratives under transference, psychoanalysis makes social ties (Lacan, *O seminário, livro 17* 40–43). In addition, Freud studied how a group exerts a categorical influence on a person's mental life ("Psicologia de grupo" 95). In the same text, Freud goes further when he introduces the unconscious element as the link of this unity called a group. In his words, "The conscious life of the mind is of small importance in comparison with its unconscious life. . . . Our conscious acts are the product of an unconscious substratum created in the mind mainly by hereditary influences. This substratum consists of the innumerable common characteristics, handed down from generation to generation, which constitute the genius of a race" ("Psicologia de grupo" 97).

Afro-Brazilian Histories and the Psychoanalytic Experience: Double-Edged Subversion[6]

Although, as we have seen, Afro-Brazilians and psychoanalysis got off on the wrong foot, they have much to benefit from one another, as one can subvert the other. Subversion, thus, is double-edged: There is the subjective subversion of the Afro-descendants who go through the experience of analysis and the subversion of psychoanalysis by Black culture and history. Subversion implies investigating and reopening conventions, confronting new possibilities, and ultimately positioning oneself differently. For psychoanalysis, subversion is liberating the subject from unconscious repetition as, during the experience of analysis, new signifying chains open up in the subject's discourse, which were previously closed/

sutured in the certainties of the Ego (Lacan, *O seminário, livro 17* 28). Furthermore, Lacan takes Hegel's Master/ Slave dialectics in *Phenomenology of the Spirit* to demonstrate how the experience of psychoanalysis subverts the place of subjugation imposed on the Slave, insofar as it points to an unconscious truth, which, we must remember, is not a totality (Lacan, "Subversão do sujeito" 808). This is the Other; the barred Other that gives no answer to the subject when they question who they are and what they want and provokes them to take a step that divides them (Lacan, *O seminário, livro 6* 404). Faced with the emptiness of the Other's nonresponse, subjects will have to summon a part of themselves. This part is the *objet petit a*, which supports the subject in the face of the lack of a signifier that situates them in the question addressed to the Other. The result of this operation with the Other is the division of the subject; its residue is the *objet petit a*, since the subject never finds an absolute answer. The subject and the *objet petit a* depend on and are always confronting each other: this is what Lacan calls the "formula of fantasy." For him, "the fantasy is nothing more than this perpetual confrontation between the barred subject and the *objet petit* a" (Lacan, *O seminário, livro 6* 404).

Yet, Lacan's "Subversão do sujeito" questions Hegel's "absolute subject," the "self-conscious, all-conscious being," since consciousness causes the "suspension of a knowledge" about "the malaise of civilization in Freud" and the unconscious (813). According to Lacan, in Hegel's work, desire works for the subject to maintain their connection with previous knowledge so that truth is intrinsic to their realization, making explicit the idea that the subject, from beginning to end, "knows what he wants" (817). Lacan points out that Freud subverts this Hegelian perspective when he resumes this question of the junction between truth and knowledge, linking the desire of the subject to the desire of the Other (817). It is in this articulation that dwells the "desire to know" about the subject's truths— exactly when the barred Other asks, "Che vuoi? What do you want?" This same question is relaunched via transference by the subject to the analyst when, even unconsciously, they inquire, "What does he want from me?" (Lacan, "Subversão do sujeito" 829). It is in the field of the Symbolic, where the subject's revolutions take place. When these revolutions emerge in the signifying chain in the discourse of the analysand, the subject abandons the certainties imposed on them. For Lacan, the discourse of the Master is the dominant discourse in the unconscious. Lacan describes the place that truth occupies in the discourse of the Master: truth is repressed and, thus, the knowledge of the divided subject of the unconscious is abolished, that is, the Master does not want to know about his division, a division that points to his cleft, his lack, and his ignorance. The Master, who wants *jouissance*, does not care about his castration and that it is this truth that organizes his relationship with the Slave. In Hegelian dialectics, says Lacan, the Slave renounces *jouissance* for fear of death and it would be through this renunciation that they would reach freedom. We understand at this point that the subversion of the Slave does not reside in leaving the masochistic pole for the sadistic pole and being violent like the colonizing Lord. The outputs of genuine revolutions, which the experience of analysis promotes, are in the way of the Symbolic. This may involve symbolically killing the White colonizer within oneself, knowing what to do with the desire to be White, and seeking the strength to rebuild oneself in one's own roots.

We could, however, ask ourselves: but how to renounce the desire to be White if the Black person is not recognized in their Blackness? How to kill, symbolically, this "White Master" if in every corner of the world, the Black person finds references and demands for Whiteness? Veríssimo cites psychiatrist and psychoanalyst Jurandir Freire Costa, who makes important articulations about the narcissism of the Black person regarding their relationship with the body (241). Costa writes about what "inhabiting a Black body" entails: "going through a range of intense affections and the violence caused by a double injunction: that of embodying the White subject's body and ego ideals – ideals incompatible with his physical structure – and that of refusing, denying, and nullifying the presence of the Black body in their concrete reality" (Veríssimo 241). This violence that the Black's psyche suffers leaves them without the possibility of thinking about their identity, a "symbolic abolition" (Veríssimo 241). Although the Black person knows that Whites have oppressed them, Whiteness becomes a fetish, an "immaculate ideal" that is the target of idealization and also of hatred. It is important to mark here that the mechanism of disavowal can be present in all three psychic structures (psychosis, perversion, and neurosis) with devastating and impeding consequences. Yet, in spite of these devastating consequences, the Black person can get out of impotence and, as a divided and castrated subject, get in touch with their conflicts and, thus, find possible and particular ways out for each one that breaks with those imposed and/or raised by the colonization process.

Let us turn now to excerpts of a clinical listening from one of Motta's clients. A Black client of neurotic structure, speaking of her dissatisfaction and experience with her body, says that when she looks in the mirror, she sees a "body that gets beat up," a "cultural, political beating . . . the other only beats," a "body beat to resist and exist" that sees herself "carrying a body, alone." When Motta asks her how she wants her body to be, she starts to describe traits (size, hair type) of a White body. Motta points to this desire to be like a White person, and she ratifies the observation by answering that "it is tiring" to have to do "so much resignification to look at herself in the mirror" when the reference throughout her life and everywhere is of exclusion of the Black person. Motta asks about the possibility of letting go of this desire to have a White body and to instead welcome her Black body. The association that then appears is the reflexive verb "to love oneself." The analyst's intervention triggers the emergence of the client's division in her narrative: the desire to be White versus her selflove as a Black person. Such division will lead to new signifying chains, which will provide access to her unconscious truths.

The discourse that leads to knowledge, therefore, is the discourse of the hysteric. Cardoza et al. claim that the foundation of psychoanalysis is deeply imbricated in the concept of the unconscious and the position of the subject in the discourse of the hysteric, for it is from the latter that Lacan develops the discourse of the analyst (Cardoza n.p.). In the discourse of the hysteric, the master Signifier

(S1) shifts to the place of the other to whom the hysteric as agent and divided sub-ject addresses this other (the analyst). The hysteric puts the analyst in the place of the Master and demands that the analyst produce knowledge about them and their symptoms. The Master, unable to answer the questions of the subject in the hys-terical discourse, reveals the impossibility to master everything (Cardoza n.p.). This is where the turn from the discourse of the hysteric to the discourse of the analyst happens: when the analysts put themselves in the place of the *objet petit a*. On the one hand, the analyst semblances this place of supposed-knowing (a nec-essary fiction) that engages the discourse of the analysand who assumes that the analyst knows about their symptom; this fiction stimulates the analysand to seek to decipher their symptom. On the other hand, the analyst knows that this is an untenable place that ends up in the place of the *objet petit a* (lost object, inscrip-tion of lack), becoming the cause of the desire of the analysand. The discourse of the analyst, the mainspring of the transference, provokes the analysand to face their division and to speak, thus producing master signifiers (S1) that point to their "truth" as unconscious knowledge. Truth as knowing, or even, knowing without knowing, is an enigma; it is from this structure that interpretation springs—inter-pretation, which indeed comes from the analysand, as a puzzle.

Lacan clarifies that the structure of the subject and the dialectics of desire incorporate the function of the object that is deepened, in the analytic experience, through the phenomenon of anguish—the anguish of castration, "an insurmount-able term" for Freud in the dialectics of the neurotic's desire (Lacan, *O seminário, livro 10* 55). However, he adds that castration anxiety is not the supreme impasse of the neurotic; it is not in the face of this that the neurotic retreats, Lacan states, but that the neurotic retreats "to make of his castration what the Other lacks," that is, to access new signifying chains through speech, in the experience of analysis, so that the symbolic works, since the function of the signifier is to bar the *jouis-sance* of the Other (Lacan, *O seminário, livro 10* 56). Barring this Other whose womb is full of other signifiers; "womb that gives, like a monstrous Trojan horse, the basis for the fantasy of a knowledge-totality . . . its function implies that from outside something comes knocking at the door, without which nothing will ever come out of there. And Troy will never be taken" (Lacan, *O seminário, livro 17* 31). In the case of Black people, we could think that they are in an imaginary ambivalent position in relation to the White person: they believe, with a certain illusory "admiration," in the discourse of omnipotence and absolute knowledge of the White person and, at the same time, they see themselves as dispossessed, which makes them enter the path of hatred and violence. In this sense, the White person stands in the place of the unbarred Other. The point is that the Black person also wants to be recognized as total and value-bearing and this has been impor-tant, to some extent, as a rescue of their self-esteem. However, we know that if they remain imprisoned, they will always end up in frustration, because we live in a society where inequality rules.

It is then necessary to make of their castration what is missing in the Other and this already implies a change in the discourse within the clinical setting: to place oneself as lacking in order to access the S2 at the unconscious level and other chains that bar the dominant "knowledge" at the imaginary level. This means accessing the barred Other, as a discursive place, which interrogates the subject at the root of their desire, as the cause of desire, and not as object. In other words, one is not to identify with the object, as, for example, when some Black clients say that they are "shit," identifying with the object feces/dejection. It is necessary to go through the fantasy that reveals in which object the subject is alienated; the analytic device promotes this movement and subverts such alienation. In this sense, Lacan diverges from Hegel, and attests to such divergence, when he states that the question of the Other is not one of recognition, because if the Other never recognizes me enough then I only possess the path of violence, and this keeps me imprisoned. Whereas by the path of the subject interrogating desire via transference—what do they (barred Other embodied by the analyst) want from me? What am I going to do?—it is possible to access, through lack itself (castration), the path of love, of the lover who speaks: this way frees the subject since they are now subverted by the signifier system.

In the process of analysis of each Black subject, to whom an inhuman condition of objectification, invisibility, vilification, and exploitation has historically been imposed, it is necessary to identify who is their barred Other and to work toward the fall of identifications and idealizations. In the dynamics of analysis, one must listen to the enunciation (the between the lines) in the client's discourse to access the Other, beyond all alienation. Who imprinted marks on them? It is important to highlight their positionality as a divided subject before their Blackness and to work with the signifiers in the narrative of each individual as a way out.

The Black's alliance with the whip and with death also comes from this place as a Slave of the White Master's *jouissance*, even as a trace of identification in the unconscious. Motta's Black analysands produce a discourse of whipping themselves in the sense of self-punishment and self-flagellation: "the skin hurts" . . . "it's inflamed," a Black client told her in a very painful moment of her analysis. The Master does not want to know, he wants *jouissance*. Lacan says that knowledge "is what makes life stop at a certain limit toward *jouissance*. For the road to death – this is what it is about, is a discourse on masochism – the road to death is nothing but what is called *jouissance*" (Lacan, *O seminário, livro 17* 16). The experience of analysis enables the client to get out of the limbo imposed by the history of oppression. Once the analysand asks themselves about their *jouissance*, psychoanalysis deals with desire in the play between the life and death drives. Lacan recalls that Freud introduced the question of the death drive as a "tendency to Nirvana" to the inanimate and adds: "Certainly, this tendency to return to the inanimate is present within the analytic experience, which is an experience of discourse" (Lacan, *O seminário, livro 17* 16). This appears in the narrative of one of Motta's Black clients, while speaking about his *jouissance* relation to life and his wanting and not wanting to know about his castration during analysis said: "*Oxóssi* [i.e., a reference to an *orixá*, a deity in Afro-Brazilian religion Candomblé] . . . dances for death . . . deceives death . . . seduces death. . . . Distrustful, he gives the right arrow." It is by considering the history, crossed by racial prejudice, culture, and religion of the patient, that analyst and analysand, in partnership, can tread new networks of signifiers other than that of the oppressor-oppressed violence. To free this subject that, accessing his unconscious knowledge, "dances to death" and "shoots the right arrow." Analysys, therefore, allows the analysand to reposition themselves before their masochism, which can be fatal.

Castration, for Lacan, "means that *jouissance* must be refused, so that it can be attained on the inverted scale of the Law of desire" ("Subversão do sujeito" 841). Therefore, desire is the law that forbids *jouissance* because desire is moved by lack. It is in the relationship of the subjects with the signifier that they are given the possibility to face their desires, to know what to do with them, and to allow one other that was hidden and suffocated to emerge and make new choices. The divided subject, marked by the bar, brings in itself the possibility of becoming. As Coelho claims, "Discourse theory shows us that psychoanalysis is the possibility for the subject to change his position in front of the Other, recover his dignity and be infinitely different from what he is" (119). Fanon, in turn, asks a fundamental question for the Black person to start their rehumanization process and free themselves from the shackles of colonization, starting from the recognition of their Blackness, their desire, and, from there, their subjective repositioning: "What does the Black man want?" (8).

In the analyst's discourse, the analyst hysterizes the discourse of the candidates for analysis and, questioning about their desire, divides them by pointing to their castration (a castrated subject) in search of wanting to know about themselves, about their *jouissance*, alienations, and desire. Thus, the analyst provokes the analysand to face their castration, to produce master signifiers (as effects of interpretation) that point to their alienations. Finally, in the place of the unconscious truth, the knowledge that is not known (S2), appears the discontent, in Freudian terms, and the Real, in Lacan's. It is around the Real that discourses circulate, and it is to the Real that analysis points. It is from this Real and from this void that something new emerges: the creation and meaning that we give to life, even if it has no meaning. In the specific case of Afro-descendants, we wonder what can be created and how they can reinvent themselves from a mark that is impossible to undo—a mark that the inhumane process of colonization imprinted and that capitalism perpetuates. The reverse of psychoanalysis is the discourse of the Master, that is, the discourse of the analyst is the counterpoint of the discourse of the Master since the discourse of the analyst reveals the object *a* as the cause of desire and not as the production of *jouissance*.

The function of the analyst in directing analysis is to help the analysand subvert the fate that was imposed on them. This has nothing to do with adjusting or adapting the subject to reality. It aims neither to remove their symptom nor to help them achieve happiness. The analyst makes a semblance of the place of object cause of desire so that the analysand can face the unconscious plots and desires to which they are imprisoned, thereby able to make new choices. It is also fundamental to remember that the experience of analysis begins when the subject asks themselves who they are, what they desire, and what they have to do with the symptom from which they suffer: "What we discover in the experience of any psychoanalysis is precisely of the order of knowing, and not of knowledge or representation. It is precisely something that links, in a relation of reason, one signifier S1 to another signifier S2" (Lacan, *O seminário, livro 17* 28).

In a two-way street, psychoanalysis is also subverted by Afro-descendants with their own peculiar language, history, and culture. This becomes evident in another example from one of Motta's clients who writes about her experience of analysis. For this analysand, psychoanalysis can be defined as the "head *ebó*" (spiritual cleansing in Candomblé):

> *Ebó* is action. In candomblé, for my elders, *ébó* is something that we do in secret to overcome hidden and declared enemies. Psychoanalysis for me is an *ebó de Ori*, that which heals inside while preparing you for war. An act that (re)placed my body in the world and changed the effects of racism on it (my body). I am not "immune" to racism, no one is, but I feel much less vulnerable to the emotional and psychic effects of violence perpetrated by an anti-Black world. . . . Maybe "discovering" that psychoanalysis existed was one of the first steps to save me from death.

From this narrative, we can infer how psychoanalysis is subverted and crossed by the culture of candomblé, by the knowledge and history of the subject that speaks. This Black woman conceives of psychoanalysis as an act that relocates her body and shows how analysis subverted her, relocated her subjectivity in the face of the world and her destiny. Moreover, according to her, analysis resituated her body as a social symptom within a history of pain and racism: the experience of analysis "changed the effects of racism on it (my body)." Thus, this excerpt also demonstrates how this client imprints her language and rewrites, from her knowledge, one of the fundamental concepts of psychoanalysis: the drive, a concept between the psychic and the somatic; libido that is born in the body and is crossed by language ("Os instintos e suas vicissitudes" 42).

Upon examining these narratives, it is telling that "scream" is a verb that comes out of the guts of Motta's Black clients; this is one of the verbs that paves the way to subvert their histories. When a person gives themselves to the experience of analysis, they are no longer the same because the process offers them a symbolic avenue of thinking to subvert the subjective place where they have been imprisoned, both in the micro social group we call "family" and in the macro sociopolitical-economic group.

In "Radiophonie," Lacan states that the subject is spoken by an unconscious knowledge (403–448). Subjects are trapped in the symbolic chain (in language) even before they are born, because speech founds the lineage before history is embroidered on it. We notice this aspect translated in the written narrative of the client to whom we referred earlier: "But I was born 'a Black woman' and I am/ was born 'Black' because racism operated in all structures of society, even before I was born. Dealing with that, defending myself from that is the biggest challenge

I have on the couch. . . . I call the miracles of psychoanalysis what happened to me." For psychoanalysis, the process of humanization begins when the child is born into language. The human being is thus caught as a whole in the language game of the unconscious, that is, they are spoken to, desired or rejected, even before the rules of this game are transmitted to them. The subject, one only-after, surprises these rules in the course of their life, and can re-signify them in analysis.

Concluding Thoughts

Psychoanalysis has been questioned in regard to its social insertion and praxis. It has been criticized as individualistic and tailored for the bourgeoisie. Yet, in *Civilization and Its Discontents*, Freud designed psychoanalysis in articulation with the collective, with culture, history, and politics. He fought for a psychoanalysis that would serve the poor population. There are no elements in psychoanalytic thought that can limit psychoanalysis's scope to any given group of people. On the contrary, it may serve everyone. It is necessary, however, to address this perception that exists in Brazil. As this essay has shown, there are enough reasons to be suspicious. These reasons, however, are not related to psychoanalysis itself but to the way the discipline has historically been manipulated and misused. As Torquato observes, the principles of psychoanalysis indeed go in the opposite direction of the one took by Brazilian twentieth-century hygienists:

> Freud differs from this pedagogy when he avoids this "uprooting of evil" proposed by doctors to "cure the moral ills" of the Brazilian people. For him, it would rather be recommended to channel, to use this sublimatory source towards higher values. It would not be possible, therefore, to build culture without going through sublimation, which rules out the presumption of eliminating the impulses of the subject proposed by the pedagogical-hygienist movement.
>
> (70)

Psychoanalysts must pay more attention to the Afro-Brazilian experience and reposition themselves to face criticism and to work according to the directions that Freud provided since the beginning of his clinical practice. In "Linhas de progresso na terapia psicanalítica," Freud explicitly demonstrates his concern for the "wider social strata, who suffer from neuroses in an extremely severe way," alluding to the importance of society becoming aware and awakened to this issue, and defending the idea that "the poor have exactly as much right to an assistance to their minds as they have now to the help offered by surgery, and that the neuroses threaten public health no less than tuberculosis . . . there will be institutions or clinics for outpatients" so that they may "become capable, by analysis, of resistance and efficient work. . . . Such treatments will be free" (210). Thus, Freud thought of a psychoanalysis beyond the walls of the consulting room, suitable to be applied in institutions and with the purpose of "meeting the enormous neurotic misery that exists in the world" (Elias 88).

Notes

1　Claudia dos Reis Motta descends from Africans, Amerindians, and Europeans. Antonio Luciano de Andrade Tosta descends from Amerindians, Arabs, Jews, and Europeans. It is from these positions that we produce this piece of writing. Motta's clients authorized the use of excerpts from their narratives and the psychoanalyst's clinical listening in this and other future publications. Tosta, the other author of this essay, did not have access to any other information about these clients, including their identity.
2　Translation is ours. Unless otherwise noted, all subsequent translations from Portuguese into English are ours.
3　Although Sperry is far from wrong in calling attention to the dearth of Afro-Brazilian psychiatrists and psychoanalysts, it would be incorrect to say that Brazilian psychoanalysts have not participated in discussions on racism at all. Noemi Moritz Kon, Maria Lúcia da Silva, and Cristiane Curi Abud, for example, co-edited the volume *O racismo e o negro no Brasil*, a book that brings together essays by an interdisciplinary group of scholars who contribute with "practical experiences and theoretical reflections" to consider the ways in which psychoanalysis might participate in a discussion about racism in Brazil (7). See also Arreguy et al.; Belo; Guerra; Pereira; Veríssimo; and Schechter and Bonfim for examples of other works that discuss psychoanalysis and racism in Brazil.
4　In Freudian doctrine, the phallus symbolizes the penis or clitoris, but it is not reduced to the organ itself. The term phallus refers to one of the phases of infantile sexual development, the phallic phase, described by Freud when the child has the conviction that all beings have a penis. When faced with the castrated mother and the paternal intervention that removes her from the position of imaginary phallus (object of desire of the mother), the child is introduced into the so-called "castration complex." Castration, therefore, is of symbolic order. From being or not being the mother's phallus, the child, further on, moves to having or not having the phallus. The phallus, now symbolic, is a signifier that represents the lack (Kaufmann 79–81). In addition, note that the concept of object, for psychoanalysis, can be a person or a partial object (the nipple, the voice, the phoneme, the look, the feces, the urinary flow, etc.). They are all representatives of the phallus.
5　The word *banzo* expresses the melancholic feeling and depression that enslaved Africans felt for missing their homeland. It also refers to resistance to their lack of freedom, mistreatment, and forced labor.
6　We would like to thank Amon de Castro for his careful reading of and suggestions for this section of the chapter. We would also like to thank Hélio de Castro for his comments and suggestions at the beginning stage of this process.

Works Cited

Abrão, Jorge Luís Ferreira. "As contribuições de Júlio Pires Porto-Carrero à difusão da psicanálise de crianças no Brasil nas décadas de 1920 e 1930." *Memorandum*, no. 20, 2011, pp. 123–134.

Andrade, Oswald de. "Anthropophagite Manifesto." *The Oxford Book of Latin American Essays*, edited by Ilan Stavans. Oxford UP, 1997, pp. 96–99.

Arreguy, Marilia, Marcelo Coelho, and Sandra Cabral. *Racismo, capitalismo e subjetividade: leituras psicanalíticas e filosóficas*. Eduff, 2018.

Belo, Fabio. *Psicanálise e racismo: interpretações a partir de Quarto de Despejo*. Relicário Edições, 2018.

Bortoloti, Karen Fernanda da Silva, and Marcos Vinicius da Cunha. "Anísio Teixeira e a psicologia: O diálogo com a psicanálise." *História da Educação*, vol. 17, no. 41, Sept.–Dec. 2013, pp. 59–77.

Coelho, Carolina Marra S. "Psicanálise e laço social: uma leitura do Seminário 17." *Mental*, no. 6, June 2006, pp. 107–121.

Console, Luciana. "'Impactos do racismo não são reconhecidos pela psicanálise', afirma psicóloga." *Brasil de Fato*, 31 July 2017, www.brasildefato.com.br/2017/07/31/impactos-do-racismo-nao-sao- reconhecidos-pela-psicanalise-afirma-psicologa. Accessed 5 Dec. 2020.

Costa, J. F. *História da psiquiatria no Brasil: Um corte ideológico.* Xenon Ed., 1989.

Da Silva, Maria Lúcia. "Racismo no Brasil: questões para psicanalistas brasileiros." *O Racismo e o negro no Brasil: questões para a psicanálise*, edited by Noemi Moritz Kon, Maria Lúcia da Silva, and Cristiane Curi Abud. Perspectiva, 2017, pp. 71–89.

De Paula, Maria de Fátima. "A formação universitária no Brasil: concepções e influências." *Avaliação*. Campinas; Sorocaba, SP. vol. 14, no. 1, Mar. 2009, pp. 71–84.

Devulsky, Alessandra. *Colorismo.* Jandaíra, 2010.

Elias, Valéria de Araújo. "Psicanálise no hospital: algumas considerações a partir de Freud." *Revista da SBPH*, vol. 11, no. 1, June 2008, pp. 87–100.

Fanon, Frantz. *Black Skin, White Masks.* Translated by Charles Lam Markmann. Grove Press, 1967.

Filgueiras, Fernando de Barros. "Guerreiro Ramos, A redução sociológica e o imaginário pós- colonial." *Caderno CRH*, vol. 25, no. 65, May–Aug. 2012, pp. 347–363.

Freud, Sigmund. *Civilization and Its Discontents.* W. W. Norton & Company, 1961.

———. "A divisão do ego no processo de defesa." *Obras psicológicas completas.* Imago, 1969, pp. 305–312.

———. *Group Psychology and the Analysis of the Ego. 1921.* Translated by James Strachey. W. W. Norton & Company, 1959.

———. "Linhas de progresso na terapia psicanalítica." *História de uma neurose infantil e outros trabalhos.* Obras psicológicas completas. Vol. 17. Imago, 1969, pp. 199–211.

———. "Os Instintos e suas Vicissitudes." *A história do movimento psicanalítico, artigos sobre metapsicologia e outros trabalhos. Obras psicológicas completas.* Vol. 14. Imago, 1969, pp. 127–162.

———. "Psicologia de grupo e análise do ego." *Além do princípio de prazer: psicologia de grupo e outros trabalhos. Obras psicológicas completas.* Vol. 18. Imago, 1969, pp. 87–179.

Garcia, Ronaldo Aurélio Gimenes. "Arthur Ramos e Durval Marcondes: higiene mental, psicanálise e medicina aplicadas à educação nacional (1930–1950)." *Educação e Sociedade*, vol. 35, no. 128, July–Sept. 2014, pp. 629–996.

Gordon, Lewis R. "Prefácio." *Pele Negra, Máscaras Brancas*, edited by Frantz Fanon, Translated by Renato da Silveira, EDUFBA, 2008, pp. 11–17.

Guerra, Andréa Máris Campos. "O papel da psicanálise na desconstrução do racismo à brasileira." *Revista Subjetividades*, no. 2, 2020, pp. 1–13.

Guimarães, Antonio Sérgio Alfredo. "Africanism and Racial Democracy: The Correspondence Between Herskovits and Arthur Ramos (1935–1949)." *Estudios Interdisciplinarios de América Latina y el Caribe*, vol. 19, no. 1, 2008, pp. 34–79.

Hegel, G. W. F. *Phenomenology of the Spirit.* Oxford UP, 1977.

Jesus, José Raimundo de. "A necessidade de mudanças no sistema educacional brasileiro: uma reflexão para T." *Portal Educação*, n. d., www.portaleducacao.com.br/conteudo/artigos/idiomas/a-necessidade-de-mudancas- no-sistema-educacional-brasileiro-uma-reflexao-para-t/67583#. Accessed 6 Jan. 2021.

Kaufmann Pierre, ed. *Dicionário enciclopédico de psicanálise – O legado de Freud e Lacan.* Jorge Zahar, 1996.

Kon, Noemi Moritz, Maria Lúcia da Silva, and Cristiane Curi Abud, eds. *O racismo e o negro no Brasil: questões para a psicanálise*. Perspectiva, 2017.

Lacan, Jacques. *O seminário, livro 6: o desejo e sua interpretação*. Jorge Zahar, 2016.

———. *O seminário, livro 10: a angústia*. Jorge Zahar, 2005.

———. *O seminário, livro 17: o avesso da psicanálise*. Jorge Zahar, 1992.

———. "Radiophonie." *Outros escritos*. Jorge Zahar, 2003, pp. 403–448.

———. "Subversão do sujeito e dialética do desejo." *Escritos*. Jorge Zahar, 1998, pp. 807–842.

Mansanera, Adriano Rodrigues, and Lúcia Cecília Da Silva. "A influência das idéias higienistas no desenvolvimento da psicologia no Brasil." *Psicologia em estudo*, vol. 5, no. 1, 2000, pp. 115–137.

Mokrejs, Elisabete. *A psicanálise no Brasil: as origens do movimento psicanalítico*. Vozes, 1993.

Moretzsohn, Maria Ângela Gomes. "Uma história brasileira." *Jornal de psicanálise*, vol. 46, no. 85, 2013, pp. 209–229.

Müller da Silva, Iúvi Yrving. "A história de uma pioneira da psicanálise brasileira: um estudo historiográfico sobre Virgínia Bicudo." *Paidéia*, vol. 22, no. 51, Jan.–Apr. 2012, pp. 141–142.

Pereira, Milene Amaral. "Virgínia Bicudo: A invisibilidade na psicanálise, racismo e as consequências psíquicas para uma psicanalista negra." *Psicanalistas pela democracia*, 21 Oct. 2010, https://psicanalisedemocracia.com.br/2018/10/virginia-bicudo-a-invisi-bilidade-na-psicanalise-racismo-e-as-consequencias-psiquicas-para-uma-psicanalista-negra-milene-amaral-pereira/. Accessed 10 Dec. 2020.

Perestrello, Marialzira. "Primeiros encontros com a psicanálise. Os precursores no Brasil (1899–1937). *Jornal Brasileiro de Psiquiatria*, vol. 35, no. 4, July–Aug. 1986, pp. 195–208.

Ramos, Alberto Guerreiro. *A redução sociológica*. Editora UFRJ, 1996.

Rocha, Francisco Franco da. *A Doutrina de Freud*. 2nd ed. Cia. Editora Nacional, 1930.

Schechter, Rosa Coutinho, and Flavia Gaze Bonfim. "Psicanálise e racismo: entre os tempos de ver, compreender e concluir." *Ayyu: Revista de Psicologia*, no. 7, 2020, pp. 1–29.

Silva, Antonio Lima da, and Volnei M. Carvalho. "Education." *Brazil: Nations in Focus*, edited by Antonio Luciano de Andrade Tosta and Eduardo F. Coutinho. ABC-CLIO, 2015, pp. 156–171.

Sperry, Luiz. "Racismo, psiquiatria e psicanálise: onde estão os negros nessa área?" *Blog do Luiz Sperry*, 08 June 2020, https://luizsperry.blogosfera.uol.com.br/2020/06/08/rac-ismo-psiquiatria-e-psicanalise-onde-estao-os-negros-nessa-area/ Accessed 7 Dec. 2020.

Teperman, Maria Helena Ingig, and Sonia Knopf. "Virgínia Bicudo: una historia del psicoanálisis brasileño." *Jornal de psicanálise*, vol. 44, no. 80, 2011, pp. 65–77.

Torquato, Luciana Cavalcante. "História da psicanálise no Brasil: Enlaces entre o discurso freudiano e o projeto nacional." *Revista de teoria da história*, vol. 14, no. 2, Nov. 2015, pp. 47–77.

Torquato, Luciana Cavalcante, and Guilherme Massara Rocha. "A *Peste* no Brasil: A introdução das ideias freudianas no Brasil a partir da medicina e do modernismo." *Ágora*, vol. 19, no. 3, Sept.–Dec. 2016, pp. 425–439.

Tosta, Antonio Luciano de Andrade. "Modern and Postcolonial? Oswald de Andrade's *Antropofagia* and the Politics of Labeling." *Romance Notes*, vol. 51, no. 2, pp. 217–226.

Veríssimo, Tânia Corghi. "O racismo nosso de cada dia e a incidência da recusa no laço social." *O racismo e o negro no Brasil: questões para a psicanálise*, edited by Noemi Moritz Kon, Maria Lúcia da Silva, and Cristiane Curi Abud. Perspectiva, 2017, pp. 233–249.

Chapter 7

The Politics of Psychoanalysis in Colombia

Social Action for the Representation of the Radical Other

Silvia Rivera-Largacha and Miguel Gutiérrez-Peláez

On September 26, 2016, after four years of negotiations and dialogue, the Colombian State and the Revolutionary Armed Forces of Colombia-People's Army (FARC-EP) signed peace agreements in Cartagena. These peace agreements were supposed to put an end to the insurgent organization and to a half-century conflict that had left a wave of pain and death. During the ceremony, women from the municipality of Bojayá, a village that had witnessed one of the bloodiest massacres in the recent history of the armed conflict, sang *alabaos*[1] to celebrate the end of the armed conflict, evoking the suffering of the victims and their hope of finding reparation, restitution of their rights, and the non-repetition of acts of barbarism: "For five hundred years we have suffered this great terror. We ask violent people: no more repetition."[2] During the ceremony, when Rodrigo Londoño, alias Timochenko, commander of the now new political party "Farc," read his speech asking for forgiveness to the victims, two warplanes sailed through the sky. Londoño looked in terror above his head holding his breath, to realize seconds after that the roar of the engines had a new meaning from that day on. They were no longer the planes chasing the insurgent group to bomb their troops, but aircrafts announcing a new chapter in history.

Just like when that afternoon in Cartagena the terror of war was drawn in Timochenko's face and body, the traces of this armed confrontation have been rooted in the memory, the territory, and the body of the Colombian population and it is part of the great difficulty to build peace that we find today. This conflict of half a century is just one of the many manifestations of the difficulties Colombia has had since colonization to be a society capable of recognizing human dignity in each citizen and giving value to the subjectivity of each person within the great social diversity that characterizes this country.

As psychoanalysts and social researchers, in our work we have sought tools to identify and understand how Colombian national history, marked by the force of trauma, becomes present in individual and collective histories, identifying the original forms that certain subjects and groups have found to face the burden of trauma and to create new ways of building social bonds that overcome the

DOI: 10.4324/9781003266211-10

crippling force and inertia imposed by violence; in other terms, a new way to become political subjects. In this journey, we have encountered the work of different researchers who have allowed us to understand part of the complex historical, social, economic, political, and psychic interactions that generated and prolonged the history of segregation and violence in Colombia. In this chapter, we describe how these theoretical elements have allowed us to understand some edges of the complex Colombian social and political reality and the impact this comprehension has given us in our work dealing with violence and trauma inside and outside the clinic.

The Segregation of the Radical Other

In her book *Civilization and Violence*, Cristina Rojas explores the strength of violence and trauma in Colombian society from a post-Marxist and intersectional perspective interspersed with contributions from psychoanalysis. Rojas proposes a critical analysis identifying the effects of different forms of violence based on segregation and the historical prolongation of trauma, particularly in the nineteenth century. Violence and segregation are explained as phenomena revealing the impossibility of achieving a representation of "the Other," of "difference," articulated as the impossibility to recognize the value of the subjectivity of individuals and entire communities, such as American natives, African slaves, *mestizos*, and women, all of whom had been marginalized from a national project on account of their gender, social status, race, and beliefs, among others. She describes this tendency to understand the identity of the Other, by the reduction of its characteristics to several trades, identified as monological (Bakhtin 23) or unchangeable and designated from a single position. Violence intensifies as a manifestation of monological representations that have been constructed in the colonization process and which prevail in our time. Rojas describes how, in the effort of this country to adopt the logic and political structure of modernity, it ends up adopting the ambivalences of the discourses of civilization and capitalism, and with this tacitly accepts the links of these discourses with violence and, we would say, with the prolongation of violence and trauma. In the twentieth century, the economical organization continues to be in force as a strategy to achieve the expansion of an economy based on extractivism (Browitt et al. 1–17), attempting against the defense of social diversity and human rights. Once again, the country dismisses what has historically been marginal: the indigenous, the afro, the mixed, the local, and the feminine.

In the mid-twentieth century, in the midst of this social and economic tension, peasants took arms to confront the elites that seized political power, land tenure, wealth, and other privileges. The privileged elites, aware of the risk of losing their social benefits, organized private armies (paramilitaries) to combat these nascent guerillas. The paramilitary groups have been allied with the state, since the elites owning the land have been also those who held power in government. President Juan Manuel Santos (2010–2018) engaged in peace dialogues with the guerrillas as a strategy to confront the bases of violence. Even though the signing of the peace agreement and the change of FARC from an armed guerrilla group to a political party were huge steps toward the construction of peace, during the presidency of Iván Duque (2018–2022) the implementation of the peace agreements has been unstable. Even when 90% of former combatants are still engaged with the peace process, a fraction of the FARC-EP has gone back to arms, different paramilitary and illegal armed groups are operating in rural areas, and the number of social leaders and former guerrilla members being murdered grows day after day. It was of course evident that the implementation of the peace agreements would not be easy, that the construction of peace is never a regular process but is, instead, a movement with constant vicissitudes. Nonetheless, the lack of clear endorsement on behalf of the government has made the country more vulnerable to the subsequent uprising and return of the same forms of violence.

The history until today has shown that the incarnations of the different forms of violence in Colombia have always affected mainly those who are not part of the privileged groups; those who have been the forgotten protagonists of a history that continues ignoring the value of difference. While armed conflict has been one of the cruelest manifestations of violence in Colombia's history, it has not been the only scenario of misrecognition of the other. The armed conflict is the public incarnation of this phenomenon, but there are also other multiple forms of violence, such as gender-based violence, class violence, and racial violence. Considering this social configuration, we wonder: What is the place of psychoanalysis in Colombia? In this essay, we answer this question by describing our own work as psychoanalysts inside and outside the clinic; a clinical work created to respond to the specific conditions of the target population.

The Experience of Psychoanalytic Psychosocial Interventions in Colombia

Our clinical experience with people affected by Colombia's armed conflict and other forms of violence has been carried out in different contexts. Some of them have taken place in classical settings, such as consultation offices, private individual interventions, and psychoanalytical treatments, as well as individual, group, or family interventions in psychiatric hospitals. Our experience in private practice has been mainly with victims and NGO workers that bring social support to victims of the armed conflict and other types of violence. To a lesser degree, we have worked with other actors of the armed conflict and other violent contexts. In psychiatric hospitals, the work has been with police officers, soldiers, paramilitaries, and ex-guerrilla members. The other forms of psychoanalytical interventions have been those carried out "outside the couch," by going to institutions and communities, in urban or rural areas, and working with different populations, amongst them: groups of victims; demobilized guerrilla members in facilities of the Ministry of Defense; work with FARC members in "Territorial spaces for training and reintegration" (ETCR for its name in Spanish: *Espacios territoriales de capacitación y reintegración*) after the signing of the peace agreement; groups of former right-wing paramilitary armed groups through government agencies; work with professionals of the different public agencies and NGOs in charge of the interventions with populations psychologically affected by war experiences and other forms of violence; and work with journalists that recover testimonies from massacres in the Colombian territory.

The clinical work with groups and in communities constituted a necessity, for it is not possible to conceive that all clinical interventions with people affected by the armed conflict or other forms of violence must pass through individual interventions in private consultation rooms. In many cases, we were able to find the benefits of going beyond the couch and allowing people subjected to different forms of suffering to have a voice. The psychoanalytical experience aims to obtain a maximum singularity, an absolute difference that would allow a subject to better cope both with their own self and with their reality. This orientation is what guides both interventions inside and outside the couch: it is not the adaptation of the subject to this reality, nor a normalizing procedure, but an effort to listen to that radical otherness of the subject, giving voice to those silenced dimensions. In what follows, we present some examples of our own clinical practice.

We will begin with an intervention we carried out before the signing of the peace agreements, with a group of guerrilla members who had fled from the group and voluntarily adhered to the government route to legalize their social status and avoid imprisonment. We met with the group in a secret and secure location disposed by the Ministry of Defense. We presented ourselves, after which we invited them to talk. They spoke about their motives to leave the guerrilla group. They had fled just a couple of days before, and most of them had not met earlier. It was not a homogeneous cluster, despite having belonged to the same guerrilla group. Some of them had a poor peasant upbringing, others belonged to different indigenous and ethnic groups, half were male, and half were female, and were of different age groups. They had joined and left the group for different reasons. As they spoke, our interest in listening to them became evident, and they perceived more clearly that we were not government officials, that we were not judging them, and that we did not want to produce a moral reflection of their actions. Most of them decided to talk and many were able to mention that what they were talking about was something they had never spoken of before. After the meeting ended, a young woman who had remained silent during the group session approached one of the psychoanalysts. She spoke urgently about what she had found moving in the session. The analyst embraced her words and suffering. A few other individual sessions followed in which she was able to isolate the motives that had led her to that moment in her life and direct her life perspectives in a clearer alignment with her own desire.

Another experience consisted of a three-day series of workshops with former combatants living in an ETCR. These activities were proposed by professors and university students with diverse theoretical and professional approaches to violence and conflict. These interventions were meant to facilitate the ex-combatants' transition to civilian life. This group of more than 30 people, mostly women, had to reconfigure a new identity in a political project, which was also a community and even family venture (since many of them began to have children, something that was limited in the context of war). Some of these workshops were tailored to the reconstruction of the historical memory of the group. Other spaces were proposed to think about the new ways of projecting their future as a group.

Our presence as psychoanalysts came because of the concern of the organizers, based on their previous encounters with this group of ex-combatants, where they identified different emotions emerging in the participants as well as in the students and teachers, which seemed difficult to face. None of the leaders of the process had training in psychological support or psychotherapy, and they often felt disoriented or even overwhelmed by the appearance of these manifestations of sadness, anxiety, fear, and other emotions appearing in certain individuals or the entire group. We were invited to support the process, containing and, as far as possible, helping to deal with these manifestations of emotions. In one of these sessions, the group worked on how their individual histories had encountered the collective history of the armed group. Most of the participants' experiences were similar. During their childhood and adolescence, in an adverse social context marked by poverty and inequality, they were repeatedly exposed to different forms of violence, both in the public and in the private context. Some of them were seized in the crossfire between different armed actors; others had been victims of paramilitary groups, the national army, and/or guerrilla groups. Some had also experienced situations of domestic violence. But the common denominator for all of them was to have faced, from a very young age, situations where they felt unprotected and vulnerable, and where they had perceived a threat to their integrity.

In these situations, they faced the impossibility of being recognized as subjects by an Other that was menacing. Then, in an adverse context where the assurance of basic rights was limited or even inexistent, the only possible way out seemed to be to embrace a collective guerrilla identity: the guerrilla promised them not to be again the target of the threats of a tyrannical Other: whether a paramilitary group, the national army or even an abusive father, a violent mother, or an aggressive sibling.

These experiences allowed us to give voice to those who had been silenced in a social context where some individuals impose their own desire over others, ignoring their subjectivity and their dignity. We talk about a context marked by this regime of representations analyzed by Rojas, where there is still a legitimation of the imposition of power of some privileged actors over the basic needs of others. Paradoxically, by engaging this identity that protected them from this tyrannical Other, they incarnate the representation of another tyrannical Other, committing massacres, kidnaping, displacing peasants from their lands, and generating forms of suffering that they had personally experienced. But this paradoxical position is not mentioned in group sessions, where they tend to validate the sense of their decisions by handling their own suffering and the sorrow from others. They justify war as a legitimate defense of those communities disregarded by the state and the privileged classes. When the collective sessions finished, some of them underwent individual psychoanalytic encounters. In these sessions, some of them talked about their sleep troubles, their anxieties, their sufferings, and even their symptoms. They recalled images and emotions from the war and from people who had suffered in these violent scenarios: comrades from their army, victims from their attacks, and themselves. It was a process where the violence of war revealed itself in its rawest presentation. We talk about psychoanalytic encounters, because we can't describe these interventions as psychoanalytic treatments. There is not a prolonged process where the analysand can identify deeply the traces of their desire. Nevertheless, these short interventions are listening spaces where these persons can talk about their own stories, taking distance from a collective identity that once offered them protection. As they talk, they can identify some elements from their own history and some traces of their own particularity. In these sessions, they can identify the character of their pain and the suffering derived from violent or traumatic episodes in their life. They recognize another way to tell their history, without using the psychic defenses incarnated by the violence of war or the hermetic signifier of a hierarchical armed group. In one of these sessions, for example, a young woman talked about how she left her home as a teenager, to enroll in the guerrilla. She describes this choice as her only alternative to escape from the mistreatment and violence from her family. In the guerrilla, she is charged to construct the bombs for the attacks. She describes her role in these terms: "I had in my hand the devices for destruction, I felt I was important for the group, for my comrades." It seems to be for her some kind of transformation in her position toward violence. She goes out from a violent home to "take in her hands" the management of violence. Some months after this encounter, she calls the psychoanalyst she talked to once, and she asks to be listened. She had left the ETCR, and she was living with her family. She was no longer seen as the young fragile girl against whom everybody could exert violence, she says. Now she was respected as an adult and as a strong woman. She found a job; she has a boyfriend, and she was trying to construct a life as a couple with him. Nevertheless, she claimed that it was not easy, because she had never had any type of affective relationships outside the guerrilla. She finally recognizes that it is her desire to engage in this new life, where she can put distance to violence by the affective world she is constructing.

As it is explicit in the work of Lacan, subjects obtain their dignity through the recognition of their desire. It is through this operation that the subject abandons the position of alienation to the Other, passing to act in conformity to that desire that inhabits within them. As the psychoanalytic experiences have taught us, getting hold of our own desire is not easy, it can take decision and time, and it can imply losses, renunciations, abandoning socially accepted positions, and restructuring everyday lives. In this sense, it requires braveness and many times the aid of an Other to face and embrace. It is different for every singularity, and it occurs in the unique logical time frame of the subject. It is this desire that gives human life its real sense and dignity (Lacan, *The Seminar of Jacques Lacan*).

After three days of intensive work, we left the ETCR and met with teachers and students to identify the emotions emerging during the experience. We mostly reflected upon the nuances of their desire to accompany this process and their connection to these ex-combatants. From their own personal history, they could identify the connection that they had with this work, recognizing the process of idealization that sometimes guided their closeness to the ex-combatants. We talked about transference and countertransference to better understand their strengths and difficulties to face the paradoxical position of these ex-combatants regarding their place as social actors.

Contrary to what happens in psychoanalytic training, where the analyst is necessarily confronted with their vital decision of choosing to train as an analyst, in other professions the decision to deal with others' emotions is frequently obscure to the subject. This has been our experience with educators, social workers, psychologists, journalists, and other professionals who work directly with victims of different forms of violence or with demobilized members of armed groups. The reasons why they have chosen to carry out that work and why they have decided to dedicate an important part of their lives to this effort have not always been clear to them. Therefore, many times, what we have found are burned-out groups and professionals, anxious and symptomatic, haunted by what they have seen and listened to. Frequently, they do not count on an "affective" infrastructure in their institutions that can aid in this matter. It is expected that they know how to deal with these emotions and that they should be able to do so. This leads, many times, to hiding anxiety. It is only in these group interventions that they have the chance to verbalize sensations and process them through words. Frequently, being able to illuminate for them something about what functions in their singularity in an articulation with their professional decisions has been crucial for their further work, with the concomitant appeasement of their anxiety and, even for some, their symptoms.

Our interest in supporting professionals who work with people and communities affected by violence and suffering has also led us to support humanitarian workers. In 2020, we engaged in a clinical intervention for workers from NGOs supporting communities in the Colombian frontier with Venezuela and the Pacific coast. These areas affected by violence due to armed groups disputing the territory and the drug trade are also the scenarios of other forms of violence, especially gender and domestic violence. When we began this intervention, we were expecting to find vicarious trauma affecting these workers. We thought that the quotidian confrontation to situations of violence, negligence, stigmatization, and suffering in others could be the main source of sorrow and anxiety to these workers. However, we soon realized that most of the professionals recruited by these NGOs belonged to these communities. In this sense, they had been directly touched by the same forms of suffering affecting the NGO clients. Despite the economic and social constraints in which most of these professionals were born and raised, they obtained college degrees hoping, among other things, to help their communities. However, in dealing with the situations of violence, inequality, and vulnerability of the people with which they work, they inevitably face their own history. In this sense, they must deal with the forms of violence, mistreatment, and negligence to which they were confronted during their childhood and adolescence and, in some cases, they continue to face within their family settings.

The work with all these actors led us to the concept of *extimité* (extimacy), Lacan's neologism to designate that which is, at the same time, most exterior and most intimate to every subject, "combining intimacy with radical exteriority" (Lacan, *Le Séminaire XVI* 206; our translation). In our work with these humanitarian workers, we helped them recognize, in their daily confrontation of other people's suffering, the *extimité* of the suffering that touched their own lives. We thus opened a space where they could be aware of their feelings, including the manifestation of anxiety. This process enables them to recognize the echo of these exterior pains in their own history, in their own sorrow. That is how the identification of their own position as subjects appears to be one of the main concerns of the psychoanalytic interventions, where they try to reach for the clues to face the intimacy and the oddness from their own suffering and desire.

To illustrate this work, we can mention the case of Miss R, a professional humanitarian worker in her mid-30s, who is deeply engaged in combating all forms of violence, especially against women. She benefits from the program of psychosocial support for humanitarian workers offered by the international NGO where she is employed. She started a psychotherapeutic process with a psychoanalyst hired by the NGO. As she started this process, Miss R was working in a small city, taking in a program of humanitarian intervention within vulnerable communities affected by different forms of violence and social isolation. But her demand to receive psychosocial support is not triggered only by the emotional challenges from the confrontation of different forms of trauma within the users of the services from the NGO. Her main demand comes from what she describes as a psychic discomfort that persists in her.

In fact, previously in her life, she looked for different forms of psychological support including Cognitive Behavioral Therapy (CBT), psychiatric treatments, and even a short psychoanalytical process that she decided to abandon. She complains of a tendency to fall into a deep and unavoidable sadness. She has felt these emotions since she was very young, nonetheless, they went out of proportions when she was 12 years old. One day, as she was looking for her birth certificate, she unintentionally found the death certificate of her father, who was kidnapped for a few days and thereafter killed, when she was four years old. These events were never clarified in a judicial process and the perpetrators were never identified. Consequently, Miss R grew up feeling the absence of her father and the dearth of justice.

She has no memories of her father or her hometown. She only remembers a lonely childhood, with a young mother who had to escape from her hometown to save her own life and her daughter's life. The violent murder made the mother think that the crime against her husband was an act of vengeance and she was especially concerned about the security of R. She received death threats and kidnapping menaces targeting her daughter. Nevertheless, the young mother could not explain herself nor her daughter the aims of these threats, because she ignored their purpose and who was behind them. Eventually, the mother renounced to look for justice in the case of her husband, prioritizing instead to protect her life and her daughter. Eight years after the murder, when Miss R read the death certificate, she discovered the violence that was inflicted on her father when he was killed. The document described the traces of torture marked on his body. She seems to remember that the body was found beheaded. This image from a wrecked and tortured body makes her think about the solitude of her father as he was kidnapped and killed, and the pain he felt during his final hours. These images incite feelings of solitude, vulnerability, and sadness. Miss R declares that it was probably from that day on, that suicidal ideas appeared in her mind, accompanied by feelings of guilt and helplessness.

This clinical vignette brings up the psychic difficulties present in a context where the role of the State is not assured as a guarantor of social justice. In the case of Colombia, the State and its institutions do not represent firmly the existence of a collective agreement between political associates who enjoy approximate equality of power. In fact, the absence of an effective political and justice system generates and prolongs social inequalities. Since the murder of her father, Miss R must face the terror of a committed crime and the threat of a new offense where there is no Other that can put a limit. There is no guarantee of restitution and reparation. There is no certainty that the brutal murder will not be repeated. The absence of the father is not recognized, explained, or repaired. Consequently, there is not a society where this absence can be represented as a painful situation and an irreparable injury. Therefore, Miss R finds many difficulties to face this disappearance and to move on.

The murder of the father both condemns her to his absence and the lack of opportunities derived from this tragedy and generates terror. Wolff states, in a reference to British philosopher Jeremy Bentham, that "the crimes that affect us most are the ones which threaten 'boundless injury' to person or property. These can induce not just fear but terror, and Bentham plausibly argues that the total fear such crimes create may be worse than their total damage" (112). In this case, the murder, the lack of justice, and the menaces generate in this woman a constant perception of being the target of violence. Paraphrasing Wolff, this situation seems to depress her life and creates a wide and deep pool of misery. What seems especially terrifying in her situation is the insecurity this whole situation creates in their life. The murder and the cruelty evidenced in the description of the death certificate, the remembrances from her mother concerning the displacement from their hometown, and the threats over their lives, generate in Miss R a perception of hopelessness, where no one can defend her from an unidentified violence: "for me there is not a face to whom to complain to. I don't know whose fault this is," she declares.

For Miss R, the psychoanalytic process has been a space to recognize the effects of the traumatic episodes she lived as a child. Once she and her mother escaped from their hometown, the menaces gradually disappeared. Nevertheless, the terror leaves from thereafter the presence of different manifestations of anguish, exhibited in various moments of her life. She gradually identifies these moments as she tries to establish some distance between the anxiety from these situations and the terror derived from the episodes related to the death of her father. She identifies the defenselessness she faced as a child when her life was menaced, and she did not have a father figure, a strong mother or even the presence of a protective Other, as the judicial system, to assure her well-being. Therefore, she tries to construct herself as an adult who can put limits to the unknown menaces producing her anxiety and to go ahead with her life.

As we have shown in these clinical vignettes and descriptions of group interventions, our work has been a laboratory to explore the complex configuration of violence in Colombian society. In this intricate constitution, it is hard and sometimes impossible to trace a line between victims and perpetrators. The actors of the different manifestations of violence seem to interact in a convoluted situation where they occupy different positions, sometimes in a paradoxical constitution. In this context, it is also difficult to imagine original alternatives to find a deadline where historical forms of violence could come to an end. The question here is if our psychoanalytical approach can help to understand and approach these multiple forms of violence and trauma.

Conclusion

As we have illustrated throughout this chapter, there is an unrecognized remainder in Colombian society. Different sectors still either erase or do not recognize this remainder. Levinas mentions the orphan, the widow, and the stranger as the places of the radical other (Gutiérrez-Peláez, *Confusion of Tongues* 87). In Colombia, this remainder has received different names, such as *indio* (Indian), *desechable* (expendable), and *gamín* (homeless child) (Fergusson 55; Gutiérrez 120).[3] Even though each term points to a different dimension, they all name something that is excluded from society, something that does not fit in. This, in turn, perpetuates the idea that, without this leftover, Colombian society would close in a perfect circle. On the contrary, the applications of psychoanalysis outside the couch that we have discussed show an effort to give a voice to that remainder. In this sense, psychoanalysis goes in the opposite direction of eradication. Psychoanalysis aims to reincorporate this remainder to society, not by constructing a closed set but, rather, by maintaining a social openness toward difference. In the same way, that the Ego is not a closed set, but permanently open and overwhelmed by the Id, societies are not constituted by pieces that fit. These pieces are precisely social *actors*: As *remainders*, they point to an Otherness that is both part of what a society is and a product of its functioning. Through psychoanalytically oriented interventions, we aim to give a voice to those excluded, to recognize their words and locus of enunciation, and to restitute their dignity.

In this sense, then, extimacy becomes a symptom that serves a crucial purpose: it is felt as something absolutely *Other* that the subject wishes to get rid of. Yet, via psychoanalytic treatment, the analysand discovers that it is precisely the otherness they want to expel from themselves what defines them most intimately, accounting for a unique form of *jouissance*. Lacan mentions that at the root of racism lies in the hate toward the *jouissance* of the Other (Lacan and Copjec 32). This is, also, what is most unbearable of us to ourselves. Congruent with Rojas's reading of Lacan, whatever is hated in the Other is that which is rejected in oneself. The most unbearable thing of the Other is the most unbearable and uncanny of each of us as speaking subjects: "The inhuman is not the outside of the human, but its inseparable otherness, its most improper interior, its extimac*y*" (Gutiérrez-Peláez, *Confusion of Tongues* 124).

Throughout this chapter, we have reviewed how this unrecognized part of the social fabric, just like the rejected and repressed parts of the psyche at an individual level, insists and returns in different ways. Such return goes against one of the main goals of the construction of peace, which is precisely to stop the cycle of violence and exclusion of the Other. The lack of recognition or representation of the Other triggers the compulsion to repetition. On the contrary, the recognition of the Other, its inscription in the social fabric, leads to a different place. Our past experiences have effects in our lives but do not determine our destiny. A psychoanalytic experience permits us to take distance from the Other who is positioned as the determinant of our destiny and allows for a decision: whether to persist in the same form of mortification or to choose something else, a path that convenes most to each of our singularities.

The Colombian national project is marked by the internal inconsistencies of a society that denies the great social diversity that constitutes it. As a nation, we are facing systematically the paradoxical position of rejecting what is so proper to us. Psychoanalytic interventions with these marginalized and forgotten populations, these people directly facing different forms of violence, segregation, and vulnerability, are an attempt to give voice to that extimacy that is part of us. Our commitment is to explore what we believe is one of the deepest roots of the existence and prolongation of violence: the naturalization of the rejection of this Other that is different. The psychoanalytic field is a space where the subject is recognized as a subject of the unconscious and a subject of the word. The decision to use psychoanalysis in Colombia as a tool of psychosocial intervention inside and outside the clinic leads to open the dialogue and identify the unconscious processes behind the acts and affections of those who have been actors in multiple forms of violence. Psychoanalytic interventions in Colombia unfold various meanings of existence that resist monological forms of representation that have dominated the manifestations of violence. In this sense, psychoanalysis in the Colombian context can be an act of resistance to the inertia of violence and the prolongation of trauma. We know from Lacan, however, that the effects of an act cannot be totally predicted. As Porge describes, "The clinic from the analytical act is the analyst's clinic produced by the analysand, in the after-the-fact and in the case by case" (35; our translation). Psychosocial interventions with a psychoanalytic orientation have the intention of introducing a space for word and language where the singularity of each subject can be recognized. But the effects of this bet can only appear in the case by case. In the applications of psychoanalytic theory outside the clinic, we propose to understand the psychic defenses of denial, silencing, and projection often used to ignore or not denounce the violence and abuses of different social groups, governments, or aggressors against certain sectors of society. Our bet is to create a space where groups participating in these interventions can question these defenses, look for new alternatives to confront violence, and create new possibilities to recognize the social diversity of this country.

Notes

1 "Declared as an intangible heritage by the Nation since 2014, the '*alabaos*' are songs – as well as prayers – that bring together many people around the death of a loved one. According to the age of the deceased, the songs tell stories narrated by a leading voice and a chorus of responding women" (Radio Nacional de Colombia). For this ceremony/ occasion, the *alabaos* were a tribute for the deaths caused by war, and a hymn of hope for peace.
2 Lyrics from the *alabaos* by the *cantaoras* (woman singers) from Bojayá on September 26, 2016.
3 In Colombian argot, the term *desechable* is a pejorative word used to refer to homeless people. It is a term that evidences the stigmatization and the violence menacing these populations who are considered socially useless and deprived of any value or right.

Works Cited

Bakhtin, Mikhail. *Problems of Dostoevsky's Poetics*. U of Minnesota P, 2013.
Browitt, Jeffrey, et al. "Colombia in the Crucible: Civil War, Citizenship and the Disintegration of the State." *Journal of Iberian and Latin American Studies*, vol. 7, no. 2. Routledge, 2001, pp. 1–17.
Fergusson, Alberto. *Accompanied selfrehabilitation*. Universidad del Rosario, 2015.
Gutiérrez, José. *Medio siglo de travesía freudiana por Colombia: contrapunto y secuencia de un analista con un antropólogo sobre la vida y obra de éste*. Spiridon, 1996.
Gutiérrez-Peláez, Miguel. *Confusion of Tongues: A Return to Sandor Ferenczi*. Routledge, 2018.
———. "Retos para las intervenciones psicológicas y psicosociales en Colombia en el marco de la implementación de los acuerdos de paz entre el gobierno y las FARC-EP." *Avances en Psicología Latinoamericana*, vol. 35, 2017, pp. 1–8.
Lacan, Jacques. *Le Séminaire XVI: D'un autre à l'Autre*. Le Seuil, 2006.
———. *The Seminar of Jacques Lacan: The Ethics of Psychoanalysis*, edited by Jacques Alain-Miller, Translated by Dennis Porter. W. W. Norton & Company, 1997.
Lacan, Jacques, and Joan Copjec. *Television: A Challenge to the Psychoanalytic Establishment*. Le Seuil, 1990.
Porge, Erik. "Clinique de l'acte psychanalytique." *La clinique lacanienne*, vol. 1, 2013, pp. 35–50.
Radio Nacional de Colombia. "¿Qué son los alabaos y los gualíes?" *Radio Nacional de Colombia*, 8 Oct. 2019, www.radionacional.co/especiales-paz/que-son-los-alabaos-los-gualies. Accessed 15 June 2021.
Rojas, Cristina. *Civilization and Violence: Regimes of Representation in Nineteenth-Century Colombia*. Vol. 19. U of Minnesota P, 2002.
Wolff, Jonathan. *Ethics and Public Policy: A Philosophical Inquiry*. Routledge, 2019.

Chapter 8

The Predictive Imaginary of Gender

Reading Lucía Puenzo's XXY (Argentina, 2007) as an Emotional Situation

Oren Gozlan

Knowledge as a Scene of Cruelty

In his review of the movie *XXY* about an intersexed teenager called Alex, The New York Times's critic Stephen Holden (1) asks: "How must the world appear to someone who has been treated as an exotic clinical specimen from birth?" To this I add, how are individuals understood inside and outside the predictive imaginary of gender? Holden's question turns the mirror on the viewer, who is invited to look into their own phantasies of sexuality, embodiment, and gender. Through the story of Alex, his family, and his community, the viewers enter an enigmatic emotional situation that teeters between curiosity and cruelty, which may also mirror the audience's potential reception to the scene—the wish to expose, control, and disavow the capacity to choose.[1] For the viewer who is also an analyst, the question takes a particular form and touches on the conundrum of having to resist predicting what one cannot imagine. How does the analyst confront a new situation in the absence of any sedimented knowledge? Is there an inner life to cruelty—hatred of what we don't know, desire to possess, control, and predict— that is inherent to the experience of being affected before we know or understand?

As an analyst who works with nonbinary and transgender patients, what draws me to the film is its presentation of gender as an ambiguous emotional situation involving questions of desire, identification, and identity. Beyond a voyeuristic desire to find out Alex's gender, I was drawn to the liminality of the gendered body and the struggles around intermediacy and indeterminacy, tensions which I also encounter in the analytic clinic.

That liminality seen in *XXY* is absent in many Anglo-American films about gender, intersexuality, and transitioning, where the emphasis is often placed on questions of identity and resolution through social recognition. With its emphasis on the "production of liminal bodies and sexualities through the opposition of nature and culture" (Frohlich 167), the film poses the dilemma of "having to choose between a binary decision and intersex as an identity and not as a place of mere passage" (Puenzo, cited in Corbatta 824). While social pressures on gender

DOI: 10.4324/9781003266211-11

identity are evident in the film, *XXY* focuses less on external expectations for conformity, and more on the play of identifications, and the inherent pressures in gender's own unfolding—its uncertainty, surprise, and unpredictability. Alex's capacity to present and explore her intersex subject position on her own terms allows the viewer to imagine more degrees of freedom in exploring and negotiating gender. Circumventing the "before and after" arrangement that typically structures many common narratives of gender transitioning—and their focus on adaptation, correction, or a return to what "should have been" one's "natural gender"—*XXY* presents gender identity as intermediate, always a *Nachträglichkeit* where what follows transitioning constitutes what precedes its.

Cruelty and the Drive to Know

The idea that something unpredictable can usher cruelty is at the film's forefront, starting with the idea that the migration of Alex's parents from Argentina to a remote and small coastal town in Uruguay is partly explained as a recourse to safeguard their child from the preying social gaze. The town is a place where Alex's protective father, Kraken, works as a marine biologist, attempting to rescue and cure wounded turtles. Holden poignantly notes how the film positions Alex's intersexed body alongside those of injured turtles who are wounded by the fishermen's nets, causing them to lose their precious fins. The marine life under Kraken's care exhibits sexual hermaphroditism: over time, they change sex, from male to female. The injured rare sea turtles with their revered fins are juxtaposed against the intersex body. Both are an object of curiosity and are vulnerable to intrusion and cruelty. The injured turtles and the intersex body are metonymically joined through the social phantasmic view of the nonnormative body as castrated, wounded, and incomplete, but also as enigmatic and threatening. Like the turtles, Alex's intersexed body is seen by the social gaze as being wounded by nature at the same time that the film's depiction of the social conception of what counts as natural addresses its cruelty.

Yet, the film also positions nature and culture in paradoxical opposition insofar as the variability that exists in nature is negated in culture. This split leads Frohlich, in her article "What of unnatural bodies?" to appeal to the limits of our thinking: "what of bodies that cannot conform to the logic of nature neither through 'curative' science nor through the visual craft of a film director?" (172), she asks, and we may add: what internal pressures impact our capacity to sustain our own uncertainty in encountering forms of embodiment which exceed our understanding? For Frohlich, the metaphor of the injured body, which links "the intersexed person with the biodiversity of the animal world is part of a larger fiction that sets the supposedly natural truth of sex in opposition to civilization within a moral framework of protection" (166). This metaphorical trope, Cabral suggests, turns intersex people into "exotic minorities" as it continues to uphold the fiction of the "truth of nature" (Frohlich 166). As Frohlich suggests, the "legitimating function of the truth of nature" (166) is a fictive discourse that does violence to supposed unnatural bodies, and refuses the possibility for the intersex, or nonbinary individual to be "loved and accepted as (s)he is" (167) without the threat of needing to be fixed or corrected.

Like an engendered animal, Alex is whisked away to a remote town to protect him from the voyeuristic social gaze and its aggressive "need to know." The migration to the remote town, however, does not offer refuge. Soon enough, Alex's ambiguous gender becomes a fervent question for the young town men, who seem aroused by his enigmatic appearance and are ruthless in their intrusive curiosity. In a near-rape scene, Alex is caught in a vulnerable situation with a mob of young men intimidatingly approaching her and aggressively examining her genitalia. She is finally rescued by an adolescent boy who is in love with her and who got punched in the nose a day earlier for asking Alex about the nature of her genitals. The previous viewing of the punching scene presents a dilemma for the viewer who gets a glimpse of another side of Alex—her omnipotence. She has many secrets, one of which, of course, is her genitalia. Whoever comes close gets punched in the nose. Alex is hard to understand. Like the effect of her gender on others, it is as if her very stance is designed to delight and agonize those around her who are eager to "make sense of her." The attempts to decipher Alex's gender fail again and again. There is no conclusive answer, no closure to Alex's enigma, and no one has access to her secret. She wants his secret revealed in her own way.

The scene of migration is an interesting starting point to the film because just like a migrant, everyone in the film, including the audience, has to adapt to a new, unfamiliar scene of gender, where femininity and masculinity become ever more opaque and inscrutable. There is a new language with which to refer to the character's gender, and a set of actions that turn what is familiar about gender into an uncanny liminality. The intersex body, like an intruder, is perceived as a threat that ruptures the doldrums of a familiar story of gender. In turn, the demand for intelligibility is crushing. Alex's indeterminate genitalia incites a parental anxiety that takes different forms: Is Alex a boy or a girl? What will be Alex's future? Can an indeterminate gender have a future?

Alex's intersex body is strange, estranging, and unsettling to the parents who consult a trans person for clues about the possibility of living in a body that appears so uninhabitable to those who feel disorganized by gender. The anxiety heightens as soon as Alex reaches adolescence, and it is at that point that the atmosphere of the film becomes restrictive and uneasy. The adults become more insistent and intrusive in their wish to know, secretly monitoring Alex's intake of effeminizing hormones. They are curious and frightened by the imagined fate of their child's sexuality and its orientation. A plastic surgeon is called by Alex's mother with the clear intention of "settling her child's gender." The line between maternal care and cruelty blurs and we are again reminded of the slippery slope we tread when we are affected by something unknown.

When settling gender is accompanied by a sense of urgency—to cure, to save, to settle once and for all—the question of consent falls by the waste side. From the point of view of the social, Alex is a baffling enigma: What is Alex's emotional logic? To refer back and fully grasp Holden's question we must also ask, how does the film give us insight into Alex's particular view of the word? Alex is secretive, quiet, and mistrustful. As his secret life is slowly revealed, his own ruthlessness gradually becomes evident through her need to test people. She eschews her parents, pushes away her friends, and teases and antagonizes her lovers. The adolescent Alex navigates social and parental demands against and through questions of desire and love. His rebelliousness also manifests in his keeping secrets. Everyone tiptoes around Alex, who refuses to respond to questions amidst the demands to select his gender. At some point, he stops taking effeminizing hormones but does not openly refuse them. He is aware of the reason for the surgeon's visit but does not confront it. Like Bartleby's "I would prefer not to," Alex's refusal to comply is quiet but forceful. By refusing to speak about his gender, he takes his time, forcing those around him to wait.

The film's capacity to present views from many frames allows us to see Alex's subjectivity unfolding within a complex psyche-social kaleidoscope. These multiple perspectives complicate sexuality by presenting a "vision of sexual desire that does not parse passivity and activity out along gender lines" (Frohlich 164). The complex relational scenarios present gender as an emotional situation that is simultaneously personal and social. It also bears on the political through the question of the child's consent: Did Alex have a say in the family's choice to move to Uruguay? How does the decision to take hormones come about? The film presents sexuality as a crowded scene, where social and individual anxieties and cruelties overlap and mirror each other in ways that are impossible to tease out. Alex's difficulty in deciding who he can trust mirrors the social mistrust of Alex's difference. Everyone gets caught up in the anxiety over indeterminacy, and what emerges through their helplessness, curiosity, and anxiety is an incompleteness, not as a property of the intersexed person but as a quality of the group's intense intersubjective exchanges. Everyone becomes unhinged by gender's disorder, and this encounter stirs great discomfort and confusion that gives rise to an aesthetic crisis—a confusion between love and hate, arousal and repulsion, interiority and exteriority.

Difficult Knowledge

The emotional situation of gender is uncanny and this strangeness is captured in a sexual scene between Alex and Álvaro, the surgeon's son, as the sexual tension between them intensifies. Their nervous flirtatiousness culminates in sex. Alex gropes Álvaro and appears to be penetrating him anally. The scene is presented as if through the eyes of Alex's father, who is watching covertly from the door. As the sexual act unfolds, the father's distress becomes intolerable. The father's reaction suggests helplessness, confusion, and anxiety, as if unhinged by something forbidden and foreboding in the scene itself and in his own self. He is visibly disturbed by what he sees and has difficulty tolerating watching the sex scene between his child and another adolescent boy. After lingering for a while, he walks away, and the audience may imagine a momentary repulsion mixed with arousal. We witness a primal scene, at the threshold between infantile polymorphism and adult prohibition, but this time in reverse: It is the adult who is confronted with the sexuality of the child and what is evoked is an encounter between the father and his own infantile polymorphous sexuality. Interestingly, the scene purposely frustrates the fantasy that gender can be inferred from the positions assumed during sex. Indeed, faced with an ambiguous situation where genitals do not confirm gender, the viewer may rely on the expectation that the sexual scene could finally release us from suspense. We may ask, what of gender is revealed to the child in the conventional primal situation when she walks into the parents' sex scene? Is gender then associated with activity and passivity, assumed sexual position, choice of object, the act of penetrating or being penetrated? The scene between Alex and Álvaro appears to reveal the crack in the fantasy that sexuality settles gender. Holden describes the effect of the scene on the audience as creating a "hyperaware sexual limbo in which you scrutinize the masculine and feminine components in the movie's other characters and recognize the degree to which everyone has both" (4). The scene, in my view, disrupts the very coordinates that organize a distinction between the elements that make up the imaginary of gender—passivity and activity, hardness and softness, orifices and protuberances—and in experiencing the coalescing of femininity and masculinity; infantile and adult sexuality; and desire, fear, and interdiction the viewer eventually realizes that the film remains inscrutable to the binary terms of gender. As we watch the father, we may imagine him wondering, "What does a penis mean when there is also a vagina? Who am I, and what is the nature of my desire, if I cannot tell who you are?"

The sexual scene, I suggest, is haunted by a "something more" that exceeds our capacity to stabilize or make intelligible, and we are left with an excessive remainder that cannot be comprehended. What the scene also animates is the traumatic perception that immediately positions hatred as a way of getting rid of disorganization when encountering something we do not understand. As an emotional scene of anxiety, Alex's subjectivity is refused because its inexplicability is central to heterosexuality's own self-recognition. The scene's reception also brings to view how, in a normative conception of gender as binary, femininity and masculinity are burdened with arbitrary attributes that are mistaken for something that is known. The conception of gender as binary is so saturated that a threat of wreckage looms when something appears as other to its saturation.

The charged emotional situation that the film animates offers the viewer a lens through which to examine their own tacit idealities of gender when encountering the nonbinary adolescent. From a normative stance, Alex's sexuality, much like that of the trans or homosexual, has no function because it is unproductive. Conceived as an error of nature, it is rendered useless, through a fantasy that appeases the normative anxiety over the meaninglessness of sexuality as such. Alex's unintelligible subjectivity, however, is presented throughout the film as a kind of resistance to the social attempt at its obliteration. He escapes, hides, slips off, then returns with a vengeance. She is seductive and triumphant. Opposing this elated subjectivity, there is the ominous and omnipresent concern with the future of Alex's gender, and here we are reminded of Edelman's contention in his book *No Future* about the parentified preoccupation with the future of the child as a mechanism of social control and a belief in sexuality's purposeful design, which renders it meaningful through the aim of procreation. In this way, heteronormativity is equated with normalcy and sexuality's polymorphous history, its unpredictability, is forgotten. In the heteronormative frame, sexuality and gender are intertwined not so much by libidinal force that incurs significance through and by way of identifications and lived experience, but by a fantasized organic law. The imaginary of heteronormative sexuality is predictive.

In attending not only to how Alex's enigmatic sexuality is the object of others' desire but also to how Alex's desire makes it difficult for others to see the world through her eyes, the film captures the difficulty of staying with intermediacy. Something in Alex's desire is unhinging the normative predictive imaginary and what we are witnessing through the uncertainty of Alex's unfolding adolescence is also the repetition of the rhythms of sexuality. Alex loves Alvaro but omnipotently pretends he does not. He is still in charge regardless of what decision he makes with regard to his gender. His desire is kept through refusal. The sway between awareness and denial, giving into and withholding gives the movie its intermediate nature and creates a lull where nothing happens. No decision is made, no action is taken, and love is endlessly deferred.

In watching the film through the lens of the parents, we are particularly struck by the way they are affected by their child's sexuality and their differential responses to the worry over her future. Alex and Álvaro's fathers are both "fixers": Both are surgeons who are deeply invested in their capacity to repair the damaged body, and yet the quality of their relationship to their work differs strikingly. There is gentleness to Alex's father, and in his way of caring for the turtles he appears to identify with their vulnerability. In contrast, the plastic surgeon treats his work in a mechanical and distant fashion. He identifies with his skills and sees surgery as a way of fixing an unruly body. For the plastic surgeon, it is this attachment to mastery and certitude that defines his way of numbing internal conflict and quieting difficult emotions. The fathers' subjective orientations toward their work echo their handling of their children's sexuality. The plastic surgeon cannot bring himself to touch his son, who he suspects is gay, and openly expresses hatred toward him. The surgeon's rigidity undermines the fantasy that he has anything under control, including his own homoeroticism. The marine biologist, in contrast, is tender and protective of his child. There is an anxious yet contained quality to how Alex's father approaches the enigma of his child's gender. He stops rushing into action and waits for something to unfold. There is a capacity, we observe, in Alex's father to give in to an experience and be affected by it.

The Emotional Situation of the Clinic

As an analyst, I am particularly compelled by the film's capacity to stay in the space of liminality and by the pressures it exerts on the audience to tolerate indeterminacy. This pressure is mirrored in the clinical setting when the analyst himself is faced with similar demands in trying to respond to something we do not understand. In *XXY*, we might say, gender and sexuality are conceptualized in the realm of affects—sensations and intensities that are effervescent, beyond words or signification, rather than as codified emotions.[2] The film captures the dilemma of the nachträglichkeit nature of understanding—of being affected, and sometimes constituted, by something we cannot grasp. Like sexuality, affects are "obtuse and erratic" (Garibotto 20), and meanings made of affects retroactively constitute their origin. The past is constituted through its reverberation in the present.

In the clinic, as in film's emotional situation, the past is reconstituted through the transference, and understanding leans upon a series of crises, moments of helplessness, rejection, and revolt. The capacity to stay with the uncertainty of affects, and hence, in the realm of fantasy, is obfuscated by the analyst's ignorance of how their own need to help affects the analytic function. As Britzman eloquently notes, "The human is always subject to the uncertainties of bios, logos, Eros, and ethnos and to the ambiguity of having to interpret reality and translate the affected psychical body, composed and compromised by health and illness and by the urgency of becoming a subject with and for others" (71). Listening analytically, that is, not to a reality of need but to psychic demands and affects, places us all in the dilemma of having to figure out, as Britzman suggests "how these ephemeral affects are transmitted and communicated not only as political positions but also more intimately and more personally, as states of mind" (63).

This dilemma is animated in the film through the encounter between the adult and the child. As Alex's sexuality erupts, the film shows the difficulty of stepping into an unknown situation through a crisis of meaning. Nobody knows the fate of gender, whether it is stable or unstable. No one can predict it, and no one imagines that it changes. Everyone witnesses the blossoming of a problem, but nothing can be done because the situation itself is not yet understood. Lots have been written in psychoanalysis about the child's unpreparedness to encounter the (dis)orienting effects of the adult's sexuality (Laplanche, "Seduction" 673). In this film however, we have an opportunity to witness the lingering aftereffects of the child's unpreparedness in the adult's confusion as she faces the child's burgeoning and enigmatic sexuality. After the heated sexual scene, as in latency, everyone's sexuality goes to sleep.

The oscillation between the cruelty of the need to know and the wish for the mind to go to sleep is not foreign to the clinic, as the analyst confronts new and unfamiliar gender formations. As we witness the film's approach to the problem of understanding the child's gender, we may wonder whether this response could orient our thinking when we are faced with the conundrum of engaging with gender embodiments we cannot imagine and whose fate we cannot predict. The emotional situation of anxiety over unpredictability returns us to the dilemma Holden raises about our capacity to imagine an other's experience. The problem of how the world appears to someone who is outside the normative phantasy of gender is a particularly interesting one in the context of the clinic because the analyst too must enter the patient's emotional logic by stepping into her world. As Bion suggests, the analyst must abandon their memory and desire in order to truly encounter the patient. But how does the analyst meet the nonbinary patient?

Seeing the world through nonbinary eyes already posits a challenge for the analyst who may have never thought of her own gender outside of the contours of normativity. At the limits of understanding, the analyst must reevaluate everything she knows. This generates resistance to that which one cannot anticipate and requires the ability to tolerate the loss of mastery as well as feelings of futility and anguish. What is at stake for the analyst is not only an ethical attempt to understand the other, but also the willingness to study one's own resistance in order to unlock one's imagination.

The Fate of Love

The analyst's dilemma of attempting to understand the new without passing to the act involves the sway between two positions: acceptance that one really does not understand and the ethical imperative to make meaning. This dilemma, I believe, takes a particular form with a nonbinary patient. The analyst comes to the scene with her own biography—their own way of inhabiting and relating to their gendered body—and may experience difficulties sustaining analytic neutrality. The analyst must think about the patient's identity as well as their own and must contend with the effects of the patient's identity claims on her own sense of intelligibility. The experience of needing to know, and not knowing what counts as knowledge, is a phantasy-laden crossroad that impacts our capacity to listen to what is being said and to understand its unconscious dimension. Learning about the patient's internal world, however, involves the capacity to tolerate experience before meaning, which hinges upon the analyst's ability to tolerate their own wish for stability and knowledge in the absence of any resources for predicting the future. The analyst must wait.

What I have attempted to transfer from the film to the clinic is the question of temporality; that is, the inherent retroactivity that defines the meaning-making process. Like the viewer, the analyst must have the capacity to hold doubts about what is being seen, and it is not until one experiences this crisis that it is possible to begin asking new questions and develop new ways of seeing. Psychoanalysis teaches us that we are inherently susceptible to impressions without meaning and that subjectivity gets configured through the process of translation and mistranslation of the other's "enigmatic messages" (Laplanche, "Seduction" 673). These enigmas, in Laplanche's view, are traumatically "implanted," (673) because their meaning exceed both the sender's conscious meaning and the receiver's capacity to interpret and integrate. The structural lack of correspondence between what we receive and what we make of it is what makes any signifying exchange an emotional situation, riddled with "the violence of interpretation" (Auglanier xxii).

Imagining our psychical world as a scene of seduction makes the analyst's capacity for listening challenging. How do we unlearn prohibitions? At stake in this question is our capacity to understand something that is experienced as forbidden. From the point of view of translation, the enigma we face can be articulated in this way: The partial nature of our own identifications gives us the possibility of variability because only parts of enigmatic messages we receive are internalized. Yet, our identifications are already subjected to adult prohibitions. As we listen to the nonbinary patient, we cannot extricate ourselves from the interdictions that shape our experience of gender, nor can we easily step far beyond the education which frames our thinking. It may be difficult, in other words, for the analyst to get out of the science of psychiatry or psychology and its desire for stability through diagnosis. There is also the potential transference crisis that may ensue upon encountering something unrecognizable, and yet familiar. In addition, the gender-nonconforming person may respond to the analyst's perceived normativity in ruthless, omnipotent, or hysterical ways, which in turn may provoke the analyst to act out in similar ways.

The opening up of gender possibilities could potentially also awake the desire of exploration in the analytical setting—the excitement over being seen or not seen, the thrill of beauty and transgression, the elation of playing with the forbidden, or a seeming carelessness about one's gender and objects of desire. How do we, as analysts, open space for these explorations? The film also offers us this space of freedom and imagination, as we too enter into a space of suspended temporality with no stable origin or predictable future. While our attempts to make sense will often meet our emotional defenses, the film strongly suggests that an ethical relation can be made without understanding—or precisely because we cannot understand—the origin and future of our sexuality.

The enigmatic situation of the film presents an aesthetic crisis for the viewer who is left holding the indeterminacy of gender and the mysterious fate of love. By suspending the question of futurity, *XXY* slows down time, and what is transposed to the clinic is the question of whether the analyst can hold time in mind and wait for things to unfold without taking action. The move from action to thinking is an approach that resembles the act of watching the film as an aesthetic situation, and it involves the analyst's capacity to hold the patient's demands as a way into an imaginary world. There is an immense psychical effort involved in bearing with uncertainty, and this emotional demand is placed on the viewers through the near-rape scene, where the gang "acts out" our individual and cultural voyeurism. We, the viewers, want to see; we want to know what Alex is. Just like the gang, we say we are not hurting her; we just want to "see and categorize" (Corbatta 828).

This difficulty of bearing with enigma is also mirrored in the psychoanalytic clinic. As I witness Alex's enigmatic subjectivity unfold, I am also considering the inevitable losses and disillusionment both analyst and patient must experience along the way for something new to be created. There will not be a perfect resolution, final answer, or totalizing understanding, and meaning-making will involve a destruction of our ties to the familiar. What is at stake for the analyst in entering a new experience is anxiety over losing mastery, and yet, what may be metaphorically described as castration is also an anxiety over separation. Separation anxiety is repeated in the afterlife of affects as a nostalgic holding on to a saturated concept that renders difficult affects intelligible and through which the analyst will have to work. Without the analyst's willingness to tear down theory with a kind of lightness, our conceptual apparatus risks becoming concrete. For separation, as Klein suggests, also involves tolerating the destruction that comes within creativity, a devastation of meaning that requires a rebuilding of new signification through reparation (311).

If reparation in the realm of gender requires the analyst to bear with difference, with queer affects—affects that are strange and estranging, even unthinkable, and at the same time familiar—the analyst must be prepared to take themselves as an unknown, to put their own gender in doubt through the possibilities of sexuality. Here we may imagine the analyst as an artist whose creativity leans upon their capacity to loosen their certainty over reality, to cease treating it as known. The creative process, Milner suggests, "is a plunge that one could sometimes do deliberately, but which also sometimes just happen[s], as when one falls in love" (31). Milner's linkage of creativity with love also reminds us that in the creative process of the analytic encounter there are two libidinal investments—one's own and the other's. The encounter of two libidos conjures an image of intense passion and, alongside, a threat of devastating wreckage. And here we may wonder, how does the analyst, who sways between openness and apprehension, moves toward the space of creativity needed to think gender beyond the claustrum of normativity?

Milner suggests that there is a necessary regression that paves the way to creativity and symbolization, not by way of defeat or destruction, but through the capacity to give in to an experience through concentration and play. When we enter an experience, she argues, we occupy an intermediate space where an illusion of a kind of fusion surfaces, allowing a return to a primary object but also a vague awareness that me and not me can come together. Something is created within the illusion of a future that cannot be anticipated but is nonetheless imagined. The link between regression and creativity also positions the transitioning of gender and the transitioning of the analyst's mind within the realm of an aesthetics—a surrendering to a process that is unknown but one that leans on the work of interpretation as a way of giving imaginative form to our enigmas.

As an aesthetic experience, the film *XXY* impresses and excites us out of our gender certainties. As we surrender to the intermediate, suspended time of the film, we also enter into an emotional situation of uncertainty, where we too, may experience ourselves as other to what we thought we were. The analyst too is required to give in to experience, to loosen their omnipotent hold over knowledge, understood as that without which I can no longer recognize myself (or the other). "Beware of understanding," Lacan warns. This loosening is predicated upon the acceptance that every act of understanding is an emotional situation, and hence, counter to the certitude of identity. *XXY* approaches the indeterminacy of gender as an inquiry into the vicissitudes of Eros in our current time. Linking the problem of temporality—the delay in understanding the retroactive construction of meaning—to aesthetics—our capacity to sustain the enigma and its affective weight—the film strongly signals that we are all implicated in the emotional situation of gender.

Notes

1 Throughout this essay, I will use the pronouns "he" and "she" interchangeably as a way to echo the very ambiguity produced by the film. My decision stems from the fact that the pronoun "they," which is never used in the film, risks stabilizing Alex's gender in a way that takes away from the character's sustained indeterminacy.
2 As Verónica Garibotto notes, Massumi defines emotion as "the socio-linguistic fixing of the quality of an experience which is from that point onward defined as personal" (20). As a result of social convention, emotion has meaning and can thus be verbalized.

Works Cited

Aulagnier, Piera. *The Violence of Interpretation*. Routledge, 2001.
Bion, W. R. *Attention and Interpretation: A Scientific Approach to Insight in Psycho-Analysis and Groups*. Tavistock, 1970.
Britzman, Deborah. *Anticipating Education: Concepts for Imagining Pedagogy With Psychoanalysis*. Myers Education Press, 2021.
Corbatta, Jorgelina. "Sexuality, Normality, and Social Terror: *XXY* by Lucía Puenzo." *Psychoanalytic Inquiry*, vol. 3, no. 8, 2015, pp. 823–831.
Edelman, Lee. *No Future*. Duke UP, 2004.
Frohlich, Margaret. "What of Unnatural Bodies? The Discourse of Nature in Lucía Puenzo's *XXY* and *El Niño Pez/The Fish Child*." *Studies in Hispanic Cinema*, vol. 8, no. 2, 2011, pp. 159–174.
Garibotto, Verónica. *Rethinking Testimonial Cinema in Postdictatorship Argentina: Beyond Memory Fatigue*. Indiana UP, 2019.
Gozlan, Oren. *Transsexuality and the Art of Transitioning: A Lacanian Approach*. Routledge, 2015.
Holden, Stephen. "Confronting the Perils of Puberty Squared." *Review of XXY*, directed by Lucía Puenzo, *New York Times*, 2 May 2008, www.nytimes.com/2008/05/02/movies/02xxy.html. Accessed 10 June 2021.
Klein, Melanie. *Love, Guilt and Reparation and Other Works, 1921–1945*. The Free Press, 1975.
Laplanche, Jean. "Interpretation Between Determinism and Hermeneutics: A Restatement of the Problem." *The International Journal of Psychoanalysis*, vol. 73, no. 3, 1992, pp. 429–445.
———. "Seduction, Persecution, Revelation." *The International Journal of Psychoanalysis*, vol. 76, no. 4, 1995, pp. 663–682.
Meltzer, Donald, and Meg Harris Williams. *The Apprehension of Beauty: The Role of Aesthetic Conflict in Development, Art, and Violence*. Karnac Books, 2008.
Milner, Marion. *On Not Being Able to Paint*. Routledge, 2010.
Winnicott, Donald. "The Theory of the Parent-Infant Relationship." *International Journal of Psychoanalysis*, vol. 41, 1960, pp. 585–595.
XXY, directed by Lucía Puenzo, 2007.

Chapter 9

Trans-transvestite Childhoods

Considerations for an Out-of-Closet Psychoanalysis in Argentina and Uruguay[1]

Translation: Veronika Brejkaln

Mauricio Clavero Lerena

In the last 20 years, both in Argentina and in Uruguay, debates on sexuality and gender relations have been at the forefront of the public sphere, spearheading the agenda in Latin America. These debates had been postponed during the military regimes in both countries. Yet, according to Dr. Diego Sempol (18), the conquest of democracy and the process of re-democratization made possible greater freedom of expression. Thus, since the end of the military regimes and especially in the last two decades, social movements around sexual diversity have gained relevance in both countries, generating institutional and cultural conditions for collective actions.

The changes are evident in the structure of opportunities, the regulation of legal situations, and the historical trajectories of the relationship between the State and peoples of sexual diversity, many of whom have become involved in activism, at times of high risk (McAdam 28). These individuals have turned their discomfort into action, producing rights and group solidarity, both of which have left an impact on a psychic level via new identification processes resulting from militancy for a common cause (Sempol 20). These social movements have successfully challenged the moral frontier that separated "legitimate" and "stigmatized" sexualities: They have increasingly displaced pathologizing views on sexual identities, made new identities visible, and made possible the recognition of their rights. In 2012, Law No. 26.8743—The Gender Identity Law—was passed in Argentina. In 2013, this law made it possible for a girl named Luana to become the first trans person in the world to have her self-perceived identity officially recognized by the State, without the mediation of judges or health professionals.

In 2018, Law No. 19.648—The Comprehensive Law for Trans People—was passed in Uruguay. It included the possibility of legal recognition of trans childhoods, as well as the elimination of discrimination and stigmatization of this population, establishing measures for prevention, care, protection, and reparation.[2]

Yet, in the cases of Argentina and Uruguay, social and institutional practices have changed faster than theories. On many occasions, psychoanalysis has not

DOI: 10.4324/9781003266211-12

adequately accompanied these new realities. Although the passing of the afore-mentioned laws alludes to an increasing public interest in sexual and gender diversity, psychoanalysts have in general failed to revise some of their long-standing conceptions on these topics and to update their clinical practices. As a result, they might be contributing to further marginalizing people of sexual diversity.

I believe that thinking psychoanalytically about trans-transvestite childhoods requires a debate so that "the invisible becomes visible and the unthinkable becomes enunciable" (Fernández, "Morales incómodas" 171). It would be neces-sary to consider a theoretical breadth both in and outside that territory, as well as to listen and learn from these presentations, to construct interventions, metaphori-cally and literally, outside the closet, attempting to incorporate aspects of what has been called an epistemology of the closet, as proposed by Eve Kosofsky Sedg-wick. This involves a review of how knowledge has been built from the sufferings of that reality, keeping in mind what we say and who we are talking about when we discuss closets of dissent, as well as the tensions around sexual and gender identities and the process of construction of dissident subjectivities within the patriarchal system that subordinates them. It also implies unraveling the methods, logics, and languages of knowledge that lie in what we understand as the closet of sexuality, recognizing that each process involves assuming a risk of ideological, political, economic, and, sometimes, physical survival.

According to Dr. Débora Tajer, the closet is a biopolitical device that unfolds in the processes of subjectivation and generates specific distresses, depressions, and anxieties ("Algunas consideraciones" 278). In the past, prior to their legal and public recognition—in the "closet stage"—people of sexual diversity would emerge publicly almost exclusively during adulthood. Expressions of sexual diversity during childhood were either inhibited or redirected to the closet. Today, in the "post-closet stage," these expressions become visible much earlier, often during childhood. This imposes a challenge to the psychoanalytic practice of rec-ognizing a post-closet stage.

Psychoanalysis and Sexual Dissidents: A Field in Tension

One of the first tensions that can be elucidated between psychoanalysis and sexual dissidence is related to the epistemological obstacle of (non-)problematization, developed by Dr. Ana María Fernández, in which theories unfold in the tension between what is possible to be thought and what is not thought. A conceptual advance develops when it is taken as a challenge to produce thought in the limits of what is not known, which undoubtedly raises uncomfortable thinking (Fernán-dez, "Morales incómodas" 171). This can prevent the unthinkable from extricat-ing itself from the order of prohibition and metaphorically institute unconscious denials of one's own field of vision. In the words of Thamy Ayouch "more than in any theory or praxis, thought in psychoanalysis happens only to the extent that it opens up to the non-thought and invites a renewal of the coordinates of thinking" (12).

It is worth highlighting the precision with which the author articulates this position, pointing out two irreducible dimensions that contribute to our understanding of the relationship between psychoanalysis and sexual dissidence. On the one hand, there is the plane of the analytical process that seeks psychic elaboration, transformation outside of repetition, conflict management, and transference relationship. On the other hand, there are the social, historical, political, and subjective transformations that exceed the analytical process and cut through it irreducibly (Ayouch 13). As such, the psychoanalytic edifice is not immune to the historical and sociopolitical, and psychoanalysts who speak of sexual dissidence often fail at contemplating dynamics of the psychic when speaking from the historical sphere. According to Ayouch,

> Speaking as a psychoanalyst and speaking in the name of psychoanalysis are two very different positions. The first, that of the psychoanalyst, involves going through a personal analysis, which could be defined as the renunciation of abusing a position of power. The second, as a claim to intercede on questions of society in transit to rework the links between subjects, is a position of power that refuses to submit the analytical discourse itself to an analytical approach.
>
> (13)

Ayouch, drawing on Merleau-Ponty (61), mentions that refusing to question categories of metapsychology based on new phenomena causes a petrification of the institution and a loss of its instituting dimension. For theory not to become dogmatic and de-centered from its narcissistic axis, it has to open up to the intersubjectivity of transference through contact with the clinic, with history, and with other theories. All fixed metapsychology is nothing more than a resistance to psychoanalysis (Ayouch 14).

One of the great psychoanalytic contributions regarding psychosexuality consists of decoupling the drive from its object. In this sense, infantile sexuality is conceptualized as a *plus de placer*, irreducible to the satisfaction of a vital function. As Blestcher has observed ("Sexualidades diversas" 19), diverse presentations of infantile sexuality challenge the limits, categories, and legitimizing practices of a conservative social apparatus. By understanding sexuality as a *plus de placer*, psychoanalysis contributed to criticizing the sexual morality of its time and to denouncing its disciplinary mechanisms. It is thus surprising to observe how, today, certain psychoanalytic developments resist an examination of the heteronormative mandates underlying their theories. Therefore, it is necessary to bear in mind the Foucauldian proposal that considers different forms of psychoanalytic discourses. The Foucauldian warning would heed not to incur in a reductionism of psychosexuality that responds to a technology and that agrees with the logic of the Christian pastoral (Foucault, *Historia de la sexualidad* 137–140), in which the prohibition of incest intends to show that children have desire thanks to their parents, and, to parents, that their children could not hate them. Psychoanalysis, in short, must examine its complicity with the normativities imposed by the technologies of sexuality.

From this theoretical assumption, and considering the conditions for the construction of knowledge in psychoanalysis, one might ask: What are the discourses of psychoanalysis regarding trans-transvestite childhoods? How are conditions of psychoanalysis able to generate discourses regarding this reality? How does psychoanalysis conceptualize trans-transvestite corposubjectivities (Clavero 84), considering that they are inserted in a historically unthinkable discursive plot?

It is observable that many positions on the subject stem from a psychoanalysis that is instilled in the tradition of medical-pastoral discourse on sexual dissidence; and, on occasion, from a psychoanalysis that presents itself with the intent of integration that stems from tensions between psychoanalytic postulates and the reality of sexual dissidents.

The latter are those that avoid the horizon of structuralism and essentialism, and think within the framework of interdisciplinary borders, asking questions, like those proposed by Dr. Silvia Bleichmar: What does psychoanalysis currently have to offer? How can it contribute to make sense of the human suffering of this century and to what extent do our thinking, our theories, our positions in the face of such suffering allow us to face the problems of current subjectivities? What is left of the psychoanalytic formulations referring to sexuality, and what is it that is no longer valid? (*Las teorías sexuales en psicoanálisis* 1). These questions propose a non-essentialist path toward considerations of the relationship between psychoanalysis and sexual dissidence, and require a critical review within psychoanalytic theory and clinical practice. Thus, the question arises as to how to produce psychoanalytic knowledge from the experience of sexual dissidence, contemplating the subjectivity of those who share their life biography, without falling into an academic extractivism that subjects the protagonists to intellectual abuse?

One possible way of addressing these questions is the rigorous theoretical distinction that Bleichmar makes between the production of subjectivity and the constitution of the psyche (59). She postulates a constitution of the psyche by referring to the processes of its functioning which persist beyond historical changes, and, in this case, beyond the existential presentations of dissident subjectivities. The production of subjectivity, in contrast, is anchored in the field of the political and the historical, such that subjects are always integrated into culture. The production of subjectivity makes a significant contribution to differentiating between the concept of extended sexuality and the concept of gender. In this sense, sexuality would be defined by autoeroticism, and understood as the extra pleasure not reducible to self-preservation. It includes, directly or through sublimatory forms, the whole of psychic life, sexuation, and the male–female attribution classically linked to anatomical sexual difference. The concept of gender, on the other hand, is anchored in historical and contextually situated ways of attributing traits to these differences (Bleichmar, *Las teorías sexuales en psicoanálisis* 124).

For Bleichmar, the moment in which the infant defines "masculine-feminine" beyond the recognition of sexual distinction is what today must be considered under the coordinates of gender. Freudian theory did not make a considerable advance in the conceptualization of diversity. Psychosexuality implies an assembly of movements and steers away from a linear vision. It is characterized instead by resignifications of psychic life and the culture where it is built, not limiting itself to a genital choice of object exclusively. In other words, psychosexuality is traversed by instinctual movements throughout the entire life of the subject, and desiring productions arise from the order of sexual identity and from the different ways in which the sexed subject belongs to an identity sector. This concept of sexuality amplifies the possibilities of listening to sexual dissidents from psychoanalysis.

In conjunction with the aforementioned, Javier Sáez believes that queer theory "has been built, from its beginnings, in a permanent debate with and against psychoanalytic theory" (16). He argues that one of the paradoxes of the history of psychoanalysis is that some psychoanalytic institutions have developed in the opposite direction to the critical potential that Freudian approaches held. In some cases, clinical perspectives led to an increasingly moralizing, hetero-centered, and normative practice and theorization, producing rejection and criticism on behalf of the groups of sexual dissidence.

Moreover, Judith Butler sees in psychoanalysis the potential to "serve as a critique of cultural adaptation and also as a theory that understands the ways in which sexuality does not conform to the social norms that regulate it" (*Gender Trouble* 31). This author is one of the referents of *queer* thought who, together with Teresa de Lauretis, has vexed the most with psychoanalysis, providing a deep and grounded criticism of the binary nature of sexuality, the pathologization of trans under the psychotic structure, the primacy of heteronormativity founded on structural bases, and the phallocentric character based on the primacy of the phallus and sexual difference.

Advancing in the postulation of these tensions between psychoanalysis and sexual dissidents, it can be affirmed that one of the greatest challenges in psychoanalysis has been the psychopathological vision *per se* of sexual diversities. Pathological readings and discourses in relation to sexual orientation were a prelude to other visions, also pathological, of sexual and generic identity. Psychosis and perversion became princeps for the alleged understanding of particular forms of presentation of sexuality.[3]

The Freudian concepts exposed in "Sobre la psicogénesis"—where the configuration of homosexuality is established, from both somatic-sexual and psychic-sexual characteristics and the type of object choice—often led to misleading bridges with perversions. Likewise, those exposed in "Puntualizaciones psicoanalíticas," along with Schreber's record, became an input for the construction of that psychopathological view.

In this regard, Facundo Blestcher ("Infancias trans" 21–40) argues that, for a long time, the transvestite has been associated with perversion, transsexualism has been homologated to psychosis, and trans childhoods have been viewed as the feminized phallus of the mother. The forms of exercise of sexuality or their identity positions do not define, by themselves or completely, psychic structuring or eventual psychopathology. Therefore, it would be a mistake to state that trans-transvestite childhoods constitute a psychopathological picture *per se* (Clavero 83). According to Blestcher, sexuality is not limited to social arrangements that guide the masculine/feminine bipartition, nor to genitality crossed by the difference of the sexes; nor is it subsumed to a harmonic unity free of conflict beyond the regulatory zeal of disciplinary regimes of the social imaginary. As such, it rescues that value of psychoanalytic praxis in which the transforming capacity of psychic suffering has been demonstrated, not because it was compatible with the subjectivity of each era, but, as the author says, because it challenged clinical practice, sustaining the fecundity of its paradigms for the resolution of conflicts and human suffering. Likewise, psychoanalytic practice considers that a diagnosis is not reduced to a sum of observable indicators or to the grouping of signs based on nosographic categories. For this reason, the depathologization of sexual diversities is imperative in order to contemplate metapsychological indicators that allow the precise localization of psychic suffering and pertinent clinical interventions. This implies considering the complexity of desiring determinations and identifying logics in the processes of constitution of sexual identity, which must be contemplated case by case and inserted in a wide spectrum of sexual subjectivities.

Pathologization, *per se*, calls for the singling out of a new point of tension within the modern sexual order. In this regard, Fernández affirms that we are heirs to a sexual order that responds to a binary, hierarchical, and attributive logic of sexuality (Fernández and Siqueira Peres 21). It is binary because it fixates on only two terms (man-woman, heterosexual-homosexual). It is attributive because it assigns certain characteristics to people who carry particular identities. Finally, it is hierarchical because it has positioned nonheterosexual sexualities as "difference." This logic has built an epistemic, political, ethical, and scientific a priori, which has unequalized sexual presentations that do not respond to heteronormative criteria. This causes naturalization of "different" people as inferior, dangerous, and sick. Deep transformations of erotic and existential modalities go beyond the stereotypes of this logic, coexisting in a new symbolic order that rejects swift identity traps and instead produces a pathway from sexual difference to sexual diversities. This transition implies the construction of philosophical and political categories that can account for these transformations.

This point is crucial for understanding the relationship between psychoanalysis and sexual dissidence. Specifically, it puts into question the instituting of difference and diversity, not with the aim of discarding or imposing one on the other, but in order to discuss the conditions of containment of the subjective suffering that both propose. This is not a question of ignoring the episteme of sexual difference, which has contributed so much to psychoanalysis. Rather, it is a question of how, from the episteme of sexual diversity, other notions of suffering may be considered, since the term diversity expands binary forms without denying the differentiation of the sexes (Fernández and Siqueira Peres 22).

It is therefore necessary to deconstruct criteria that make psychosexuality invariable and to approach the problem as part of a sociohistorical field (Fernández and Siqueira Peres 25). In other words, it is necessary to consider the complexity and specificity of successive transformations, as well as the ties with erotic practices in agreement with these definitions, in which a modern sexual order is sustained. This reminds us that the modern device of sexuality, as described by Foucault, built a specific imaginary that channeled desires, bodies, and practices of subjective formation under logo-phallocentric and heteronormative logics (Fernández, *Las lógicas sexuales* 19).

For Fernández, notions such as gender, gender identity, sexual identities, and sexual diversities are at odds with classic psychoanalytic terms such as sexuation, sexual difference, and sexual identification. This discrepancy, which is both clinical and conceptual, needs to be further examined in order to better understand the subjective positions presented by sexual dissidences. It is necessary to support the visibility of diversities as well as to build a new conceptual framework that avoids reducing these existentiaries to the formulas of sexuation proposed by Lacan. "Sexuation" refers to a logic whereby enjoyment is limited to a specific conceptual field. Fernández (*Las lógicas sexuales* 23–26) points out that the two logics regarding collective sexuality are far from being synonymous and that conflating them into one would be a mistake. In this sense, it is necessary to implement methodologies that make it possible to sustain a tension between sexual logic and the logic of sexuation. These methodologies should allow for interrogation and uncertainty and should ensure that we do not explain what we do not understand about sexual dissidence based on prior knowledge that stems from a different logic. Relying on the idea that psychoanalysis is grounded in a politics of listening on a case-by-case basis is not enough. It is of course imperative for clinical practice to be based on the singularity of listening. But listening is not something by itself (Fernández, *Las lógicas sexuales* 24). Indeed, recent social changes, their new collective logics, and the concepts that accompany them demand an examination of the modern episteme of identity/difference that provides the conceptual framework on which listening is based. According to Fernández, if we disregard this epistemological level, we run the risk of being unable to understand what the latter conceptual framework considered impossible to be understood.

The modern sexual order has been enriched by contributions of gender studies and sexual diversity which have become a transdisciplinary horizon calling for coordination between metapsychology and the psychoanalytical clinic. This enrichment is not sustained through the reduction of trans-transvestite childhoods to a view of gender identity, but in viewing gender as a dimension of articulation with metapsychology. In the words of Blestcher, sexual drive is not subsumed to gender representations, nor is it reduced to the difference of the sexes ("Infancias trans" 25). From a conceptualization of subject formation, the exchange with gender studies allows us to consider the ways in which statements, mandates, and ideals, constructed according to the historical-social imaginary, are psychically inscribed. Considering the complexity of the processes of constitution of the psyche and the production of subjectivity, it is possible to recover a boldness that challenges the efforts to normalize the apparatuses of sexual discipline.

Trans-transvestite childhoods and their corposubjective presentations come to question. In many cases, they challenge and dislocate that sexual order, demanding psychoanalytic listening outside the psychoanalytic closet and destabilizing a certain status quo of psychosexuality. The various presentations of sexed bodies expand and disturb the stereotypes of traditional devices, building a field of tension problematization.

Thinking about these trans-transvestite corposubjectivities (Clavero 85) implies considering the psychosexual constitution of these childhoods, their life biographies, discourses of culture, and parental desire production, thus appealing to the intersectionality and transversalization of trans-transvestite bodies in childhood as an opening to the problematization of its political dimension.

The above brings us, once again, to consider that these childhoods will be crossed by paradigms in crisis. As such, we must reflect on the emergence of actors reclaiming distinct rights and for whom certain referential theoretical frameworks available in analysis to date have proven ineffective. This implies a wager on intertextuality that is not simply quantitative but is based on the order of complex multiplicity in which it is not only a question of weaving different strands of reality but also of highlighting the differences as a specific issue in itself—as mentioned by William Siqueira Peres (155–167)—in other words, to propose "cartographies of the trans-contemporary," which would make it possible to trace connections of emancipatory processes in opposition to practices that maintain binary, universal, and ahistorical thinking.

It is pertinent to cite the question that Butler asks—true to her political-philosophical vision—of psychoanalysis regarding the trans: "How could the excluded return, not as psychosis or as the figure of the psychotic within politics, but as that which has been silenced, that which has been excluded from the domain of signification?" (*Cuerpos que importan* 270).

For the philosopher, the mechanisms through which a subject is structured are determined by certain normative aspects of psychoanalysis. This calls for thinking about theory from a political point of view and, at the same time, not excluding certain social and sexual positions, since to do so would imply being "at the service of the normalizing law that it seeks to question" (Butler, *Cuerpos que importan* 270).

Trans-Transvesti Existenciaries in Childhood

There are several tensions that have unfolded within psychoanalysis in relation to the conceptualization of trans-transvestite childhoods. I have noticed that some analysts prefer to talk about the "trans in childhoods" while others about "trans childhoods." There are also those of us who prefer to speak of "trans-transvestite childhoods." The various theoretical orientations, the totems of our libraries, the new texts, the theoretical-clinical training, the perspectives on the modes of sexual subjectivity, and the erotic-existential events will, perhaps, build a toolbox for those psychoanalysts who ponder these realities. Thus, the discourse of "those patients do not come to us" echoed by some colleagues becomes a question of "why don't these patients come to us?" If we can truly build and uphold such questions, perhaps we can understand that it is not about *what we have to say*, but rather *what we have to listen to*.

Those of us who have had the opportunity to follow up clinically and/or investigate empirically these realities have found that it is a matter of recognizing the richness of knowledge that has been produced exclusively outside our disciplinary borders, particularly from groups of diversity and sexual dissidence. These collectives have constructed theories that many of us, from our cis-sexuality, have not been able to adequately engage (Clavero 84).

To intervene psychoanalytically with these realities implies accompanying the crossing of borders, as proposed by Paul B. Preciado. Such crossing practices, which question the political and legal architecture of patriarchal colonialism, sexual difference, and the nation-state, place a living human body within the limits of citizenship and even of what we understand by humanity—a radical path not only for the traveler but for the human community that welcomes or rejects it. This crossing is the place of uncertainty, of nonevidence, of the strange, all of which is not a weakness, but a strength (Preciado 29).

The notion of border crossing makes it possible to visualize central and peripheral sexualities; as if using a geographical simile, not with the aim of maintaining a locus of belonging, as mentioned by Raquel Lucas Platero (82), but with the aim of outlining the position that a sexual practice, experience, or identity occupies with respect to the vectors of power that compose it, so as to show its constitutive fissures. In this sense, it is a territory to be known, produced in the cartographic movement itself—a parallel process where that which is found is also established, as proposed by Gilles Deleuze and Félix Guattari. In this sense, it is pertinent to dwell on what Marlene Wayar rigorously describes as "mutual empathy" (*Travesti* 24). This mutual empathy would favor the consideration of the nostalgia of childhood as time and cartography for inquiry, transformation, and identification. This will make it possible to empathically listen to exploratory childhoods that, when not swiftly pathologized, can be used as reference models that offer the possibility of producing new knowledge (Clavero 85). As Wayar points out,

> Childhood as that time and cartography where we can add a third option to the dichotomy proposed between identity/I and Otherness, with the power to build Ourness, a valuable possibility to raise our voices. Humanity is until today understood as the heterocentric man-woman systemic reality. From

such binary understandings, we have results such as those enunciated in the first law: "Thou shalt not kill." In macro terms, death has been the most productive business of the binary system: heterosexual civilizations against heterosexual civilizations. And at the micro level, heterosexual families and homes have been forcing, expelling and even killing, by action or omission, these childhoods. So, from the Latin American Trans Theory we affirm that "We no longer want to be this Humanity" (Susy Shock). And when we say this, we attempt to get out of the systemic binary: "I am not a man, I am not a woman, today *I am being transvestite*." The gerund explains the *only for today*, but it does not close it off from crisis or transformation. I will see whether from my commitment and responsible love I am able to leave the topography of the other, alien and oppressive, in order to produce, from my place and time and with all those records that I have, a critique from which to confront any theory in order to situationally ratify or rectify any theoretical construct, the all-knowing.

(Wayar, *Travesti* 25)

In a similar manner, Dr. Eva Giberti in a personal communication from May 5, 2019 mentions:

A world that has always existed and has been able to make itself see and seek recognition against any current that has marked what is normal and what is not. A reality that has been hidden and concealed, suffering, confused . . . closely defined by the outside . . . where cultural violence tries to force one to behave as desired . . . where children who are discovering their gender identity perceive themselves as mystified, putting into play elements of being as identity and of the existence of that being.

The words of Wayar and Giberti introduce us to the passage from "identities" to "existenciaries," with the aim of contemplating a possible cartography around these trans-transvestites childhoods while recognizing their uncatchable character in terms of their definition and the fluency of their locations. "Existenciaries" echo a constructive perspective of trans identity, a construction not finished but open to temporality and contingency (Arfuch 28), emerging from positions of the subject without being fixed in time or reduced to a few key signifiers. Thus understood, they refer, rather than to being, to the process of becoming (Arfuch 28) and operate as a game of representations that work within the framework of specific symbolic and material contexts. This assumes that there are no existenciaries without a narrative of the self, without a discourse or a network of social intersubjectivities that serve as a framework of intelligibility (Clavero 85).

Existenciaries make possible apparently discordant "identity" forms, as mentioned by Blestcher ("Infancias trans" 40), with the assigned anatomical sex or with generic binary representations that define the difference between masculine and feminine in accordance with devices for production of subjectivity, proving that it is never about the wrong body.

The notion of existenciaries follows the thought of Martin Heidegger and is articulated alongside current developments of Fernández, and Fernández and Peres, as well as with the notion of trans existenciaries, coined by Lohana Berkins (91), who urges us to go beyond the nomination trans as an "umbrella" term that groups transsexuality, transgenderism, and transvestite.

The notion of trans existenciaries not only considers identities as diverse but also claims that they are masculine or feminine enough (Butler, *Gender Trouble* 76), thereby wagering on a transvestite identity that summons us to wonder what it is to be *transvestite enough*. In this regard, identity is not merely a matter of a theoretical order. It is a manner of existing, seeing, and being seen in ways that allow or prevent recognition, enjoyment, and access to rights. Being a transvestite is not being gay. It is not being transsexual. Being a transvestite is a political act, typical of a southern movement and not, as Europeans used to say, a step toward transsexuality. Being a transvestite is a way of life. It is to give a nomination to what you want to be, embedded in an order that challenges such nomination. In Wayar's words "it is to pass theory through the body" (*Diccionario* 68–69).

These trans-transvestite existenciaries are enriched with the notions of nomadic itineraries and nomadic subjectivities, proposed by Rosi Braidotti (25) as figurative styles and political fictions that allow us to think through, and beyond, established categories. Nomadism enables a type of critical consciousness that resists the settlement of socially encoded forms of thought and behavior. The nomadic subject is the changing and multilayered product of a dynamic outside. The nomad is also an eminently critical fiction; hence the author affirms, "what defines the nomadic state is the subversion of established conventions, not the literal act of traveling" (31). During childhood, trans-transvestite existenciaries take on, from Braidotti's position, corporeality as a construction of desiring subjects, where the will for rational self-perceived change is in tune with desire.

The passage from the notion of identity to that of trans-transvestite existenciaries in childhood addresses what is here proposed in that it adheres to the dialogues between psychoanalysis and queer theories, upholding the notion of hybridization as a way of breaking with homogenizing processes. This concept, developed by Donna Haraway (18) and taken up by William Siqueira Peres (162), refers to the uses and abuses of the category of identity category. Likewise, there is a critique of identity from an anti-essentialist position that challenges attempts at naturalization and fixation from a totalizing perspective. As Siqueira Peres says, "identity presents at its core a dimension of exclusion and denial of any differential vector, dosing the sex/gender/desire system and its binary and universal determinations" (163). Furthermore, he mentions that "all identity is constructed through the effects of a relationship of knowledge-power-pleasure, where the process of identification represses, excludes, denies, and prohibits other possibilities for the subject's position" (163).

Final Reflections

Trans-transvestite existenciaries in childhood, legally recognized, materialize the expansion of rights and put into discussion conceptual categories that until a few years ago were not up for debate. Questioning these categories does not mean subjecting them to full revision and modification, but rather to promote the coexistence of traditional and novel discourses at a time of transformation of our clinical practice. This process of coexistence is traversed by prejudices that, at times, become more visible in waves of neoconservatism or in discourses that strongly advance a depathologizing position.

Psychoanalysis finds itself challenged by being summoned to consider the changing presentations of psychosexuality. As mentioned by Dr. Leticia Glocer (215–216), this is not necessarily an attack on a symbolic order. Rather, order and disorder coexist, and it is out of moments of disorder that new symbolic orders emerge. Likewise, the concept of sexual difference in psychoanalysis becomes obsolete when it is sustained within a binary logic. The new order allows for a rethinking of categories that consider lines of flight with greater complexity, accounting for a psychoanalytic porosity that appeals to the construction of theory and clinical practice from intersectionality and interface. "Intersectionality" alludes to the different dimensions that constitute the dissident subject's singularity and that go beyond sex-gender to include age, race, social class, economic position, and access to formal education, among others. These dimensions bring us closer to a situated subject whose heterogeneity cannot be subsumed under only one category. Ignoring intersectionality can result in the erasure or in the lack of recognition of the similarities among certain sectors of dissidences and diversities. "Interface" refers, in a theoretical and clinical level, to the ability to think psychoanalytically across disciplinary fields. This makes it possible for us, as involved analysts, to accompany the psychic suffering of dissident childhoods by inviting us to overcome normalization and to position ourselves against current demands for social adaptation.

Psychoanalysis is a theory that occupies a particular place of medical-hegemonic knowledge. From this place, psychoanalysis can engage in interdisciplinary dialogue in order to identify which position, in relation to psychoanalytic theory and clinical practice, a psychoanalyst assumes when thinking of trans-transvestite existenciaries. This dialogue is of utmost importance not only in order to understand the psychoanalyst's intervention but also in order to repair and rebuild a bond relegated during the process of dissident subjectivation.

To conclude, I turn to a quote from Débora Tajer,

> We must be aware that a discipline (or field) such as psychoanalysis, which was a pioneer in dislocating the relationship between psychosexuality and biology, does not re-knot sexuality and biology anew . . . since we may become part, without wanting to, of the conservative thought and practice

that psychopathologizes all sexuality outside the heteronormative. . . . Perhaps it is more honest to admit that, at present, the clinical and theoretical tools that we have are mostly built to alleviate human suffering, albeit from a heteronormative perspective, with a naturalization of sex and an essentialization of gender. Therefore, we know very little about how to diagnose in order to decouple aspects of production of subjectivity and historical sexuation from the psychopathological ones in the field of sexual diversity practices. And that is part of our current challenge.

("Diversidad y clínica psicoanalítica" 142)

In this sense, and in line with Tajer's words, trans-transvestite existenciaries in childhood are a new challenge for psychoanalysis.

Notes

1 This article is part of an ongoing research project, titled "Psychoanalytic Perspectives on Trans-transvestite Childhoods." The project is part of the Doctorate of Psychology in the Faculty of Psychology of the University of Salvador and is affiliated with the Argentine Psychoanalytic Association in the city of Buenos Aires.
2 For further details on this topic, see Saldivia; Mansilla (*Yo nena, yo princesa* and *Mariposas libres*); and Pavan. These texts expand on the case of Luana and are the first antecedents in Argentina on trans childhoods.
3 The texts of Didier Eribon expand on this point, criticizing psychoanalysis as the bearer of homophobic and heterocentric discourses. Both texts are worked on by Javier Sáez in his text *La teoría queer y el psicoanálisis* (2008). Moreover, Sáez's text reveals the latent content of homophobia that underlies political correctness in certain psychoanalytic discourses.

Works Cited

Arfuch, Leonor. *Identidades, sujetos y subjetividades*. Prometeo Libros, 2005.
Ayouch, Thamy. *Géneros, cuerpos, placeres. Perversiones psicoanalíticas con Michel Foucault*. Letra Viva, 2015.
Berkins, Lohana. "Los existenciarios trans." *La diferencia desquiciada*, edited by Ana María Fernández and Wiliam Siqueira Peres. Biblos, 2013, pp. 91–96.
Bleichmar, Silvia. "La atribución de identidad sexual y sus complejidades." *Actualidad Psicológica*, vol. 29, no. 320, June 2004, n.p.
———. *Las teorías sexuales en psicoanálisis. Qué permanece de ellas en la práctica actual*. Paidós, 2014.
———."Sostener los paradigmas desprendiéndose del lastre. Una propuesta respecto al futuro del psicoanálisis." *Aperturas Psicoanalíticas. Revista Internacional de Psicoanálisis*, no. 6, 2000, www.aperturas.org/articulo.php?articulo=130. Accessed 15 June 2021.
Blestcher, Facundo. "Infancias trans y destinos de la diferencia sexual: nuevos existenciarios, renovadas teorías." *Psicoanálisis y género. Escritos sobre el amor, el trabajo, la sexualidad y la violencia*, edited Irene Meler. Paidós, 2017, pp. 21–40.

———. "Sexualidades diversas e identidades nómades: incidencias sobre el psicoanálisis." *Entrelíneas, Revista Digital del Centro Oro*, no. 11, 2017, pp. 19–27.

———. *Transidentidades, transexualidades, transgéneros. Una lectura sintomática de la clínica psicoanalítica*. Topía, 2009.

Braidotti, Rosi. *Sujetos nómades*. Paidós, 2000.

Butler, Judith. *Cuerpos que importan. Sobre los límites materiales discursivos del «sexo»*. Paidós, 1993.

———. *Gender Trouble*. Routledge, 1993.

Clavero, Mauricio. "Infancias trans. Interpelaciones en la figura del psicoanalista." *Equinoccio, Revista de Psicoterapia Psicoanalítica*, no. 1, 2020, pp. 79–100.

Deleuze, Gilles y Guattari, Félix. *Mil mesetas*. Pre-Textos, 2006.

Eribon, Didier. *Reflexiones sobre la cuestión gay*. Anagrama, 1999.

———. *Una moral de lo minoritario*. Anagrama, 2001.

Fernández, Ana María. "Composiciones actuales de las diversidades sexuales." *Revista Generaciones*, vol. 4, no. 4, 2015, pp. 2–20.

———. *Las lógicas sexuales. Amor, política y violencias*. Biblos, 2009.

———. "Morales incómodas. Algunos impensados del psicoanálisis en lo social y lo político." *Revista Universitaria de Psicoanálisis*, no. 2, 2000, pp. 171–189.

Fernández, Ana María, and Juan Carlos De Brasi, eds. *Tiempo histórico y campo grupal. Masas, grupos e instituciones*. Nueva Visión, 1993.

Fernández, Ana María, and William Siqueira Peres, eds. *La diferencia desquiciada. Géneros y diversidades sexuales*. Biblos, 2013.

Foucault, Michel. *Historia de la sexualidad*. Vol. 1. Siglo XXI, 1976.

———. *Vigilar y castigar. Nacimiento de la prisión*. Siglo XXI, 1984.

Freud, Sigmund. "Algunas consecuencias psíquicas de la diferencia anatómica entre los sexos." *Sigmund Freud. Obras completas*. Vol. 19. Amorrortu Editores, 1925, pp. 259–276.

———. "Puntualizaciones psicoanalíticas sobre un caso de paranoia (Dementia paranoides) descrito autobiográficamente." *Sigmund Freud. Obras completas*. Vol. 12. Amorrortu Editores, 1911, pp. 1–76.

———. "Sobre la psicogénesis de un caso de homosexualidad femenina." *Sigmund Freud. Obras completas*. Vol. 19. Amorrortu Editores, 1920, pp. 137–164.

Giberti, Eva. "Maternidad travesti." *Revista Actualidad Psicológica*, vol. 25, no. 281, 2000, pp. 6–10.

———. "Transgénero, travestis y bioética." *Bioética y bioderecho*, edited by Luis Blanco. Editorial Universidad, 2002, pp. 88–109.

———. "Transgéneros, psicopatología y/o bioética." *Revista Actualidad Psicológica*, no. 260, 1998, pp. 5–11.

———. "Transgéneros, síntesis y aperturas." *Sexualidades migrantes*, edited by Diana Maffia. Feminaria, 2003, pp. 31–58.

Glocer Fiorini, Leticia. *La diferencia sexual en debate. Cuerpos, deseos y ficciones*. Lugar Editorial, 2015.

Haraway, Donna. *Ciencia, cyborg y mujeres: la revolución de la naturaleza*. Cátedra, 1991.

Heidegger, Martin. *Ser y tiempo*. Fondo de Cultura Económica, 1951.

Kosofsky Sedgwick, Eve. *Epistemología del armario*. Ediciones de la Tempestad, 1998.

Mansilla, Gabriela. *Mariposas libres. Derecho a vivir una infancia trans*. Universidad Nacional de General Sarmiento, 2018.

————. *Yo nena, yo princesa. Luana, la niña que eligió su propio nombre.* Universidad Nacional de General Sarmiento, 2014.

McAdam, Doug, John McCarthy, and Mayer Zald. *Movimientos sociales: perspectivas comparadas.* Istmo, 1999.

Merleau-Ponty, Maurice. *Résumés de cours. Collège de France, 1952–1960.* Gallimard, 1968.

Pavan, Valeria, ed. *Niñez trans. Experiencia de reconocimiento a la identidad.* Universidad Nacional de General Sarmiento, 2017.

Platero, Raquel Lucas. *Intersecciones: cuerpos y sexualidades en la encrucijada.* Bellaterra, 2012.

————. *Transexualidades. Acompañamiento, factores de salud y recursos educativos.* Bellaterra, 2014.

Preciado, Paul Beatriz. *Un apartamento en Urano. Crónicas del cruce.* Anagrama, 2019.

Sáez, Javier. *Teoría queer y psicoanálisis.* Editorial Síntesis, 2008.

Saldivia, Laura. *Subordinaciones invertidas. Sobre el derecho a la identidad de género.* Universidad Nacional de General Sarmiento, 2017.

Sempol, Diego. *De los baños a las calles. Historia del movimiento lésbico, gay, trans uruguayo (1984–2013).* Sudamericana, 2013.

Siqueira Peres, Wiliam. "La psicología, lo queer y la vida." *La diferencia desquiciada. Géneros y diversidades sexuales,* edited by Ana María Fernández and William Siqueira Peres. Biblos Sociedad, 2013, pp. 155–167.

Tajer, Débora. "Algunas consideraciones éticas y clínicas sobre las infancias trans." *Psicoanálisis y género. Escritos sobre el amor, el trabajo, la sexualidad y la violencia,* edited by Irene Meler. Paidós, 2017, pp. 277–295.

————. "Diversidad y clínica psicoanalítica: apuntes para un debate." *La diferencia desquiciada. Géneros y diversidades sexuales,* edited by Ana María Fernández and William Siqueira Peres. Biblos, 2013, pp. 123–139.

Wayar, Marlene. *Diccionario travesti, de la T a la T.* Página12, 2020.

————. *Travesti: una teoría lo suficientemente buena.* Muchas Nueces, 2019.

Wittig, Monique. *El pensamiento heterosexual y otros ensayos.* Egales, 2006.

Popular Reception and Public Circulation

Transnational Perspectives

Chapter 10

Anarchists, Socialists, Communists, and Freudians

The Working Class in Chile and Their Reception of Psychology and Psychoanalysis (1920–1950)

Mariano Ruperthuz Honorato

Acknowledgments

This article discusses the findings of the research project ANID-CONICYT-FON-DECYT N° 1190226 titled "El Rol de la Higiene Mental en la Definición del Modelo de Asistencia Psiquiátrica en Chile (1917–1954)" directed by Dr. Mariano Ruperthuz Honorato.

Introduction

The objective of this work is to discuss the protagonists of the history of psychoanalysis in Latin America from a new perspective that includes other actors and protagonists. I aim to extend the frontiers of the history of the discipline, offering new ideas about the worldwide social and cultural impact of psychoanalysis. In this sense, my approach differs from typical thinking about the spread of Freud's ideas centered on professional associations, their analysts, and their patients. This focus has resulted in a canonical history based on a linear conception of time that underscores the role of pioneers who paved the way for "a true history of psychoanalysis"; a history whose origins can be traced to remote European and North American practices and that culminates in the founding of local branches of the International Psychoanalytical Association (IPA). The most famous examples of the history of psychoanalysis from this approach stem, indeed, from the work of Sigmund Freud himself in 1914 (933): Freud supposedly founded a whole new way of understanding the world, which was born as an *ex nihilo* product and inspired in his own creative genius. Later, the hagiographic style of Ernst Jones, in his monumental biography of Freud, reinforced a canonical perspective linking psychoanalysis to Freud's personal life. Many later works followed this lead and engendered a scientific myth around the "Freud event," as Alfredo Eidelsztein (42–43) calls it, which focuses on the creator of psychoanalysis without much focus on the particularities of the different contexts to where Freudian ideas arrived.

DOI: 10.4324/9781003266211-14

Researchers such as Thomas Glick and Mariano Ben Plotkin have been especially critical of this narrative, which reflects a clear strategy of self-legitimization while simplifying the complex processes of the reception of Freud's theories in Latin America. Indeed, in the last 20 years, several historical works have validated the existence of multiple, diverse, and intricate implementations of psychoanalysis in Latin America, long before the local introduction of psychoanalytic organizations. In this sense, psychoanalysis, as an object of historical research, has become less centralized and more diffuse, with a more penetrating presence in many sectors of Latin American societies. As Hugo Vezzetti (7–13) states, it is indeed more fitting to use the term "Freudism," as opposed to "psychoanalysis," when attempting to elucidate the power of this discourse in reconfiguring the fields of social medicine, psychiatry, education, and criminology, to name but a few. These ideas have prompted a whole series of research on the different processes of cultural reception of Freud's ideas in our continent, where these processes are indeed more important than the cultural capital of psychoanalysis's "legitimate" representatives. Researchers who have engaged in this latter perspective include Mariano Ben Plotkin, Hugo Vezzetti, Alejandro Dagfal, Cristiana Fachinetti, among others. Their historiographical style offers many more options for understanding psychoanalysis as connected to social fields like politics, education, social medicine, other international movements in health care such as mental hygiene, the media, and mass culture.

Drawing from this perspective, my chapter focuses on the first half of the twentieth century, specifically the process whereby a portion of the Chilean organized working class began to incorporate "psy knowledge" (Rose 39): a heterogeneous set of knowledge including psychology, psychiatry, and psychoanalysis. Working-class people shaped their own understanding of the pain and suffering of the working classes of the continent through a novel appropriation and reformulation of ideas about the mind. Until now, and in line with the more canonical view of the history of psychoanalysis referenced above, the history of mental disciplines has largely adopted a vertical, top-down approach with an almost exclusive focus on the "official" representatives of science as the only legitimate source of knowledge (Scull 1–19). Such historical accounts tend to privilege a narrative whereby knowledge descends upon the common population, brought by physicians, psychologists, psychiatrists, government agents, etc. to guide and illuminate their lives. Yet, the fundamental thesis of my study is that anarchists, socialists, and communists configured an incipient culture of care, or rather self-care, in mental health matters and dedicated significant space in their publications to discuss psychological theories and principles that would explain the impact of working-class life on mental health, relations with the ruling class, and their own sociopolitical projects. In contrast to the top-down approach which does not consider the Chilean working class as anything other than passive objects of state medical attention and intervention, I contend that they were active protagonists in the appropriation and reformulation of psychological insights that they integrated with relevant political ideologies. The evidence presented in this chapter, then, also helps to establish a new approach for the history of the working class, calling attention to the importance of the mental variable in the middle of the political struggle and to how the Chilean working class thought about the psychic effects of the capitalist way of life; for instance, how they thought about labor exploitation, the technification of life, and strategies of political repression that used psychological categories to pathologize workers' demands.

The idea of the prevention of mental illness was a paramount objective for these social groups, and this prompted a movement that was no longer exclusively medical and brought together a coalition of various civil society actors (Campos 101–106). Mental hygiene constituted, especially in the interwar period, a transnational health movement geared toward the prevention of mental disorders, not just treatment, which was considered belated (Thomson 283–304). The mental hygiene approach informed important reform movements in asylum psychiatry and influenced the creation of different Pro-Hygiene Mental Leagues in various countries, thereby promoting popular education programs in psychological health. In this sense, this chapter aims to provide a discourse on how people adopted a type of psychological culture that corresponded to their political ideas. Mental illness and its treatment became important to demonstrate the need to resist the productivity requirements of the owners of factories and manufactories. Diagnoses like neurasthenia, which popularly circulated in Western societies, underlined the relationship between psychology and social discourses on physical and mental energy and work performance. Some important examples are the works of David G. Schuster, and Marijke Gijswijt-Hoftra and Roy Porter.

The historical evidence of my work is based on several statements about psychology, psychiatry, and psychoanalysis found in metropolitan workers' journals and newspapers during the period 1917–1950 in Santiago de Chile. These entries revealed how ideas by Sigmund Freud, Ivan Pavlov, Richard Von Krafft-Ebing, Santiago Ramón y Cajal, and many others, were used to read into the experience of class and pay testament to a psychological culture (Illouz 1–21). Considering this, it is interesting to look at how workers viewed themselves in relation to history:

The way history has been written distorts the true moral character of those men of bourgeois identity, and therefore must be annulled. At all times, human history should be written by those who suffer the most. The moral history of men should be written by prostitutes and wartime histories should be written by the inhabitants of the villages occupied by the enemy and refugees from the villages that are burned down. This would ensure we always know the reality of how it felt to be there and the truth of what happened.

("Psicología integral" n.p.)

Workers decided to rethink their role in the history of Chilean society, precisely when their movement, in the first decades of the twentieth century, gained increasing representation in national politics. Researchers such as Raymond Craib show

how the Chilean oligarchy used their political power against groups they considered dangerous. It was a time when the social State began to develop in Chile, and the popular sectors became a concern for the political oligarchy (Craib 1–13). From this point of view, by considering the workers' journals as historiographical documents produced by nonexperts—in this case Chilean workers, who are thought of as a subaltern group (Guha 17–32)—this chapter seeks to demonstrate the impact and significance of this material, as an "archive from below," in reframing the history of the development of psychological knowledge and psychoanalysis in Latin America. These past years, especially since October 2019, Chile has been confronting the consequences of neoliberal economics and its political regime in the lives of the population. The "social awakening" in Chile under the slogan "it's not depression, it's capitalism" shows how the psychological dimension of social pain has been an important focus of debate for many years. Chilean workers have always valued aspects such as instinctual drives, the channeling of sexual energy, and the role of the mechanism of sublimation. Although there are ideological differences among anarchists, socialists, and communists, all of them agreed on the establishment of a culture of mental self-care, solidarity, and self-management. It is precisely the history of this culture that my chapter illuminates.

Metropolitan Anarchists, the Society of Death, and the Psyche

The presence of anarchist groups in Chile dates back to the end of the nineteenth century. Based on the idea that the power of any state organization would end up being detrimental to individuals, anarchists stimulated the libertarian self-management of communities. The labor organization had as a principle that no one but the workers themselves should take care of their own health. Piotr Kropotkin's ideas of mutual support and those of the International Brotherhood of Mijaíl Alexandrovich Bakunin, for instance, were instrumental for Chilean anarchist groups. In their publications, Chilean anarchists called on their supporters to know well how capitalism dominated and exhausted workers both physically and mentally. The Chilean national crisis of the 1920s was reflected in the anarchists' diagnosis of their challenging social reality and the increasing manifestation of mental stress associated with exploitation, unemployment, and alcoholism. Without any hope of assistance from the state, church, or military, the workers declared that they needed "direct action" as a unique method of subsistence. A new order would come from workers organizing themselves. Chilean society was viewed as a set of murderous forces guided by raw self-preservation and offering no protection for the weakest: "Rather than an ode to death, present society seems like a campaign of mutual extermination. Killing the stomach, heart, and brain. . . . Drowning us in economic misery, religious preoccupation, authoritarian farce, and the collective mourning of the battlefields" ("La sociedad de la muerte" n.p.).

The anarchists were critical of the prevailing legal-political system and of the power networks of the military, the church, the banking system, and those working on building a formal nation. For them, these kinds of organizations violated people, enriching themselves off the efforts of the working class ("Sin trabajo" 7). The elites were seen as degenerates in a society that suffered—in psychopathological terms—from a "macabre obsession: the preservation of the 'social order,' an obsession sowing its own downfall, with the ongoing thievery inflaming the people who will inevitably explode like gunpowder" ("Represión y orgía" 1).

Anarchists had promoted educational work as a central axis of training. Thus, for example, the "Grupo Universitario Lux" ("El hogar común" n.p.), "projected illumination" via education as a means of improving the conditions of the exploited. "Education" was a big umbrella that included sex education, which was considered fundamental to control birth rates and, therefore, to deny children to an unjust and exploitative system. With the help of sex education, the decision to have a child would become the result of a rational and measured decision between parents engaged in fluid and harmonious dialogue. Young children would no longer be the cannon fodder of capitalism; the workers could not pay such a high price for their reproductive irresponsibility ("Sobre educación" n.p.).

In the mid-1920s the periodical *Tribuna libertaria* published a column titled "Psicología integral" touching on topics of general psychology and self-help, offering preventative recommendations that would encourage harmony between body and soul, though always emphasizing the idea that only well-prepared and balanced individuals could withstand the risks and challenges brought on by passions ("Psicología integral" 4). Prevention meant, for example, that "Nervous people who tend toward melancholy need to put into practice a basic principle of mental hygiene, to flee from sadness. They must avoid pessimistic environments which may overwhelm them with their heavy and dark atmosphere" ("Psicología integral" 4). The environment could be modified to facilitate desired mental health outcomes. As a result, deterministic ideas of the nature of individuals' psychological makeup would be avoided. In this sense, subjects should "stay away from threateningly neurotic or melancholic environments. Pessimistic environments formed by dark language, sad writings, gloomy friendships, and vulgar spectacles" ("Psicología integral" 4).

Based on this psychological perspective, childhood was valued as a critical period of human existence, especially for the adult personality. For this reason, psychoanalysis became an integral part of pedagogical orientation and social design. Thus, for example, in the journal *La voz del metalúrgico*, the Chilean psychoanalyst Ramón Clarés used the ideas of the renowned French psychoanalyst Marie Bonaparte and of Angelo Hesnard to speak about childhood development. Bonaparte's ideas helped to understand infantile sexuality: "the adults enlightened by the discoveries of psychoanalysis should stop claiming a monopoly over sexuality. The child also has their own sexuality and they have a right to it. This sexuality is part of the natural order and cannot be considered an exceptional vice" (n.p.).

Likewise, other referents of the movement were the Spanish physician Santiago Ramón y Cajal, winner of the Nobel Prize in Medicine in 1906, and the endocrinologist Gregorio Marañón, who supported the idea that scientific knowledge would eventually become a prominent force of the modern man's character:

> The time will come when science enlightens our conscience and uplifts our hearts. And, therefore, when the fetishism of capital is banished and man has assimilated the laws of evolution, has scrutinized and exploited the natural forces. . . . the cosmos will work for us by putting into action many machines to manufacture goods at ridiculous prices. [The time will come] when well-earned leisure time permits the universalization of science and art, and everyone can savor the ineffable harmonies and beauties that pulsate in the depths of nature; when, finally redeemed by solidarity and love, we all feel waves of the same vital current, sister cells of the same body. [When that time comes] what meaning will the words rich and poor, lord and slave, happy and miserable have?
>
> ("La sociedad futura" n.p.).

For his part, Marañón referred to how the nervous system suffered from excessive stimulation in modern urban environments and suggested that personal hygiene should include adequate amounts of rest: "For most civilized peoples, life is such that the nervous system is often overly excited. These are people who lead an excessively hurried life, hardly having time to eat during working hours" ("Cartilla de higiene personal" n.p.).

Embracing a communitarian spirit, the Chilean doctor Juan Gandulfo inaugurated in 1923 a *Políclinico Nocturno* to attend to the deepest felt needs of the labor sector. Organized by the *Comité Sanitario* of the International Workers of the World (IWW), the *Policlínico* was a confirmation that "we, workers, are capable of organizing our medical services without the support of the State or philanthropic institutions, thanks to this free initiative" ("La salud es vida" n.p.). Additionally, the IWW published *La hoja sanitaria* to address physical and mental hygiene issues. This publication disseminated contributions of notable physicians, such as Richard Von Krafft-Ebing and his work *Psychopathia Sexualis*, in which he claimed that "The sexual instinct drives one of the most important urges of the human organism. Few are those who comprehend the powerful influence that our sexual life exercises on the feelings, thoughts, and the individual and collective actions of humanity" (*La hoja sanitaria*, December 1924, n.p.).

Women were a crucial target audience for the anarchists' discursive strategies, which underscored women's control over their sexuality for the purpose of denying children to the capitalist exploitative system: "Again I address the poor and to them I say: DO NOT MARRY, DO NOT PROCREATE, HAVE NO CHILDREN. . . . Sabotage capitalism by denying it your children" ("La huelga de vientres" n.p.).

Also, metropolitan anarchists declared the need to overcome the "social anemia" that drained the people's productive energy, producing a sort of "criminal lethargy" ("Anemia Social"). The fatigue and tiredness born from exploitation, which the doctors call *surménage* (overwork or burnout), should be denounced to counteract its pernicious effects. To that end, people had to stop acting as a form-less mass of subjects, asleep in their unconsciousness and pain ("Boletín de los trabajadores" n.p.).

Finally, anarchists, not unlike their bourgeois peers, proposed their own set of "commandments," promulgating "rules for healthy living," which promoted food hygiene, cleanliness, adequate rest and sleep, exercise and proper physical posture, and, in particular, mental hygiene: "Mental hygiene: It is perhaps the most important: Avoid stress and hurrying. Keep calm. Control your emotions, otherwise they will control you. Be cheerful. Be kind. Be independent. Follow the advice of Emmerson and work with your own hands, stand on your own feet and formulate your own thoughts. In this way, you acquire self-control, which is the defining characteristic of the true man" (*La hoja sanitaria*, January 1926, n.p.).

The Socialist Appropriation of Psychological Knowledge: Between Impulses and Conditioned Reflexes

The idea of a socialist state that validated representative democracy and was capable of listening to the needs of the poor working and middle classes gave way to the birth of the socialist party in Chile. The country had experienced the effects of the global depression of 1929 and had thus greater sensitivity to the reception of socialist ideas that advanced strategies for the working world. Newspapers were both a way of keeping supporters informed of doctrinal issues and a source of moral training. If, according to anarchists, "social anemia" was one of the main social diseases to be fought, socialists saw the country as a "republic of vaga-bonds" in which poverty and misery caused children to roam in the streets and turned them into potential victims of vice and crime.

The socialist formation, from its beginnings, had women as a key piece for the new social design. Women also had to expand their knowledge about themselves, be aware of their potentialities, and be responsible for their physical and mental development. Socialists worked to redefine the role of women in improving the health and hygiene conditions in their families and communities. One interesting strategy was to actively encourage them to participate in sports. The labor periodical *El sindicalista*, for instance, published a letter in 1935 that invited women to participate in the *Club Deportivo*. Using the metaphor of the "human motor," physical exercise was considered as important as healthy eating and sleeping habits:

> If food produces enough calories to keep our human motor alive, systematic exercise eliminates through perspiration the slag and toxins that accumulate bit by bit inside our body. In addition, exercise strengthens the lungs,

toughens the muscles, and balances the nervous system . . . for these many reasons, it is essential for you to practice some form of sport.

("A mis compañeras" n.p.).

"A healthy mind in a healthy body" was the slogan that socialists encouraged in their supporters. The struggle for knowledge about human nature generated a process of secularization, where private life began to be the subject of a series of discourses on good habits, healthy behaviors, the fight against alcoholism, sexuality—especially venereal contagion—and training in labor rights. The demands of everyday life and mental work in the face of various stimuli were something to start worrying about. Daily life in the case of women should be a battleground for everyone's habits—those who live in "poorly ventilated offices, workshops with their noises produced by machinery, shops with the movement of the public ever-present, etc., have contributed to an enormous percentage of nervous infirmities and other disorders in general. Especially the female sex is victim of great evils: neurasthenia, hysteria, tuberculosis, and anemia" ("A mis compañeras" n.p.). Labor exploitation, according to this point of view, increased the probability of contracting nervous diseases. The poor material conditions of existence were seen as facilitators of mental disturbances. Therefore, the social struggle had to be based on the denunciation of these conditions, which turned them against the owners of the factories and different workplaces.

Union life was one of the most vital strategies of the movement, where language learning was also based on the development of sensitivity toward different aspects of life that were considered healthy. This argument, for example, helped to deepen the role of art as a powerful source of well-being and "emotional liberation." Art was also promoted, particularly as a channel of social transformation that could offer an aesthetic outlet for the pressures imposed by capitalist oppression. ("Función social del arte" n.p.). Workers' publications mobilized a rhetoric of self-fashioning as a means of personal and political resistance and emancipation. The newspaper *El despertar traviario* of January 1941 said,

REEDUCATION—The pedagogic system of reeducation is one of the gifts given to humanity through the development of Experimental Psychology, and according to which adults of any age can resume their schooling to brush up their knowledge and stay up to date. In this matter, one would be able to march in unison with progress and avoid being left behind, for indeed, and as the proverb says, reinvent yourself or die, for stagnation is death.

("Auto-cultura integral," n.p.)

The author of this series of columns was the socialist Arturo Grove, who demonstrated the state of the discussion about the possibility of human change. At this time, the social function of the discourses of pedagogy, psychology, psychoanalysis, and experimental psychology was to support the hope for greater behavioral flexibility. The dominance and determinism of August Morel's theory of mental degeneration in the Chilean local scene forced these sectors to look for new references to take on their political challenges. The appeal of psychological discourses was that they were capable of generating a whole discursive battery for social change through individual change. Concepts such as the unconscious, independent of its exact appropriation in academic terms, helped to reinforce the idea that a component existed in each of the subjects that, although unknown, could be analyzed and used in their favor thanks to certain mechanisms. Consciousness and will were the main factors of achieving human development. Introspection was the most powerful mental tool, since it provided a contact method with the inner self. It was French psychologist Théodule Ribot who presented this initial idea of the unconscious: "Referring to the mind, medical science has undeniable proof of simultaneous functions that develop independently from each other, around certain particular ideations, and many times these activities are beyond the control of consciousness and come to produce serious disturbances" ("Auto-cultura integral," June 1941, n.p.).

The human being, according to this framework, was a complex cellular system that connected mind and body. The mind was a network of biological particles programmed to achieve more complex configurations. The idea of the unconscious allowed for the transmission of messages of behavioral and emotional malleability. Individuals could change thanks to the procedures that psychology and psychoanalysis outlined. The socialist side reinforced the idea of the "inner man" whose will was the key to personal improvement. These hypotheses had to be spread among a broad partisan public who needed to be cultivated in psychological terms. The unconscious—or subconscious mentality, according to its French descendance (Ruperthuz 109–110)—in this sense, began to be observed as an important source for life information, as it presented a mysterious aspect of the "self": "According to biological knowledge, we can see that the subconscious mentality can be the 'sum' or coordinated meeting of the smaller 'psyches' or minds of each constitutive cell of the body" ("Auto-cultura integral," June 1941, n.p.).

The will, from this perspective, conflicted with unknown aspects of the subconscious. Specifically, the act of psychotherapy was explained as

> Psychotherapy. I said earlier that part of the mind's activity is to automatically regulate and control the functioning of the organs corresponding to digestion, blood circulation, respiration, and cellular life. Indeed, the mind creates a set of organized ideas in all its modalities, creating an 'evidence-energy' concept in a way that restores health. It is not wrong to think that the mind works in this way under its own direct influence to affect diseased organs or tissues in such a way that it benefits them by restoring their functions.
>
> ("Auto-cultura integral," June 1941, n.p.)

Thus, socialists were preoccupied with defending the idea that the human mind is both a source of wealth and anxiety. Socialists, like anarchists, proclaimed that the strength of capitalism, which was in turn supported by fascism, lied in its ability to lull or hypnotize the workers, converting them into a formless and influenceable mass of subjects. For this reason, it was important to educate oneself on these matters: "The most certain agent of hypnotization is SUGGESTION; already working directly in the mind of another person through orders and concepts. Being already in a state of receptivity, . . . the subconscious mind no longer obeys the 'higher psychic center,' that, according to Dr. Grasset, is the center of the conscious and responsible personal ego" ("Auto-cultura integral," June 1941, n.p.).

The leftist public strongly worked on the will/suggestion dichotomy. Principles about the will reinforced the idea of a human being aware of their potential to transform themselves and society. Consciousness was opposed to the darkness of "torpor" (i.e., sleep), a product of suggestion and fatigue that resulted from labor exploitation. Exhausted individuals were easy prey for fascism. Psychological strength was hence a precious commodity to resist these pressures. The worker who blindly obeyed their captors was the one who fell asleep in the torpor of their lethargy. Using the ideas of Karl Marx and Sigmund Freud, among others, socialists saw the risks of religion and childish thinking that dragged subjects toward domination. Real liberation required the awakening of consciousness, dissipating the effects that religion had imprinted on humanity ("Pueblo y religión" n.p.). Superstition and childlike thinking were denounced as neurotic rudiments. When the workers took power over the means of production, they would be replaced by feelings of economic security. Sigmund Freud, in this sense, was seen as someone who could help uncover deception. Yet, his approach had serious limitations, since it neglected to psychologize material conflicts:

> The psychoanalytic school teaches the genesis of religion. It shows how in many religions the main deity is a representation of 'the father' and emerges from this figure. The bottom line is that religious beliefs are, at their root, a generalization that adults make of children's attitudes toward their parents. Feelings of helplessness, the need for protection, fear, the need to love and evoke love, when mixed with religious beliefs, are in complete disagreement with socialist criteria.
>
> ("Pueblo y religión" n.p.)

If God was the father, individuals remained like children in front of him, obeying whatever opposed the idea of a society without privileges. On the contrary, if all human beings were equal in their union, they were developed adult beings and were capable of moving away from childish submission and dependency. In this sense, sexual drive energy was recognized as a source of development and steered away from the discourses of the conservative sectors of Chilean society. The latter tended to paternalistically see workers as destitute, derailed, and ungrateful children. Yet, sex life ceased to be part of family private life and became a subject of public debate thanks to the discourses of progressive sectors of society. Psychoanalysis contributed, from this point of view, the idea that sexuality was vital energy and that individuals were left with the task of taking charge of it. The healthy conduction of this vital energy allowed it to be directed toward purposes of social improvement such as work, education, sports, and art. These ideas made the sublimation mechanism highly valued across sectors of the left in Chile. They wanted to contest against conservative sectors, recognizing the inherent nature of being human and therefore the relevance of universal education in these aspects. For instance, Dr. Luis Lara Pardo responded in regard to the relevance of sexual education: "Much more effective is what psychoanalysts call the 'sublimation' of impulses: it consists of providing the individual with useful, pleasant, and healthy derivations that liberate them from 'sexual obsession'" ("¿Es necesaria la educación sexual?" n.p.).

Education, therefore, was a therapeutic resource and sublimation was a dynamic energy that enabled people to redirect their impulses and satisfy them via socially valued products, such as art, work, sports, intellectual pursuits, among others. On the contrary, vices such as alcoholism were seen from a transgenerational perspective ("Maldito alcohol") and condemned within the labor movement, since they sapped force away from the movement and the development of the country. Vices were a social weight that was not at the height of progress. People needed to cultivate themselves to achieve their own physical and mental mastery. For the socialists, reading books and pamphlets—vital to self-help—was the most viable means of breaking into the working class.

Alcoholism, in particular, helps explain the psychoanalytic language present in these statements. This language was combined with a treatment based on the administration of rewards and punishments inspired by Russian psychology: "The system of REFLEXIVE CONDITIONING, to which I refer, will have beneficial results not only for the rail workers, since their example means that other workers will not wait to put into practice in other unions or industries the consequent improvement of general living conditions of those who submit to it, but also for the Chilean family and our country's economy that will see, in form, considerably reduced absenteeism from work and other consequences inherent to alcoholism" ("¿A quién se les puede llamar alcohólicos?" n.p.). For socialists, Freud provided a rhetoric of greater plasticity for human change while Pavlov, with his theory of conditioned reflexes and behavioral change, offered a seemingly effective and economical method of administration that yielded good results. This kind of Freudo-Pavlovism was a therapeutic system that focused on alcoholism as the main problem, but also implied comprehensive training positing a series of disciplines that workers should consume: Philosophy of History, Economic Geography, Mental Hygiene, Comparative Religion, Literary History, and Linguistics.

Communists and Psi Knowledge: Educating the Masses to Avoid the Hypnosis of Fascism

Communist publications during the period were less receptive to psychological ideas. Yet, the dramatic structure of the communist narrative also alluded to the importance of the mental state as a critical unit of inequality and class struggle.

Russia was held up as a great example of revolutionary values for Chilean communists: "Live for the day. Acquire revolutionary convictions and longings. If you do not renew yourself morally, you will vegetate like cobblestones! You must respond to the times, to the degree of evolution reached. Live for the day, take in the influence of the Russian revolution" (*El comunista*, August 6, 1921, n.p.). Under this direction, communists wagered a bet on educational and political formation to try to generate strength of character for the social struggle: "We must instill in the brain of the populace everything that tends to dignify and beautify life. . . . All will fail who, through the force of ignorance, are insincere and full of vice" (*El comunista*, September 3, n.p.). In order to successfully lead masses of workers, character had to be adequately formed through scientific and artistic training. Workers needed to have ambition, so that, when they obtained machines, they could use them in favor of the people, overcoming the manifest shortage.

Moreover, the anguish of the working class in relation to capitalist exploitation can be seen in a letter from Sofía Méndez published as a testimony:

> At six in the morning, I am on my feet and since I do not have time to prepare myself a cup of coffee, I must go without having taken a bite and so I must endure until break time, which is at noon. And, after lunch, I return at one thirty and leave at six. During all that time, I am in the factory leaning over and putting more and more shoes in boxes under the watchful eye of the boss. If you rest a moment, you will be growled at and threatened to be thrown out on the street like a dog.
>
> (Méndez, n.p.)

This publication showed how economic dependency, long hours of working on your feet, tiredness, and frustration made the working class sick, both physically and mentally. Later, in 1936, communists observed the death of Ivan Pavlov with a likening: "When Pavlov died, he was one of the most enthusiastic defenders of the Proletarian State. Pavlov, like other scholars, intellectuals, and artists, discovered that the revolution had opened the doors to unimpeded progress. The full resources of the Proletarian State were theirs" ("Ha muerto Pavlov" n.p.). Pavlov's death served as a strategy to consecrate the relationship between science and revolution. The idealization of the scientist, and Soviet progress, continued to reinforce the idea that enlightened men are charged with spearheading great social changes. Like anarchists and socialists, communists denounced the hypnotic effect brought on by capitalism along with fascism. For this reason, the working class needed to be attentive to hysteria, used as a synonym for hypnotism and suggestion caused by, for example, Nazism: "Our Chilean populace have demonstrated their vigorousness, righteousness, and virility. We will not permit fascistic Nazi demagoguery to emasculate our human dignity. The obscurantism and hysterical sentiment of the Nazis undermines the ability to think, reason, and the free use of intelligence, which are indispensable elements of a free and cultured people" (*Bandera roja* n.p.).

In short, communists sought to get subjects to be conscious of social rights through their politicization in order to gain privileges from the bourgeoisie. The use of metaphors related to hypnosis reflects the call to "awaken" class consciousness and understand the concrete limitations of the people's absence of power over the means of production. The struggle, seen from this perspective, was actively fighting over the mental territory of the working class that, thanks to the cultivation of intelligence, could discover the tricks of capitalism and fascism and be a real health cordon, to borrow the language from mental hygiene, that would facilitate the advent of a new social subject.

Conclusions

Referring to the capitalist workday, Karl Marx declared the following, advancing an important allegory about working-class living conditions in the capitalist system: "Capital is dead labor, that, vampire-like, only lives by sucking living labor, and lives the more, the more labor it sucks. The time during which the laborer works is the time during which the capitalist consumes the labor-power that he has purchased from the laborer" (279–280). In this line, the theft of physical and psychic energies was a perfectly recognizable argument in the workers' newspapers in Santiago de Chile at the beginning of the twentieth century. Indeed, Marx's idea has recently been regarded as common sense by people invested in the class struggle, who have turned these original words into a representative fight around the world of the consumer, trying to find an active resistance method against the alienating fetishization of capital (Veraza 9–54). Authors such as Wilhelm Reich had already noticed the psychological threat that the bourgeois system posed for the working class and had denounced how a strong sex impulse was morally drowning, guaranteeing the presence of neurosis (Reich 13–40)—an assertion that actually led to Reich's expulsion from orthodox psychoanalysis in 1934 (Higgins and Raphael 255–260). Similar to Reich, revolutionary politics considered that capitalism drowns its subjects, turning them into a formless, classless, and manipulatable mass. The popular class is dominated via social control, the implantation of stereotypes, and values in accordance with the bourgeois political and economic system (Parker 7–14).

Consistent with this framework, historical sources show how in Santiago de Chile anarchists, socialists, and communists sought psychological insight, with a particular vision of mental hygiene, to manipulate "the spirit," soul, or psyche (depending on each particular rhetoric) in order to give individual and social sustenance to their respective political projects. They detected, as did the doctors and other state officials, that the working class had a positive view on the use of these insights. In this way, anarchists, socialists, and communists believed that they were also protagonists in a great psychological struggle, alongside the fight over the material conditions of existence. Using the analytical categories of psychology, they denounced with firm conviction that the bourgeoisie sought to "hypnotize" the working class, plunging it into a kind of social anemia, like the vampire mentioned by Marx. Therefore, their mission was to "awaken the consciousness" of their compatriots, instructing them in the principles of how the mind works, the strength of instincts, and the role of education to overthrow the exploitative economic system. They also redefined the parameters of "normal" sexuality, mainly influenced by religion, and exposed their people to spreading sexual education, a new role for women, and the control of pregnancy. In this sense, anarchists, socialists, and communists could see their capacity as proletariat. This awareness distanced them from traditional psychology, which viewed them as "objects" of study. Social collaboration thus also meant resisting a hegemonic use of psychology that described them as degenerates, full of vice, and lazy. This hegemonic view was held in parentheses and psychology was in turn used for their own political and social projects and to illuminate their human reality. By the same token, Freud's psychoanalysis was valued as a conceptual tool that reinforced mental dynamism to guide and dominate personality's most dangerous aspects. As the publication in my article shows, psychoanalysis's use was conditioned by the political vision of the workers, who combined psychoanalytic concepts and made them compatible with their respective left-wing ideologies and with other psychologies, such as Pavlovian principles on human behavior. For this reason, the conscious/unconscious dichotomy—as a synonym both for the instinctual human dimension and for capitalism's hypnosis—was one of the central rhetorical axes of that period's psychological knowledge.

The historical account in my article, then, enables an alternative, "from below" understanding of the Ibero-American historiography of the dissemination of psychological knowledge. Traditional historiography has typically ignored the participation of the working class in standing apart from their conventional portrait at the hands of "reputable scientists." The historiographic approach in my article hence questions the ethical position from which we view the past, its protagonists, and the actions they carry out. An anthropologically inspired history is necessary in order to bring "native" voices to the fore, instead of infantilizing them as poor examples with a mistaken reading of psychological science. Deepening this direction to further demonstrate the people's agency and capacity to detect, understand, and solve their own psychological problems remains a promising focus for future examination.

Works Cited

"A mis compañeras." *El sindicalista*, 1 Sept. 1935, n.p.
"¿A quién se les puede llamar alcohólicos?" *El despertar traviario*, May 1944, n.p.
"Anemia social." *Acción directa*, 2 Oct. 1934, n.p.
"Auto-cultura integral: anomalías de lo personal." *El despertar traviario*, Apr. 1941, n.p.
"Auto-cultura integral." *El despertar traviario*, Jan. 1941, n.p.
"Auto-cultura integral." *El despertar traviario*, June 1941, n.p.
"Auto-cultura integral: el sueño hipnótico." *El despertar traviario*, Apr. 1941, n.p.
"Boletín de los trabajadores industriales del mundo." Apr. 1920, n.p.

Campos, Ricardo. "La psiquiatría en la ciudad. Higiene mental y asistencia psiquiátrica extramanicomial en España en la década de 1920." *Frenia* vol. 4, no. 1, 2004, pp. 101–111.

"Cartilla de higiene personal. Cuidado del sistema nervioso. Necesidad del descanso." *La hoja sanitaria*, Sept. 1926, n.p.

Craib, Raymond. *The Cray of the Renegade. Politics and Poetry in Interwar Chile*. Oxford UP, 2016.

Dafgal, Alejandro. *Entre París y Buenos Aires. La invención del psicólogo (1942–1966)*. Paidós, 2009.

Eidelsztein, Alfredo. "No hay que salvar a Freud." *Imago Agenda*, no. 205, 2019, pp. 42–43.

El comunista, 6 Aug. 1921, n.p.

El comunista, 3 Sept. 1921, n.p.

"El hogar común." *Acción directa*, May 1922, n.p.

"¿Es necesaria la educación sexual?" *El despertar traviario*, Mar. 1941.

Facchinetti, Cristiana, and Dias de Castro, Rafael. "The Historiography of Psychoanalysis in Brazil: The Case of Rio de Janeiro." *Dynamis*, vol. 35, no. 1, 2015, pp. 13–34.

"Función social del arte." *El despertar traviario*, Oct. 1940, n.p.

Freud, Sigmund. "The History of the Psychoanalytical Movement." *The Basic Writings of Sigmund Freud*. The Modern Library, 1938, pp. 931–977.

Gallo, Rubén. *Freud's Mexico: Into the Wilds of Psychoanalysis*. The MIT Press, 2010.

Gijswijt-Hoftra, Marijke, and Roy Porter. *Cultures of Neurasthenia: From Beard to the First World War*. Rodopi, 2001.

Glick, Thomas. "Precursores del psicoanálisis en la América Latina." *Episteme*, no. 8, 1999, pp. 139–150.

Guha, Ranajit. *Las voces de la historia y otros estudios subalternos*. Crítica, 2002.

"Ha muerto Pavlov." *Bandera roja*, May 1936, n.p.

Higgins, Mary, and Chester Raphael. *Reich Speaks of Freud. Wilhelm Reich Discusses His Work and His Relationship With Sigmund Freud*. FSG, 1967.

Illouz, Eva. *Saving the Modern Soul. Therapy, Emotions, and Culture of Self-Help*. U of California P, 2008.

Jones, Ernest. *The Life and Work of Sigmund Freud. Volume 1*. Basic Books, 1957.

La hoja sanitaria, Dec. 1924, n.p.

La hoja sanitaria, Jan. 1926, n.p.

"La huelga de vientres." *Acción directa*, 1 May 1925, n.p.

"La salud es vida." *La hoja sanitaria*, July 1926, n.p.

"La sociedad de la muerte." *Acción directa*, Jan. 1921, n.p.

"La sociedad futura." *Acción directa*, Aug. 1924, n.p.

La voz del metalúrgico, 4 Oct. 1949, n.p.

"Maldito alcohol." *El despertar traviario*, June 1941, n.p.

Marx, Karl. *El Capital*. Book I. Vol. 1. Siglo XXI, 2008.

Méndez, Sofia. "Carta." *El comunista*, 17 May 1921, n.p.

Parker, Ian. *La psicología como ideología. Contra la disciplina*. Catarata, 2010.

Plotkin, Mariano Ben. *Freud in the Pampas: The Emergence and Development of a Psychoanalytic Culture in Argentina*. Stanford UP, 2001.

"Psicología integral." *Tribuna libertaria*, Oct. 1924, n.p.

"Psicología integral: el ambiente pesimista." *Tribuna libertaria*, Nov. 1925, p. 4.

"Pueblo y religión." *El despertar traviario*, May 1941, n.p.

Reich, Wilhelm. *La revolución sexual*. Le Diable Érotique, 1984.

"Represión y orgía." *Agitación*, 14 June 1925, p. 1.

Rose, Nikolas. *La invención del sí mismo. Poder, ética y subjetivación*. Pólvora, 2019.

Schuster, David G. *Neurasthenic Nation: American's Search the Health, Happiness, 1869–1920*. Rutgers UP, 2011.

Scull, Andrew. *Psychiatry and Its Discontent*. U of California P, 2019.

"Sin trabajo." *Acción directa*, Feb. 1922, p. 7.

"Sobre educación." *Tribuna libertaria*, Dec. 1923, n.p.

Thomson, Mathew. "Mental Hygiene as an International Movement." *International Health Organisations and Movements, 1918–1939*, edited by Paul Weindling. Cambridge UP, 1995, pp. 283–304.

Veraza, Jorge. *Marx y la psicología social del sentido común: contribución a una teoría marxista del sentido común*. Itaca, 2018.

Vezzetti, Hugo. *Aventuras de Freud en el país de los argentinos: de José Ingenieros a Enrique Pichon-Rivière*. Paidós, 1996.

Von Krafft-Ebing, Richard. *Psychopathia Sexualis: Eine Klinisch-Forensische Studie*. Stuttgart, 1886.

Chapter 11

The Early Expansion of Psychoanalysis in Latin America.

The Key Role of the Argentine *Revista de Psicoanálisis.*[1]

Alejandro Dagfal

From a critical perspective, a history of psychoanalysis in Latin America as a whole is still a necessary project. In spite of all the existing publications about specific countries, the works adopting a global approach about the region tend to be very rare (Plotkin, "Dossier"; Plotkin and Ruperthuz). This article would like to contribute in this direction. Most historical accounts on the expansion of psychoanalysis in Latin America generally take the organization of the Argentinean psychoanalytic movement as a milestone. However true that may be, celebratory histories, usually written by psychoanalysts, emphasize the atypical biographies, the outstanding personalities, and the original ideas of psychoanalysts whom they consider "pioneers" (Cesio; Doria Medina Eguía; Rascovsky; Lisman-Pieczanski and Pieczanski). The problem of placing so much emphasis on the "founding fathers" (and "mothers") is that the contextual factors—like the material and social conditions of possibility—tend to be overshadowed by individual personal traits, such as intelligence and perseverance. I do not imply that those qualities did not play an important role; however, they are not sufficient to understand the complex mechanisms involved in the establishment and dissemination of a new discipline such as psychoanalysis. For that purpose, it is necessary to take other explanatory factors into account—i.e., social network construction, self-legitimation, professional identity building, psychoanalytic training, funding, advertising, etc.

Therefore, in this chapter, I focus on the deliberate strategies and thoughtful mechanisms used by the founders of the Argentine Psychoanalytic Association (APA) to organize this institution as a continental reference regarding Freudian discourse and practices. Established in 1942, the APA was not the first official analytic association to be founded in Latin America. Nevertheless, I argue that it became the most influential given its impact on the training of analysts, not only from neighboring countries (such as Brazil, Chile, and Uruguay) but also from other countries (such as Mexico, Colombia, Venezuela, Peru, Spain, and even France). Thus, the APA became a "mother association" and role model for many others.

DOI: 10.4324/9781003266211-15

The reasons for the acquisition of this central position in the 1940s and 1950s were certainly multiple, but not fortuitous. Every organizational step taken by the founding group was carefully calculated in terms of development, diffusion, and self-legitimation. Even the financial aspects were evaluated in light of those criteria. In that context, the *Revista de Psicoanálisis*—an in-house organ of diffusion created in 1943—was conceived from its very beginning as an ambitious dissemination tool with an international scope. The wide distribution of the journal—the first publication in Spanish on the subject—also gave publicity to the sociocultural and professional activities of the APA. Thus, in most Latin American capital cities, the rumor quickly spread that, in Buenos Aires, it was possible for physicians to be trained as psychoanalysts recognized by the International Psychoanalytic Association founded by Sigmund Freud.

In order to illustrate how the journal shaped the early life of the APA—and that of potential psychoanalysts in other cities and countries—I focus my inquiry on the *Revista* itself, and in particular, on the many miscellaneous anonymous notes published throughout the 1940s and 1950s. These sources, neglected by other historians, provide valuable data about a complex sociability network, which included trips, conferences, seminars, fund-raising events, and celebrations, as well as announcements about new candidates, visiting specialists, loans for training, etc. In addition, information about new foreign authors and works available in translation as well as on topic preferences among local contributors and upcoming books is helpful to understand the progressive establishment of a Kleinian hegemony, which was simultaneously produced and reflected by the *Revista*. In this way, a new professional identity was forged and even exported. In this transnational circulation and dissemination process, the *Revista de Psicoanálisis* played a key role that I examine in this chapter.

The Beginnings of the Argentine Psychoanalytic Association and Its House Organ

The Argentine Psychoanalytic Association, the first official Freudian institution of Argentina, was created in December 1942 by a small group of physicians with different origins (Cesio; Balán; Plotkin, *Freud in the Pampas*). For more than a decade, this group developed as a sort of secret society limited to a few well-off *porteños* (that is, people from Buenos Aires). In the 1960s, however, psychoanalytic discourse had become all-pervasive. On the one hand, it represented an important training component in many public psychology programs, such as those in Buenos Aires, Rosario, Córdoba, and La Plata, where the most popular professors were generally APA psychoanalysts. On the other hand, psychoanalysis became a powerful tool in the developing mental health services in public hospitals that adopted an interdisciplinary approach (Visacovsky).

By the 1960s, psychoanalytic theories and practices became central in academic, professional, and intellectual debates, not just as a medical or clinical discourse but as a sociocultural lens. Understanding the rapid success of Freudianism in Argentina would require a complex history, including the astonishing socio-cultural renewal produced in the second half of the 1950s. This would take us outside the institutional life of psychoanalysis and into its influence on cinema, literature, and popular culture in general, a topic that exceeds the scope of this chapter. Instead, I focus on previously neglected aspects of "the official history of psychoanalysis" via the *Revista*.

Several books and articles have already examined the process leading to the founding of the APA (Grinberg, "Reseña histórica"; Cesio; Balán; Plotkin, *Freud in the Pampas*). The organization of the first psychoanalytic association of the Spanish-speaking world began at the end of the 1930s. The first Latin American association, however, had already been established in 1927, in Sao Paulo: the *Sociedade Brasileira de Psicanálise* (SBP). That association edited its own journal in 1928, before being recognized by the IPA in 1929, in the international congress held at Oxford. However, given the fact that it had no training members, this society had a very short life. The Portuguese-Spanish Society would only be created as late as 1954 and recognized in 1959 (Roudinesco and Plon; Muñoz).

By contrast, the most prosperous psychoanalytic association of Latin America almost began as a family matter of a few *porteño* physicians. Arnaldo Rascovsky, a young and well-reputed pediatrician, and Matilde Wencelblat, a schoolteacher interested in the visual arts, had a nice apartment in Santa Fe avenue. Beginning in 1937, they held informal meetings every Sunday evening dedicated to the study and discussion of the works of Sigmund Freud. Rascovsky's brother and cousins (Luis, "Lucio"; Rascovsky; Jaime Salzman and Flora Scolni), and his wife's brothers and sister (Simón, Raúl, and Betty Wencelblat) also took part in the group's meetings. Soon later, other young physicians joined (Alberto Talla-ferro; Teodoro Schlossberg; Guillermo Ferrari Hardoy; Luisa, "Rebe" Gambier). In 1938, a newlywed couple also began to attend: Enrique Pichon-Rivière, who was training as a psychiatrist in the Torres asylum, and Arminda Aberastury, a schoolteacher still in training as a pedagogue (Balán).

After 1938, thanks to the arrival of Ángel Garma and Celes Cárcamo (two med-ical doctors of Basque origins, married to French women and trained as psycho-analysts in Berlin and Paris, respectively), this amateur group started to change its character. In contrast to the Sao Paulo case, several participants had the pos-sibility of beginning a training analysis with recognized members of the IPA. For example, Teodoro Schlossberg, a young gynecologist specialized in endocrinol-ogy at Harvard, began his treatment with Garma, "the Spaniard." He was followed by Rascovsky and Pichon-Rivière. Matilde Wencelblat and her brother Simón (a lawyer) as well as Arminda Aberastury would soon follow. Cárcamo (trained as physician in La Plata before leaving for Paris) became the analyst of Guillermo Ferrari Hardoy (an otolaryngologist specialized in phoniatry in Berlin, Vienna, and Paris), Tallaferro, and Gambier.

In short, the members of this group, composed of young, cosmopolitan, illus-trated professionals (mainly physicians, most of them Jewish), belonging to immigrant families, with artistic and literary interests, embraced psychoanalysis on intellectual, professional, and personal levels. They were worried about their own well-being as much as they wanted to assuage the griefs of others. At that precise moment, they had the unusual opportunity of choosing between two training analysts who had all the required international credentials and who spoke Spanish as their mother tongue. Moreover, they had plenty of available time in their office agendas. It would be difficult to think of a more favorable context for the beginning of the institutionalization of psychoanalysis in Argentina.

In 1942, when Marie Lisbeth Glas Hauser de Langer arrived in Argentina, the founding of a national association seemed imminent. Not only were there two available training analysts who guaranteed international recognition but there was also a group of potential members who had been in training analysis for quite a while. This local group was well-established in various hospitals and departments, with multiple social contacts. While the arrival of Langer, trained in Vienna and analyzed by Richard Sterba, was not indispensable to the association's creation, she became the first female training analyst in the group.

The APA was finally founded on December 5, 1942, by Garma, Cárcamo, Langer, Pichon-Rivière, Rascosvky, and Ferrari Hardoy. Teodoro Schlossberg could not sign the founding act, for he had been invited to London by the British Council to do some training in psychoanalysis and endocrinology. After his return, however, he gave an emotional account of the event's significance:

> What an emotion and what a joy, in London, when I received, between the hard work and the hustles of war, the news about the official constitution of the association. I received compliments from E. Glover, Anna Freud, S. Payne, W. Hoffer, Melanie Klein, and others, who also admire our journal. To those who have worked so hard in both undertakings, I bring the compliments of our colleagues in England.
>
> ("Regresó de Londres" 206)[2]

Evidently, in the eyes of Schlossberg and of his British colleagues, the founding of the APA could not be separated from the publication of its journal, which would become a presentation card in many different countries.

The *Revista de Psicoanálisis* Is Published With the Aid of a Sponsor

The publication of the first issue of the *Revista* (presented in its very cover as "the official organ of the Argentine Psychoanalytic Association, branch of the International Psychoanalytic Association") was a crucial event for a little private association willing to go public on the local level as well as on an international scale. This small group, organized by around half a dozen of atypical physicians, badly needed the recognition of the specialized circles, but also of society as a whole. While psychoanalysis was rapidly expanding in different ways, the APA tried to create a monopoly over its legitimate uses, establishing a "cultural jurisdiction"

(Abbott 280–314). This explains why, in the first place, the association had been carefully organized according to international standards. In the second place, all the necessary steps had been taken to found and publish a journal modeled on the quality standards of its predecessors in the northern hemisphere.

Most likely, the person responsible for these institutionalizing strategies was Ángel Garma, who was elected president of the first board of directors. (Celes Cárcamo was appointed scientific secretary and Arnaldo Rascovsky editorial director). At the end of 1943, when the APA celebrated the acquisition of its headquarters, Garma summed up the process leading to that achievement:

> Four years ago, a few physicians present here, thought of establishing the Argentine Psychoanalytic Association. . . . In fact, it was decided not to establish it at that time, but to wait for a certain number of physicians to obtain extensive knowledge in the psychic treatment of neurotic subjects and also, to be well trained to elaborate theoretically what they had to do in their practice. Quietly, over the past four years, such fundamental scientific work has been done. It was a very satisfying period. Apparently, nothing was happening, but every day several doctors gladly submitted to a training psychoanalysis to deepen their knowledge, thus following international standards. In addition, they eagerly read the works of Freud and his disciples and carried out controlled treatments of neurotic patients. All of this without worrying about the opinions of the environment, which sometimes ridiculed their efforts.
>
> ("Inauguración nueva sede" 500–501)

This quotation makes it clear that, for Garma, in order to build an association on solid foundations, it was just as important to avoid wild analysis as lay analysis. This is why he placed emphasis on theoretical preparation and the training analysis of the candidates, which he explicitly defined as medical doctors. In addition, he insisted on the question of international standards, thus highlighting the inclusion of the APA in a much larger institutional order, and implying an affiliation that, thanks to the IPA, could be traced back to Freud himself. At the same time, it was clear that the analyst from Bilbao was satisfied with the progress achieved in the first year of the association: In the same speech, he details all the courses that had been taught in the association and the multiple topics covered in scientific meetings: schizophrenias, epilepsy, psychic impotence, infantile sexuality, female homosexuality, the role of the self in the judgment of reality, sterility, and Bergsonian philosophy from an analytical perspective ("Inauguración nueva sede" 500–501).

However, what seemed to have made Garma most proud was the association's growing editorial activity—under the direction of Arnaldo Rascovsky— as reflected in the pages of the *Revista*. In fact, the association's entire editorial project was quite ambitious, involving the translation of foreign books and the publication of manuscripts written by local members (distributed through El Ateneo bookstore). At the same time, the *Revista* published foreign articles in Spanish translation, contributions by local members, as well as book and journal reviews. In short, although Garma was mostly in charge of the institutional strategy—and even the "foreign affairs"—Rascovsky's leading of the editorial strategy was of similar importance.

> The Secretary, as Editorial Director, states that communications have already been sent to medical psychoanalysts living abroad and to all physicians in this country and in the region, announcing the constitution of our institution, the start of the *Revista* and the subscription offer. It is clearly stated that this Board of Directors has decided to offer the first issue free of charge to all those who request it, so that this publication has a wide reception among medical doctors, and in order to stimulate future subscriptions. This Board of Directors has also decided that the Journal be published quarterly, that is, at a rate of 4 issues per year. The subscription price has been fixed: $ 12 for local subscribers and $ 18 for foreigners. The first issue will appear in July, according to the budget proposed by the publisher Sebastián Amorrortu & Sons, who has set the amount of 5000 copies, with 144 pages, for the sum of $ 7,348.
>
> ("Asociación Psicoanalítica Argentina" 17–18)

Nothing seems to have been left to chance in the diffusion of this publication, which, as I have shown, was specifically aimed at a specialized medical public. In the back cover of the first issue (which was accompanied by a subscription form), there was an ad announcing the articles that would be published in the following issue, a mention of the books already published in the series "Library of Psychoanalysis," and the books that would be published in the future. The six founding members of the APA—who made up the journal's editorial committee—participated in this task. So did other members, less notorious at the time, who had taken part in the Sunday meetings and now translated books or wrote reviews, such as the lawyer Simón Wencelblat and the pedagogue Arminda Aberastury. In other words, as Garma explained, editorial activities drew a good part of the attention of the entire institution:

> It is common to say that parents prefer the children who cause more trouble. If this is so, it can also apply to the *Revista de Psicoanálisis*, because its writing requires constant work, which does not tolerate periods of rest. Choosing manuscripts, correcting them, reviewing books and journals, gathering psychoanalytic news, and proofreading require continuous work from all of us, and mainly from Dr. Arnaldo Rascovsky, who is the one in charge of everything related to publications.
>
> ("Inauguración nueva sede" 502)

Once again, Garma is well aware of the importance of this work and the immense effort it required, including in financial terms. He understood that the *Revista*, as a strategic undertaking, could not be self-sustaining or profitable in the near future, even if profitability was not its purpose:

> For the moment, the number of subscriptions to the journal is quite small. No more than three hundred and fifty, although the number goes up every week. We did not expect to do better, given the world situation and the communication difficulties, even with other countries in this continent. Becoming a prophet in one's own land is hard to achieve. . . . We know that our journal will gradually succeed due to its scientific value. For us, it has been a very pleasant surprise to find that a large number of friends not only noticed the price of the subscription, but also contributed periodically to support the journal and psychoanalysis in Argentina. Despite their efforts, and despite their effective, kind, and selfless help, the *Revista de Psicoanálisis*, as an economic undertaking, is largely disastrous.
>
> About the "Library of Psychoanalysis" we can say, without exaggerated optimism, that it will even produce a surplus, since its books will surely be sold. The same will not happen with the journal. Its economic balance will continue to be negative for a long time, especially if we intend to keep it, as up to now, as perfect as possible, both in substance and form.
>
> ("Inauguración nueva sede" 503)

This feverish editorial activity, more than a mere complement, was a condition of possibility for the development of the association. It was a means of projecting it toward a broader public who had to be trained, persuaded, and "made loyal." This strategy did not only depend on the will of its members—it had other supports. The footer on the bottom of the back cover of the journal's first issue stated that it was published "under the scientific patronage of the APA and the financial sponsorship of the Francisco Muñoz Foundation." Francisco "Paco" Muñoz (1889–1965) was not a psychoanalyst but an entrepreneur—like Max Eitingon or Marie Bonaparte, who played similar roles in the development of the Berlin and Paris societies, respectively. This businessman born in Béjar, Salamanca, had built his fortune in the 1920s when he, along with his brother Emilio, established an important men's clothing business, in the heart of Buenos Aires: the traditional *Casa Muñoz* (Grinberg, "Necrológicas").

The interest of this Spanish businessman in psychoanalysis arose somewhat accidentally. According to one version of the story, Pichon-Rivière would have analyzed the manager of one of Muñoz's companies (at the time, his close friend), who suffered from an incapacitating agoraphobia. The success of this treatment would have generated immense gratitude on the part of the Salamancan, who created the "Fundación Muñoz" to finance the activities of the APA (Balán 122). Other versions mention a nephew who suffered from a very intense phobia and an accountant from Casa Muñoz, who would have been treated for headaches (Winkler and Wolff Reyes). Whatever the origin of that debt of gratitude, Muñoz himself referred to it, indirectly, in his end-of-year speech in December 1943, when he was declared "honorary protector member" of the APA:

> Yes, my friends, I emphatically affirm that the practical results of psychoanalysis are not alien to me. I have had the chance to see them very closely. This practical verification of a scientific truth is what has made me a passionate and frank admirer of this new branch of science, leading me to offer it all the support that my position in life allows me. That is to say, the "Foundation," to which Dr. Garma has referred so finely and with so much praise.
> ("Inauguración nueva sede" 504–505)

For this Spanish executive from a family of tailors, his role as a sponsor was not limited to financial support. He also participated very actively in the life of the association. This can be verified by his attendance at social events, such as the annual dinners at the Alvear Palace or at the Plaza Hotel (which celebrated the anniversary of the journal or the end of the year). All events were carefully recorded in the "notes and information" section ("Homenaje a Muñoz" 415; "Cuarta comida anual" 407; "Comida anual" 277–278; "Cena anual" 337; "La tradicional cena" 594). He was also present in several trips abroad, for example, accompanying Rascovsky to Sao Paulo and Rio, in April 1945 ("Viaje al Brasil" 377), or the entire APA delegation, in September 1946, to the Inter-American Congress of Medicine, which took place in Rio de Janeiro ("Primer Congreso Interamericano" 405–406).

Furthermore, the role of the Foundation was so important that Muñoz had Emilio Antona, the general accountant of his company, appointed as administrator of the journal. Until his death in 1965, at the age of 76, Francisco Muñoz played an essential role in the financial viability of both the APA and the *Revista* (Grinberg, "Necrológicas"). By the time he passed away, his contribution was no longer essential for an association that, in less than two decades, had become the most important and prosperous in Latin America. However, without his presence in those first years—made possible by a fortuitous encounter—it would have been difficult for the APA to afford the financial resources needed to achieve the standing and visibility it would eventually enjoy.

The Revista and the International Projection of the APA

From its very first issue, the journal showed an internationalist vocation. Of the four central articles, two were written by the first training members (Cárcamo and Garma) and two by international figures (Melanie Klein and Franz Alexander). Indeed, Kleinianism and the so-called Chicago school, with their focus on unconscious fantasy and psychosomatics, were to have a predominant place in that first decade of the APA, characterized nonetheless by the plurality of theoretical and practical approaches. At the same time, in the "Book Review" section,

Pichon-Rivière commented on a book by Garma, another by French & Alexander (published by the "Library of Psychoanalysis"), and one by René Laforgue. For his part, Rascovsky commented on Emilio Mira y López's psychotherapy manual, while Garma commented on *A History of Medical Psychology*, by Gregory Zilboorg. In other words, of the five books discussed, only one was written by a local author (even if of Basque origins).

Regarding the "Journal Review" section, of its 14 reviews, only two dealt with articles by local authors: Garma and Cárcamo. This ratio is completely understandable given that most of the founding members had just finished their training analysis, and they would require more time to begin writing and publishing. The ratio of local versus foreign authorship did change over the course of the journal's publication. If all the contributions to the first volume are taken into account, there were 14 articles by foreign authors and 7 by local authors. In the second volume, however, the ratio was 19 to 7, and in the third one, 20 to 10. Only in the fifth volume, in 1948, the proportion was reversed: 18 articles by Argentine authors were published and 15 by foreign authors.

For such a young publication, it is outstanding how, from the very first issue, the *Revista* positioned itself as a publication with a transnational audience. Indeed, from the "Presentation" and the "Greetings messages" (from Ernest Jones, president of the IPA, and Karl Menninger, president of the American Psychoanalytic Association) to the "Psychoanalytic Information" section, one idea repeats itself: an association was born in Argentina. This association is the local branch of an active international movement that has given it its recognition. As such, this local branch is committed to contributing to the expansion of the movement in an area and in a language in which it is a pioneer. The journal, likewise, is depicted as an ideal medium of promotion and diffusion. Thus, before stating the "cultural plan of the APA for 1943," an anonymous author presented the APA as follows:

> The Argentine Psychoanalytic Association has been chosen as a subsidiary to the International Psychoanalytic Association. . . . Given this agreeable news, the Argentine Psychoanalytic Association sends a cordial greeting to all the other psychoanalytic associations. . . . Considering the fact that it is the first psychoanalytic association internationally recognized in the Spanish language, it is our goal to dedicate special efforts to support the creation of similar associations in Spain and the Americas.
>
> ("Asociación Psicoanalítica Argentina" 143)

The reversal in the order of events is worth noting: it was not the APA which, after being constituted, requested—and obtained—provisional recognition (which would not be final until 1949). In this account, the APA seems to have been "chosen as a subsidiary" in "recognition and appreciation of the work carried out in recent years by Argentine psychoanalysts" ("Asociación Psicoanalítica Argentina" 143). This official recognition seems to have been obtained without being requested, based solely on merit. A few months later, Garma would reiterate the same account about the origins:

> While we were seriously considering creating the *Revista de Psicoanálisis*, we received a letter from Dr. Ernest Jones, president of the International Psychoanalytic Association, informing us that the Argentine Association had been admitted as its branch. It brought us extraordinary joy. This admission was the best award we could expect. It implies a wide recognition of our work while at the same time it carries great practical significance. It authorizes us to create and direct an Institute of Psychoanalysis and to issue diplomas for psychoanalysts that will be recognized throughout the world.
>
> ("*Inauguración nueva sede*" 504)

Even if psychoanalytic credentials never had any professional qualifying significance for governments, they did have a great symbolic value within the framework of the IPA. Having or not having those credentials made all the difference between a prestigious analyst—who could aspire to a career with international projection within the Freudian community (congresses, conferences, seminars, publications, etc.)—and a "wild analyst" who, medical doctor or not, was destined to practice psychoanalysis without the support of an important training and accreditation circuit. This was also very clear to the candidates who patiently underwent their training analysis. The same happened to those aspiring practicians in other countries who have found out about the existence of the APA—generally through its journal—made preparations to settle in Buenos Aires for the duration of their training.

The Reception of the Revista in Brazil and in the Rest of Latin America

In the Latin American context, the journal's reach was amplified by the work of dissemination carried out by the association's founding members who, from the very beginning, traveled and made contacts across Latin America, building bridges with diverse groups of interest. As early as 1945, Arnaldo Rascovsky accepted an invitation to liaise with the psychoanalytic groups of São Paulo—at that point, undergoing restructuration—and Rio—still in its formative stages. The journal reported,

> The president of the Argentine Psychoanalytic Association, Dr. Arnaldo Rascovsky, made a scientific trip to Brazil. Invited by the National Service of Mental Health and the "Juliano Moreira" Study Center of Rio de Janeiro, by the Society of Medicine and Surgery, by the Neuropsychiatry Section of the São Paulo Association of Medicine, and by the "Franco Da Rocha" Study Center of São Paulo, he presented a series of conferences in important scientific forums in these cities. On this tour, he was accompanied by Mr.

Francisco Muñoz, promoter of the "Muñoz Foundation" for the development of psychoanalysis.

("Viaje al Brasil" 377)

After this first contact, psychoanalytic relations between the two countries would become increasingly close, including a visit by Garma, in January 1946, before the First Inter-American Conference on Medicine in the month of October.[3] In that convention, the 17 papers presented by the Argentines contrasted with the three communications of the recently reconstituted group of San Pablo (read by Durval Marcondes, Virginia Bicudo, and Darcy de Mendoça Uchoa), and with the only communication from Montevideo, by Valentín Pérez Pastorini (who was already in analysis with Garma). At this medical congress, the influx of the psychoanalysts was so significant that the establishment of a specific section on the subject was approved for future iterations of the congress ("Primer Congreso Interamericano" 406). Rascovsky and Garma even had to decline invitations to settle in Rio as training analysts. Instead, the APA promoted the training of Brazilian candidates in Argentina. Matching the enthusiastic reception of the association in Brazil, the Muñoz Foundation offered generous loans: the 1949 balance sheet accounted for 14 loans, which were equivalent to almost 50% of all the association's assets ("Balance General" 179).

The first candidates from Rio arrived in Argentina right after the war. Alcyon Baer Bahía began his training analysis with Cárcamo in 1945; Danilo and Marialzira Perestrello would do the same in 1946 (with Cárcamo and Pichon-Rivière, respectively). Walderedo Ismael de Oliveira would follow, with Marie Langer, in 1947. When these four young psychiatrists returned to Brazil, in 1957, they founded the *Sociedade Brasileira de Psicanálise do Rio de Janeiro* (SBPRJ). The first Porto Alegre psychoanalysts were also trained in Argentina. Between 1945 and 1947, Mário Álvarez Martins did his analysis with Garma, while his wife Zaira chose Arminda Aberastury. The psychiatrist and writer Cyro dos Santos Martins arrived later and trained between 1951 and 1954. Along with José Lemmertz, who had also been trained in the APA in the late 1940s, and Celestino Prunes (analyzed in Rio), they formed the nucleus that, in 1961, would give rise to the Porto Alegre Psychoanalytic Society (Ferraz Lima). Once again, none of this would have been possible without the catalytic presence of the *Revista* and without Muñoz's financial support. According to the testimony of Cyro dos Santos Martins,

> Mário [Martins] and I were in our office, taking a pause, chatting, when a well-dressed man, who spoke Spanish, showed up. He was a visiting psychiatrist with a subscription gift: the first issue of the *Revista de Psicoanálisis*. In reading this issue, we learned that it had become possible to undergo analysis and to do psychoanalytic training and fulfill all its requirements without having to travel very far. This was very important considering that traveling far, at that time, was forbidden by the war. Buenos Aires was close. That visit had an impact on both of us. I was the most affected, because, at that

moment, I could not leave Porto Alegre, due to a relative's serious illness. The same was not true for Mário. He read the journal over and over again and concluded that he would go to Buenos Aires. The first essential step was to write to Garma asking for an appointment. The answer was positive. The preparations took about a year. He even had to request a leave from the Army, since the country was at war. That visit, which appeared to be a simple business formality, proved to be of consequential importance. Its effects went beyond the practice of these two young psychiatrists' who, until then, had little clinical experience and an uncertain future. That afternoon, the seed of the psychoanalytic movement was planted in Porto Alegre.

(Martins and Slavutsky, qtd. in Martins 145)

The number of Brazilian doctors who were trained as psychoanalysts in Argentina throughout this period is remarkable. The institutional impact of this migratory movement can hardly be overstated. It was the direct consequence of the journal's aggressive diffusion strategy in that country, similar to the one used by medical sales representatives (the journal was regularly offered in doctor's offices). It is very likely that similar strategies were used in other Latin American countries, such as Mexico and Colombia. Beginning in 1945, José Luis González Chagoyán, Santiago Ramírez, Ruth Ramírez, Avelino González, Jaime Tomás, José Remus Araico, and Estela Remus Araico arrived from Mexico to Buenos Aires. Upon their return to Mexico, as early as 1957, González Chagoyán, S. Ramírez, A. González, and J. Remus Araico played a significant role in the creation of the Mexican Psychoanalytic Association (APM).

After the "Bogotazo" of 1948, Carlos Plata Mujica, Guillermo Arcila, Guillermo Ángel Gutiérrez, Adolfo Dorbuch, Hernando Pastrana, José Correal, and Hugo Campillo arrived from Colombia to Buenos Aires. Upon their return, Plata Mujica and Arcila joined, as training analysts, the Colombian Group of Psychoanalysis that would establish the Colombian Society of Psychoanalysis in 1961. Hernando Pastrana chose to stay in Buenos Aires, where he would eventually become Colombian ambassador, as well as the brother and uncle of two conservative Colombian presidents (Misael Pastrana, 1970–1974 and Andrés Pastrana, 1998–2002).

The *Revista* in the United States, England, and France

The account in this section does not intend to be exhaustive. Its aim is to show how, from the very beginning, in the 1940s, the journal played a key role in positioning the APA in the central place it was to occupy among the Ibero-American associations. If we were to extend our period of study to the 1950s, we would have to add a significant number of analysts from the already mentioned countries as well as from new ones, such as Venezuela, Uruguay, Spain, Peru, and Chile. Returning to the 1940s, it is clear that the APA's network of foreign relations was not limited to Latin America. As reported in the *Revista*, in January 1946, Garma and Ferrari Hardoy embarked to the United States:

> The trip of these two qualified members of the Argentine Psychoanalytic Association will undoubtedly reinforce the scientific and friendly ties that bind us with the great northern country, and it is to be hoped that it will produce a certain reciprocity allowing us to count on the visit from some of the great figures of contemporary psychoanalytic thought.
>
> ("Viaje de estudio a EEUU" 858)

The announcement turned out to be prophetic. Ferrari Hardoy, whose stay at the New York Institute was expected to last a year, would not return until the 1960s. From time to time, until 1950, Hardoy would send chronicles on North American scientific meetings to the journal ("Reunión de invierno" 460–462). Garma, for his part, established close ties with the various institutes he visited (New York, Chicago, and Topeka), which he was able to capitalize for the APA's benefit. Furthermore, and as the journal had foreseen, Garma's visit to New York would be reciprocated, in 1947, by the visit of Gregory Zilboorg to Argentina—[4]the first member of a U.S. association to do so. His one-week stay, which included a series of five lectures, was considered a "transcendental event" ("Gregory Zilboorg" 604).

There is still more evidence that the *Revista's* reach extended beyond Latin America. In 1944, Theodor Reik—who had been Garma's analyst in Berlin—sent a letter to the editor of the *Revista* explaining that his article on Freud and Mahler had been published in the third issue (Reik, "Sigmund Freud y Gustavo Mahler"), but that he had only received two copies of the second issue: "Please, would you be so kind as to send me two copies of the journal in which my article was published?" (Reik, "Letter"). It could be said that, by 1947, the *Revista* was visible to Northern publishers. That year, Celes Cárcamo received a letter from John Rodker, co-director—with Martin Freud and Barbara Low—of the prestigious British *Imago Publishing Co.* (IPC).[5] Rodker's letter, addressed to both Cárcamo and the *Revista*, accompanied Marie Bonaparte's book, *Mythes de guerre*, published by IPC in 1946. Rodker suggested, "We would be happy to see a review published in the *Revista de Psicoanálisis* and in other places that may seem convenient to you. We would like copies of the reviews to be sent to us" (Rodker). Cárcamo, however, seems to have kept the book for himself, and no reviews were ever published.[6] As these examples show, from the journal's very beginning, well-known and reputable authors and publishers in the Anglo-Saxon psychoanalytic world were not only aware of the existence of the *Revista* but also interested in the possibilities it gave them.

Everything indicates that Rascovsky wanted the *Revista* to acquire a similar relevance in the Francophone territory, which was in a process of reorganization after the War. In 1947, a very young staff member of the *Revista* sent a momentous letter to Daniel Lagache. It was Willy Baranger, a French philosopher born in Algeria, who had arrived in Argentina with his wife Madeleine, in 1946, as Roger

Caillois's successor at the French Institute of Higher Studies. Baranger had met Pichon-Rivière at that Institute, when he was giving his first lectures on the Count of Lautréamont. Pichon made a deep impression on Baranger, which prompted him to write to Lagache—a rising star in the French movement:

> While settled in Buenos Aires, I have taken advantage of the presence of an active and serious psychoanalytic movement in this city, and have decided to start a training analysis with Doctor Pichon-Rivière. This opportunity, as you know, did not exist in the provincial towns where I used to teach in France. I now follow the training courses of the Institute of Psychoanalysis—particularly those offered by Dr Garma—and work regularly at the hospice Las Mercedes.
>
> Perhaps you will agree to help me in a completely different way: I have recently become a member of the editorial board of the psychoanalytic journal of Buenos Aires. Dr Arnaldo Rascovsky, the journal's director, has tasked me with summarizing all available psychoanalytic and psychological documentation in the French language (books and journals). All the abstracts that I write, or that are sent to me, shall appear in the Argentine journal. In addition, the journal will publish a record of the activities of the *Société française de Psychanalyse*.
>
> If you find this project interesting, I will send you some issues of the Argentine journal so that you can see that it has nothing to envy the best psychoanalytic publications in the world. Likewise, it would be possible to publish French-authored articles in the journal (it currently publishes many articles by foreign authors, mainly from North America, and a few articles excerpted from the *Revue française*. When the *Revue française* reappears—I hope soon—we could also consider establishing inverse relations: I could send French translations of the best articles published by Argentine authors and, maybe, of all the abstracts.
>
> (Baranger 1–2)

These lines, most likely written on the advice of Rascosvsky, show the extent to which the "founding fathers" longed to extend the *Revista's* reach in all directions and languages. To achieve this purpose, they had to devise specific strategies for each country, assuming the normalization of European societies—and publications—in the postwar context. As I have discussed elsewhere, Baranger's letter to Lagache was relatively successful (see Dagfal, "Entre París y Buenos Aires," "Psychanalyse et Psychologie"). The truth is that, by the 1950s, Baranger became a central figure in the circulation of Kleinianism between London, Buenos Aires, and Paris, translating both Garma and Klein into French. In this task, he collaborated with his wife, Madelaine Coldefy, but also with Marcelle Spira—a Swiss-born psychologist who had been trained at the APA (and analyzed by Marie Langer) before returning to Geneva in 1955, where she became the disseminator of Melanie Klein in Switzerland (Quinodoz). Overall, as Baranger pointed out, at the end of the 1940s, Buenos Aires was already very well-positioned on the international psychoanalytic circuit, next to cities such as Paris, London, and New York. If Argentine authors were not often referenced or quoted in those metropolises, it was not due to lack of commitment on the part of the journal's editors but because of cultural and language barriers, which tended to be very great for peripheral countries. The *Revista*, notwithstanding, always served as a vehicle for the dissemination of local psychoanalytic knowledge and practice as well as a recipient of various foreign traditions and developments.

Final Comments

The Zurich congress of 1949 would mark a milestone for the APA. On the one hand, at the institutional level, it meant its definitive recognition as an association affiliated with the IPA. On the other hand, and in terms of its theoretical orientation, the congress marked the official adoption of Melanie Klein—whom the Garmas and the Rascovskys had the chance to see for the first time—as their main reference. Indeed, everything indicates that the APA's initial position, equidistant between Anna Freud and Klein, had radically changed within a few years. In 1943, the publication of seminal works by both authors was announced in the first issue of the journal—where chapter 8 of *The Psychoanalysis of Children* (1932) was translated. By 1949, however, everything had changed. Klein's book had been published in Spanish in 1948, translated by Aberastury, who had established a regular correspondence with her since 1945. On the other hand, *The Ego and The Mechanisms of Defence* (1937), by Anna Freud—translated by Celes Cárcamo and Yvonne de Cárcamo—would only be published in 1949. However, it was not edited as planned, by the "Library of Psychoanalysis," but by another publisher, which seems significant. Everything indicates that, since 1949, Klein gradually acquired an almost exclusive status. In the early 1950s, this trend became even more prominent with the visits to London of the Pichon-Rivière-Aberastury, and Garma-Goode couples. They established a personal and an epistolary relationship with Melanie Klein that almost led to her visit to Argentina in 1952 (Dagfal, "Entre París y Buenos Aires"; "Psychanalyse et Psychologie").

Beyond this significant theoretical shift that other authors have also noted (Etchegoyen and Zismann), I would like to emphasize the role of the *Revista*, throughout those early years, in transforming the APA from a small and private psychoanalytic group to a flourishing association with multiple international connections. I have already underlined the importance of its ever-increasing diffusion, but the role of the journal in helping establish a collective professional identity among analysts is also worth noting. The *Revista's* exhaustive recording of all aspects of the association's institutional life not only gave it legitimacy; it also showcased the association's progressive expansion and inclusion within a transnational community. I would argue that these miscellaneous notes, apparently insignificant, not only helped attract foreign candidates but were also the bricks with which the members of the APA constructed a mutual interest, an *affectio societatis*, a common identity. In other words, as a new group, looking at themselves in the mirror of the *Revista de Psicoanálisis*, they constructed a narrative about who they were, where they came from, the knowledge and skills they had, and the mentors and role models they admired. In other words, they managed to establish a professional identity as psychoanalysts. This identity, in general, was related to medicine, the primary discipline for most of them. More specifically, however, this identity—reinforced through the workings of the journal—implied the fact of belonging to an international association that made them heirs of Sigmund Freud.

It is also important to recognize how successful this founding group was in establishing psychoanalysis as a new "cultural jurisdiction" (Abbott 280–314), not only in Argentina but also in other Latin American countries. For nearly two decades, the official association was able to claim for itself the monopoly of the legitimate uses of Freudianism. Even after the 1960s, when this exclusive status began to be contested by many other "unofficial" training institutions—including university psychology programs—the APA managed to present itself as the only genuine Freudian offspring, thus extending its legitimacy to other IPA associations. This was partly possible because of the rare fortune of counting, from the very beginning, with three training analysts who underwent analysis in Berlin, Paris, and Vienna. However, this fact alone would have not been sufficient to assert such a strong influence in the region. In addition to that, as I have shown, there was a very ambitious and deliberate politics of diffusion, mainly channeled through the *Revista de Psicoanálisis*. This achievement was not merely the product of the "founding fathers" individual capacities, but mostly the result of effectively implemented institutional strategies that progressively positioned psychoanalysis as an enormously influential discourse in the cultural life of Argentina and the Latin American region as a whole.

Notes

1 A shorter and modified version of this work was published in a special number of *Revista de Psicoanálisis*: "Los inicios de la *Revista de Psicoanálisis*. Difusión e identidad." *Revista de Psicoanálisis*, vol. 75, no. 1–2, 2018, pp. 19–35.
2 All translations from Spanish into English are mine, unless otherwise noted.
3 The Argentine mission included Garma, Cárcamo, Arnaldo and Luis Rascovsky, Pichon-Rivière, Langer, Schlossberg, Tallaferro, Arminda Aberastury, Matilde Wencelblat, Eduardo Krapf, Flora Scolni, and Horacio García Vega, in addition to the inevitable Francisco Muñoz.
4 In 1943, Garma had reviewed Zilboorg's book *A History of Medical Psychology*.
5 Rodker was a poet and publisher who had been contacted by Sigmund Freud in 1938, after his arrival in London. Concerned about the loss of the *Internationale Psychoanalytische Verlag* in Vienna, after the Nazi takeover, Freud wanted to create a new psychoanalytic publishing house in England, which became a reality between 1939 and 1962.
6 Only Marie Langer was going to cite that book in the third number of the seventh volume, regarding the interpretation of the "myth of the roasted child" (Langer). However, it is likely that she used the copy that is currently kept in the APA library, and not the one sent by Rodke to Garma.

Works Cited

Abbott, Andrew. *The System of Professions: An Essay on the Division of Expert Labor.* U of Chicago P, 1988.

Asociación Psicoanalítica Argentina. *Actas de Reuniones de la Comisión Directiva,* no. 4, 22 Apr. 1943, Archives of the Asociación Psicoanalítica Argentina, Buenos Aires, Argentina. Accessed 12 Mar. 2021.

"Asociación Psicoanalítica Argentina." *Revista de Psicoanálisis,* vol. 1, no. 1, 1943, p. 143.

Balán, Jorge. *Cuéntame tu vida. Una biografía colectiva del psicoanálisis argentino.* Planeta, 1991.

"Balance General de la Asociación Psicoanalítica Argentina." *Revista de Psicoanálisis,* vol. 7, no. 1, 1949, pp. 176–179.

Baranger, Willy. Letter to Daniel Lagache. 14 Oct. 1947. Éva Rosenblum's personal archive, Paris, France.

Bonaparte, Marie. *Mythes de guerre.* Imago Publishing Co., 1946.

Borensztejn, Claudia. "La revista de psicoanálisis. Una historia en construcción." *Revista de Psicoanálisis,* vol. 70, no. 4, 2013, pp. 713–727.

"Cena anual de camaradería en honor de los señores Francisco Muñoz y Emilio Antona, festejando el VII año de aparición de la Revista de Psicoanálisis." *Revista de Psicoanálisis,* vol. 7, no. 2, 1949, p. 337.

Cesio, Fidias. "Historia del movimiento psicoanalítico latinoamericano." *Revista de Psicoanálisis,* vol. 38, no. 4, 1981, pp. 695–713.

"Comida anual de camaradería en honor de los señores Francisco Muñoz y Emilio Antona, festejando el sexto aniversario de la 'Revista de Psicoanálisis'." *Revista de Psicoanálisis,* vol. 6, no. 1, 1948, pp. 277–278.

"Cuarta comida anual de camaradería de la Asociación Psicoanalítica Argentina." *Revista de Psicoanálisis,* vol. 4, no. 2, 1946, p. 407.

Cucurullo, Antonio, et al. "La psychanalyse en Argentine." *Histoire de la psychanalyse,* edited by Roland Jaccard. Hachette, 1982, pp. 453–511.

Dagfal, Alejandro. *Entre París y Buenos Aires. La invención del psicólogo.* Paidós, 2009.

———. *Psychanalyse et psychologie. Paris-Londres-Buenos Aires.* Campagne Première, 2011.

Doria Medina Eguía, Roberto, ed. {XE "Doria Medina Eguia R."} *Grandes psicoanalistas argentinos,* Lumen, 2001.

Etchegoyen, Horacio Ricardo, and Samuel Zysman. "Melanie Klein in Buenos Aires: Beginnings and Developments." *International Journal of Psychoanalysis,* vol. 86, no. 3, 2005, pp. 869–894.

Ferraz Lima, Jeremias. "Considerações sobre o conceito de mobilidade na cultura brasileira e seu papel na introdução da psicanálise no Brasil." *Verbo de Minas,* no. 3, 2002, pp. 111–121.

Freud, Anna. *The Ego and the Mechanisms of Defence.* Hogarth Press, 1937.

"Gregory Zilboorg." *Revista de Psicoanálisis,* vol. 5, no. 3, 1947, pp. 604–606.

Grinberg, León. "Necrológicas." *Revista de Psicoanálisis,* vol. 22, no. 1–2, 1965, pp. 120–122.

———. "Reseña histórica de la Asociación Psicoanalítica Argentina: discurso pronunciado por el doctor León Grinberg el día 29 de junio de 1961." *Revista de Psicoanálisis,* vol. 18, no. 3, 1961, pp. 299–303.

"Homenaje a los sres. Francisco Muñoz y Emilio Antona." *Revista de Psicoanálisis,* vol. 2, no. 2, 1944, p. 415.

"Inauguración de la nueva sede de la Asociación Psicoanalítica Argentina." *Revista de Psicoanálisis*, vol. 1, no. 3, 1944, pp. 500–506.

Klein, Melanie. *The Psychoanalysis of Children*. Hogarth Press, 1932.

"La tradicional cena de la Asociación." *Revista de Psicoanálisis*, vol. 8, no. 4, 1951, p. 594.

Langer, Marie. "El mito del 'niño asado'." *Revista de Psicoanálisis*, vol. 7, no. 3, 1950, pp. 389–401.

Lisman-Pieczanski, Nydia, and Alberto Pieczanski, eds. *The pioneers of psychoanalysis in South America: An Essential Guide*. Routledge, 2014.

Martins, Cyro, and Abrão Slavutsky. *Para início de conversa*. Movimento, 1990.

Martins, Roberto Bittencourt. "Depois de uma tarde sombria." *Fronteiras culturais. Brasil-Uruguai-Argentina*, edited by María Helena Martins. Ateliê Editorial, 2002, pp. 143–148.

Muñoz, María Luisa. "Contribución a la historia del movimiento psicoanalítico en España: Formación de la Asociación Sicoanalítica de Madrid." *Revista de Psicoanálisis de Madrid*, special issue, 1989, pp. 121–152.

Plotkin, Mariano. "Dossier: Psychoanalysis in Latin America." *Psychoanalysis and History*. vol. 14, no. 2, 2012, pp. 227–235.

———. *Freud in the Pampas: The Emergence and Development of a Psycho-analytic Culture in Argentina*. Stanford UP, 2001.

Plotkin, Mariano, and Mariano Ruperthuz. *Estimado Dr. Freud. Una historia cultural del psicoanálisis en América Latina*. Edhasa, 2017.

"Primer Congreso Interamericano de Medicina." *Revista de Psicoanálisis*, vol. 4, no. 2, 1946, pp. 405–406.

Quinodoz, Jean-Michel. "Melanie Klein's Letters Addressed to Marcelle Spira (1955–1960)." *International Journal of Psychoanalysis*, vol. 90, no. 6, 2009, pp. 1340–1365.

Rascovsky, Raquel, ed. *Asociación Psicoanalítica Argentina 1942–1992*. APA, 1994.

"Regresó de Londres el doctor Teodoro Schlossberg." *Revista de Psicoanálisis*, vol. 2, no. 1, 1944, pp. 206–208.

Reik, Theodor. Letter to the *Revista de Psicoanálisis*. New York, 20 July 1944. APA Archives, Buenos Aires, Argentina.

———. "Sigmund Freud y Gustavo Mahler." *Revista de Psicoanálisis*, vol. 1, no. 3, 1944, pp. 315–318.

"Reunión de invierno de la Asociación Psicoanalítica Americana." *Revista de Psicoanálisis*, vol. 7, no. 3, 1950, pp. 460–462.

Rodker, John. Letter to Celes Cárcamo and the *Revista de Psicoanálisis*. London, 23 Apr. 1947, Imago Publishing Co. LTD. Celes Cárcamo Collection, Biblioteca Nacional, Buenos Aires, Argentina.

Roudinesco, Élisabeth, and Michel Plon. *Dictionnaire de la psychanalyse*. Fayard, 1997.

"Viaje al Brasil del presidente de la Asociación Psicoanalítica Argentina." *Revista de Psicoanálisis*, vol. 3, no. 2, 1945, pp. 377–378.

"Viaje de estudio de los doctores Guillermo Ferrari Hardoy y Ángel Garma a los Estados Unidos." *Revista de Psicoanálisis*, vol. 3, no. 4, 1946, p. 858.

Visacovsky, Sergio. *El Lanús. Memoria y política en la construcción de una tradición psiquiátrica y psicoanalítica argentina*. Alianza editorial, 2002.

Winkler, María Inés, and Ximena Wolff Reyes. "El Buenos Aires kleiniano. Vida y obra de Arminda Aberastury (1910–1971)." *Acheronta*, vol. 22, 2005, www.acheronta.org/acheronta22/winkler.htm. Accessed 20 Mar. 2018.

Chapter 12

A Voice Behind the Curtain

How Mexican Psychoanalysis Helped Shape the Work of Oscar Lewis

Ricardo Ainslie and Neil Altman

Years ago, while one of us was attending the annual meetings of the Asociación Mexicana de Psicoanálisis, Ramón Parres, one of the founders of the association, remarked that in the 1950s Oscar Lewis had met regularly with a group of Mexican psychoanalysts to discuss his work in the poorest *vecindades* (low-income neighborhoods) of Mexico City and Tepoztlán. The comment was astonishing for two reasons: First, Oscar Lewis makes no reference to this collaboration with the exception of a very brief (one sentence) acknowledgment in *Five Families: Mexican Case Studies in the Culture of Poverty* (1). Second, the notion that psychoanalysis would have substantive interest in the lives of those living in dire economic poverty and on the margins of society will come as a surprise to most readers. Our interest in this chapter is to document the heretofore all but unknown contribution of Mexican psychoanalysis to Oscar Lewis's work in Mexico and, by implication, their role in Lewis's then emerging controversial ideas about the culture of poverty or at least of this concept's Mexican contours. We are also interested in exploring the ways in which Oscar Lewis's collaboration with Mexican psychoanalysts sheds light on the historic and highly problematic clinical and theoretical silence on the part of mainstream psychoanalysis when it comes to understanding the lives of people living in economic poverty. In so far as Mexican psychoanalysis informed the work of Oscar Lewis, that work, in turn, stands as a commentary on the possibilities of an enlightened psychoanalysis in relation to the lives of those living on the margins of society.

Positioning Oscar Lewis

One of Lewis's more controversial points is his coining of the terms "culture of poverty" (*Anthropological Essays* 69): the notion that living in poverty tends to create character traits that reproduce poverty aside from the effects of material deprivation per se. In his *Anthropological Essays*, Lewis describes the culture of poverty as follows:

> The culture of poverty is both an adaptation and a reaction of the poor to their marginal position in a class-stratified, highly individuated, capitalistic

DOI: 10.4324/9781003266211-16

society. It represents an effort to cope with feelings of hopelessness and despair which develop from the realization of the improbability of achieving success in terms of the values and goals of the larger society. Indeed, many of the traits of the culture of poverty can be viewed as attempts at local solutions for problems not met by existing institutions and agencies because people are not eligible for them, cannot afford them, or are ignorant or suspicious of them.

(69)

It is the inference that chronic poverty yields character traits which in turn tend to reproduce poverty itself, implying that perhaps the poor were ultimately responsible for their own condition, that put the work of Oscar Lewis in the crosshairs of criticism from various quarters.

   In some of his writing, Lewis sought to distinguish the culture of poverty from poverty itself. As a Marxist, Lewis valued class-consciousness as essential for resistance to oppression. He thought that passivity and lack of a historical perspective worked against such resistance and therefore contributed to the reproduction of oppression and poverty. Lewis argued that

> When the poor become class conscious or active members of trade-union organizations or when they adopt an internationalist outlook on the world, they are no longer part of the culture of poverty although they may still be desperately poor. Any movement, be it religious, pacifist, or revolutionary, which organizes and gives hope to the poor and which effectively promotes solidarity and a sense of identification with larger groups, destroys the psychological and social core of the culture of poverty.
>
> (*Anthropological Essays* 74)

Lewis sought to distinguish between poverty per se and the culture of poverty, giving examples of peoples living in dire poverty who do not manifest the attributes described under the culture of poverty:

> Many of the primitive or preliterate peoples studied by anthropologists [such as food gathering and hunting tribes] suffer from dire poverty . . . but they do not have the traits of the subculture of poverty. In India lower castes . . . may be desperately poor both in the villages and in the cities, but most of them are integrated into the larger society and have their own *panchayat* organizations which cut across village lines and give them a considerable amount of power. In addition to the caste system, which gives individuals a sense of identity and belonging, there is still another factor, the clan system . . . [which] gives people a sense of belonging to a corporate body which has a history and a life of its own and therefore provides a sense of continuity, a sense of a past and of a future.
>
> (*Anthropological Essays* 74–75)

Michael Harrington (*The Other America*) and Daniel Patrick Moynihan (*The Negro Family*) picked up on Lewis's term to define a constellation of dysfunctional character traits, centering on lack of future orientation and initiative. Without the Marxist framework, Lewis's term spoke to the cultivation, in poverty, of personal failure rather than the disabling of a potentially revolutionary class. With the framework thus shifted, the idea of a culture of poverty seemed to blame the victim of an oppressive social structure, to stereotype people, rather than to encourage the kind of complex, multidimensional look at the lives of people in economic poverty that Lewis had, in fact, undertaken. As Lewis noted,

> Some of my readers have misunderstood the subculture of poverty model and have failed to grasp the importance of the distinction between poverty and the subculture of poverty. There is nothing in the concept [of culture of poverty] that puts the onus of poverty on the character of the poor. Nor does the concept in any way play down the exploitation and neglect suffered by the poor. Indeed, the subculture of poverty is part of the larger culture of capitalism, whose social and economic system channels wealth into the hands of a relatively small group and thereby makes for the growth of sharp class distinctions.
>
> (*Anthropological Essays* 79)

In this chapter, it is not our interest to relitigate the concept of the culture of poverty. As an anthropologist in the 1940s and 1950s, Lewis no doubt suffered the limitations of his time when it came to understanding the ramifications of poverty. Whether one sees Lewis's proverbial theoretical glass on this front as half full or half empty, our interest is to document the ways in which his work was influenced by Mexican psychoanalysts and by psychoanalysis more generally and show how that influence played a role in Lewis's interest in the subjective experience of poverty, in its phenomenology, which led to his in-depth engagement with his participants. Lewis sought to understand their experiences through their own words and, by spending considerable time in their homes and in their communities, and by favoring in-depth, open-ended interviews, creating an interpersonal space that was receptive to understanding their relationships and their formative life experiences.

What is underscored in our chapter is the little-known fact that Lewis sought substantive input from Mexican psychoanalysts to make sense of his material. These psychoanalysts' views were no doubt shaped by their own personal histories, their own class position within Mexican society, and by the theoretical frameworks that governed the discipline of psychoanalysis in the 1950s. Nevertheless, their commentary, captured in the "Mexican Psychoanalysts" transcripts, reveals an interest in and sensitivity to the inner lives of Lewis's participants who were living at the bottom of Mexican society, marginalized and economically impoverished.

In "Bordering on Anthropology: The Dialectics of a National Tradition in Mexico," Claudio Lomnitz describes a shift in Mexican anthropology beginning in the 1940s toward the *indigenista* model, by which he means an anthropology that was in the service of the Mexican government's agenda of uniting the various elements of Mexican society under the umbrella of the state and its modernizing goals. This was in contrast to the work of foreign and, especially, U.S. anthropologists working in Mexico whose priorities were studying indigenous groups. Lomnitz cites Robert Redfield as a prime example of the latter. Redfield was critiqued in Mexico for romanticizing the lives of Mexican indigenous peoples while ignoring their plight as among the poorest and most marginalized of Mexicans. Lewis's work doesn't fit either mold. For example, he did not focus on the study of indigenous peoples (though his Tepito and Tepoztlán families were Nahuas), and he unambiguously critiqued Redfield as an example of the problematic cultural idealism movement within anthropology that Lewis sought to dethrone. In fact, Lewis's work was neither the "colonizing" anthropology nor the *indigenista* anthropology critiqued by Lomnitz as a tool of the Mexican state. With regard to the latter, one need only to look at the Mexican government's response to *The Children of Sánchez*—the book was declared obscene and Lewis was accused of defaming Mexican institutions and the Mexican way of life. He was accused of being a subversive and of inciting social dissolution (and therefore punishable by a 20-year jail sentence), among other things. Indeed, the Geography and Statistics Society filed formal charges against Lewis with the Mexican Attorney General. This reflects the extent to which Lewis's work broke with the Mexican government's *indigenista* project. Neither was Lewis of the same cloth as the typical foreign anthropologist. His use of the Mexican psychoanalysts to inform his readings was an effort to ground his work in a local understanding. Similarly, Lewis's team included a Mexican psychologist who helped administer the psychological tests as well as many Mexican students from the national university who helped conduct interviews among other activities. Lewis's work simply doesn't fit the two paradigms within the anthropology of the time as captured by Lomnitz. He was a foreign anthropologist who decidedly did not romanticize the lives of the poor; a foreign anthropologist who nevertheless brought the views of Mexicans into his work not only as participants but also as experts. Finally, he was an anthropologist who was not co-opted by the Mexican government's *indigenista* agenda and was therefore vilified and threatened with incarceration for shedding light on a sector of Mexican society that no one wanted to see.

Oscar Lewis's Work in Mexico

Oscar Lewis's Mexico work centered around two primary projects: Tepoztlán, in the state of Morelos, and Tepito, an economically impoverished *vecindad* in Mexico City. His first work was "Tepoztlán Restudied," where he blew apart Robert Redfield's original study of the community from the 1930s—an iconic if idealized reading of life in the village. Lewis viewed his Tepoztlán work as illustrating "the roots of my methodological and theoretical dissent from the anthropology of cultural idealism. . . . I took issue with Robert Redfield for his failure to describe the conditions of poverty and landlessness of the peasants and the effects of these conditions upon their lives and their character" (*Five Lives* ix). Lewis's critique was formative—it led the anthropologist straight into the ideas for which he is best known: his theory of the culture of poverty.

While working in Tepoztlán, Lewis became aware of the migratory patterns of villagers into Mexico City, which led to his second project. In Mexico City, Lewis studied 100 families that had moved from Tepoztlán, with a particular interest in those living in Tepito, one of the poorest neighborhoods in the city. Of these families, 67 were interviewed at least twice and 7 became the objects of in-depth, multidimensional study. One of the latter became the subject matter for *The Children of Sánchez*, Lewis's best-known work.

Lewis arrived in Mexico for his initial work in Tepoztlán already committed to a deeply psychological methodology. In Tepoztlán, Lewis sampled from each of the village's seven neighborhoods for those living at the high (families that owned their land and had cattle, for example), medium, and low (those surviving at a subsistence level) economic strata. But beyond data related to economic status and related practices—the typical domains of anthropology—Lewis conducted in-depth interviews and family histories, he interviewed all the members of some families and these interviews included explorations of family relationships. He administered psychological tests such as the Rorschach Inkblot Test, and he collected dreams. In short, Lewis was clearly interested in the subjective experience of poverty, not only its structural components. He was interested in the inner life of his participants in ways that were unprecedented in anthropology at the time.

Lewis subsequently brought these methodological tools to Tepito, in Mexico City. Here, he again administered a battery of psychological tests—the Rorschach, the Thematic Apperception Test, the Semantic Differential—all considered the leading edge of psychological assessment at the time. He collected dreams, and, as he'd done in Tepoztlán, conducted extensive interviews with a subset of families that were decidedly psychological in their tone and intent. As we will illustrate below, the result was that Lewis's Mexico material had a psychological depth and complexity that had never been seen in the annals of anthropological work or, for that matter, in the annals of psychological research either. It was the combination of in-depth psychological investigation coupled with a singular focus on the experience of poverty and the impact of poverty on the "character" of those living within it, that made Lewis's work so distinctive and powerful.

The influence of psychoanalysis on Lewis's Mexico projects is obvious, notwithstanding the fact that these works contain no references to psychoanalysis or psychoanalytic writings. For example, in discussing his concept of the culture of poverty, Lewis's notes that the culture of poverty can be studied from a variety of perspectives, such as the relationship between the subculture and the larger society in which it exists, at the level of the community itself, and, finally, at the level of the individual in terms of attitudes, values, and character structure

(*Anthropological Essays* 2). With respect to the latter, Lewis points to the following characteristics as the lens through which an individual's functioning might be described:

> a high incidence of maternal deprivation, orality, weak ego structure, confusion of sexual identification, a lack of impulse control, a strong preset-time orientation with relatively little ability to defer gratification and to plan for the future, a sense of resignation and fatalism, a widespread belief in male superiority, and a high tolerance for psychological pathology of all sorts.
>
> (73)

These descriptors for assessing psychological functioning come straight from the primary paradigm that governed psychoanalysis in 1950s, namely Ego Psychology. With the exception of the idea of "belief in male superiority" and "resignation and fatalism," the remaining descriptions are precisely the rubrics used to evaluate and diagnose human functioning by psychoanalysts at the time. They map very closely to the writings of Anna Freud (*The Ego and the Mechanisms of Defense*) and Heinz Hartmann (*Ego Psychology and the Problem of Adaptation*) on how to assess human psychological functioning, for example.

It is not surprising that Lewis's work was influenced by psychoanalysis since it was the reigning paradigm of the time. In addition, there was significant interplay between the anthropology department at Columbia University where Lewis received his doctoral training and the psychoanalytic institute at Columbia. Abram Kardiner, a godfather of U.S. psychoanalysis and a founding member of that training institute, was extremely interested in the relationship between psychoanalysis and culture and co-taught a seminar in the department of anthropology at Columbia with the anthropologist Ralph Linton on how culture is transmitted from generation to generation. While we can't document that Lewis attended this seminar, there is correspondence in the Oscar and Ruth Lewis Archive at the University of Illinois Urbana-Champaign between Oscar Lewis and Kardiner's wife, Ethel, also a psychoanalyst, regarding the interpretation of some of the psychological tests he was administering in Mexico.

Given the years that Lewis trained at Columbia and the preeminence of psychoanalysis at the time, it is to be expected that psychoanalytic ideas seeped into Lewis's work. Notwithstanding the absence of references to psychoanalysis in Lewis's writing, these ideas are clearly reflected in his methodology (about which we speak more specifically below). However, few are aware of the fact that Mexican psychoanalysts played a substantive role in helping Lewis think through the possible meaning of the material he was collecting in his work on the experience of poverty in these two Mexican communities; that is to say, in the work that would make Oscar Lewis one of the best-known anthropologists of his time.

Exposure to the psychoanalysis of his time gave Lewis the tools to illuminate the subjective experience of his subjects. The attribution of complex inner lives to economically impoverished people, along with attribution of interest therein, was uncommon at the time, and still is. People in economic poverty were, and often are, thought to lack psychological mindedness. Lewis did not make this point explicitly, but his case studies, described and quoted below, clearly illustrate a high level of psychological insight and awareness of psychological conflict on the part of his subjects. It seems to us that Lewis, almost inadvertently, opened the door to exposing the potential of psychoanalysis to disprove stereotypes of economically impoverished people as insensitive to psychic pain and conflict. We are still learning this lesson, swimming upstream against powerful cultural currents justifying inattention to the oppression of economically poor people based on their supposed incapacity for psychic suffering.

The Psychological Experience of Poverty

We are acutely aware that there is a glaring blind spot in psychoanalytic writing around the suffering of the economically impoverished and the culturally marginalized, and that vivid and fine-grained depictions of experiential lives have largely been reserved for the white and well-to-do. Until rather recently, it was assumed in descriptions of clinical encounters in case reports that both patient and analyst/therapist were white and middle to upper-middle class. Psychoanalysts have rarely turned their eye to considering, much less understanding, the lives of those occupying the bottom rungs of society. Indeed, extended meditations on the lives of the marginalized have appeared mostly in fiction (think Toni Morrison, for example), film (*Parasite* by the South Korean director Bong Joon-ho, or Luis Buñuel's *Los Olvidados* are examples), and various forms of sociological documentary, as in Nicole LeBlanc's *Random Family: Love, Drugs, Trouble, and Coming of Age in the Bronx*, the product of the author's ten-year-long residence among families in the South Bronx. Psychoanalysis is, at its core and at its best, the disciplined study of subjectivity. Yet, as a discipline, it has shown little interest in understanding the subjective experience—the phenomenology—of lives lived in the grips of economic poverty.

Among the classic works that *have* examined life in poverty, Oscar Lewis's *Five Families: Mexican Case Studies in the Culture of Poverty* (1959) and *The Children of Sánchez: Autobiography of a Mexican Family* (1961) stand as remarkable for their strikingly detailed descriptions of life in severe economic poverty. However, it is Lewis's attention to the nuances of relationships and emotional life that make his work distinctive and groundbreaking. The fact that Lewis saw psychoanalysis as a potential resource in his efforts to illuminate the subjective experience of his participants was novel within anthropology, but it was also novel within psychoanalysis to have its concepts and methodology used to explore the lives of people whose experience is shaped by economic poverty. Six decades later, psychoanalysts are themselves just beginning to actualize that potential.

The Martínez family, one of the five families that comprise Lewis's *Five Families*, lived in Tepotzlán, while *The Children of Sánchez* focuses on a family living in Tepito, both were economically impoverished communities, the former rural, the latter urban. Both books move along the same axis: lives recounted in the subjects' own words, providing a window not only into the practices and material aspects of dire economic poverty (that is, the traditional interests of anthropology) but also, and for our purposes most importantly, into the emotional realities of life under such difficult circumstances. That is, Lewis was interested in the psychological experience of those whom he studied; his concern was not only to map the material life-shaping consequences of poverty but also to map its psychological consequences.

Then, as now, psychoanalysts all too often dismiss people like the members of the Sánchez and Martínez families as "unanalyzable" because of economic or educational "deprivation," or the priority of "concrete" problems. A few pages into *The Children of Sánchez*, Lewis makes it undeniably clear that his participants are people with inner lives as rich and fascinating as that of the differently socially positioned reader.

Listen to Consuelo, talking about her life after her mother died and her father remarried:

> I don't remember my father came to school a single time in all the years I spent in primary school. He knew nothing of the things that happened in school, and he never asked. I had begged my father to come to the graduation exercises but he never appeared. I kept sticking my head over the balcony to see if he had come. . . . Some of the fathers came in their work clothes but they were there anyway with their daughters. . . . And that was my life as a little girl. Ignored when I would do well in school or when I would ask questions at home, or answered sharply by my family. This made me feel stupid or it made me think they didn't love me. But I never knew why.
>
> (*Children of Sánchez* 215–216)

Oscar Lewis listened and people talked, in detail and self-reflectively, about emotions and relationships. When people listen in a certain way, with focused attention on emotional experience, what has come to be called "active listening," the other person speaks, and hears herself, in a special way. Self-awareness evolves and, with it, a sense of ownership and authorship of one's life. This kind of listening is the bedrock of psychoanalytic praxis. This is the kind of listening that the field of psychoanalysis tends to deny to the economically besieged and culturally nonmainstream; that is, to people such as the Martínezes and the Sánchezes. We do not hear the voice of Oscar Lewis in the background of the comments of Consuelo but we can infer the kind of presence that would tend to make it possible for her to speak this way. What is clear in his work, in other words, is that Lewis deployed a psychoanalytic sensibility in his engagement with these families living in conditions of extreme poverty in Mexico. The tones of these engagements, Lewis's methodological style when it came to his relationships and interviews, are part of what made his work congenial to psychoanalytic reflection.

Consuelo's sister Marta speaks bluntly of the violence and brutality in the neighborhood:

> Every day someone was robbed, or murdered, or violated. There is a story about a girl in Tepito who had a boyfriend. He was one of the worst kind. Once he invited her to the movies. He had prearranged with some other boys to take her home through the market, and there they grabbed her, dragged her into one of the stalls and they all raped her. They say that there were so many of them that her anus came out and then they killed her.
>
> (*Children of Sánchez* 146)

Marta has a deep psychologically informed understanding of bullies and a sense of responsibility toward their victims:

> When you enter a gang, if you do not defend yourself, you can only cry. In any gang there is at least one girl who has a reputation for being mean, for fighting rough. The others begin to be afraid of her and give in or run away. But – if you stand up to her, the fury often turns out to be a phony, nothing but a mirror, reflecting the weakness or strength of the others. I never liked to see anyone take advantage of timid girls, so I often stood up for them.
>
> (144–145)

The harshness of Marta's life does not rule out a poetic sensibility:

> The year I joined my gang there was a heat wave among the girls, and one by one they were shelled like corn. It started with the older girls and ended with the younger ones – it got so, we asked each other, "Well, where did you lose it, on a bed or on a *petate*.
>
> (straw mat)?" (145)

Here is Manuel talking about violence as a defense against fear. Referring to his brother Roberto, he says,

> I attribute a lot of his trouble to the mistaken idea we have that it is a matter of self-respect or pride to show no fear. Roberto really didn't know what fear was and he was incapable of running away from trouble. If somebody pulled a knife, he pulled one too, and used it. I have said to him ' . . . if you have so much anger in you why don't you let me make a boxer out of you?' At bottom, I believe he was afraid of something. In my poor judgment, it was his subconscious at work, trying to defend itself from something indeterminate.
>
> (174–175)

Manuel, in this passage, is taking the opportunity provided by an empathic and psychologically minded listener to develop his own psychological mindedness.

In this way, Lewis's approach to the participants in his projects in Tepotzlán and, later, in Tepito, has an unmistakable psychoanalytic voice. His psychological aims—to understand the phenomenology of their lives—to coincide with the psychoanalytic aims of understanding subjective experience in all its complexity. Ironically, in his mobilization of psychoanalysis, his work stands as a counterpoint to the historical and systematic failure or refusal by psychoanalysis as a discipline to be receptive to the experiences of people living on the economic margins of society; an egregious denial of their humanity. Second, those of us who are comfortably situated in the world, occupying situations of economic privilege, do not want to be reminded of the fact that for many such comfort and privilege is utterly beyond reach. Indeed, perhaps beyond the bounds of ordinary middle-class imagination. Oscar Lewis's work was highly subversive in both of these respects.

Psychoanalysis, Oscar Lewis, and Mexico

As noted, Oscar Lewis's work was profoundly innovative and transformative within the field of anthropology for its interest in communities of people living in economic poverty, whether in the United States, Mexico, Puerto Rico, or India. Two things make Lewis's work stand out. The first was his insistence that anthropologists focus their work to understand the lives of those closer to home. He chastised his discipline for its preoccupation with the remote and the "exotic" while neglecting the lives of people living in contemporary nations or in their own cities, noting that anthropologists, as well as the public at large, knew more about cultures in faraway places than they did about those closer to home.

> It is ironic that many Americans, thanks to anthropologists, know more about the culture of some isolated tribe of New Guinea, with a total population of 500 souls, than of the way of life of millions of villagers in India or Mexico and other underdeveloped nations which are destined to play so crucial a role in the international scene.
>
> (Lewis, *Five Families* 1)

The second thing that makes Lewis's work stand out is his interest in the psychology and phenomenology of poverty itself. As noted above, he refused to see the poor as people without an inner life. That interest is partly what led Lewis to work in ways that were deeply psychological and unique within anthropology.

Lewis viewed his work as a "frank experiment" in anthropological research design and reporting (*Five Families* 3) in large part because of its psychological character. This "experiment," driving Lewis to prominence, allowed him to engage the subjectivity of individuals who found themselves trapped in the undertow at the bottom of Mexican society. As clinicians, we wish to emphasize that his subjects felt seen, recognized, and respected within that delicate, relational engagement that undergirds our own work. Lewis shows how such productive respect for the objects of study can also undergird the work of the anthropologist.

One of Lewis's axioms was that personality and culture are deeply intertwined. He had a keen sense of the ways in which culture forms and shapes psychological experience. Lewis also recognized that there was an enormous gap in our knowledge of the lives of those living on the economic margins of society. At the time of his work in Mexico, Lewis noted that almost 80% of the world's population lived in conditions of rural or urban poverty and that their lives were little understood, much less a source of interest. "We know little about the psychology of the people, particularly of the lower classes, their problems, how they think and feel, what they worry about, argue over, anticipate, or enjoy," Lewis noted (*Five Families* 1). This was the goal of modern anthropology, Lewis argued, "To serve as students and reporters" of this experience (*Five Families* 1).

The acknowledgments in Lewis's *Five Families* is only one page in length but it contains the following: "I am also grateful to my friends in the Asociación Psicoanalítica Mexicana (APM)—Dr. Ramón Parres, Dr. José L. Gonzales, Dr. Santiago Ramírez, Dr. José Remus, and Dr. Luis Feder—for their stimulating discussion of the materials on the Martínez family" (xi). The deeply psychological nature of Lewis's methodology and sensibility (as noted, he collected extensive autobiographical accounts and conducted ongoing, open-ended interviews, even collecting dreams, in addition to using instruments such as the Rorschach Inkblot Test, the Thematic Apperception Test, and the Semantic Differential—all respected contemporary assessment techniques for his time) reflect the fact that Lewis's interests were deeply psychological. What is less well known, though pointed to in the brief acknowledgments to *Five Families*, is the role that Mexican psychoanalysts played in shaping Lewis's understanding of the psychology of the people whom he was studying in Mexico. The psychoanalysts noted in the acknowledgments to *Five Families* had mostly trained in the United States and Argentina before returning home to Mexico, where they were poised to found the Asociación Psicoanalítica Mexicana (APM).

Ramón Parres was arguably the most critical member of this group. It is no accident that Lewis lists Parres first in acknowledging the Mexican psychoanalysts. Parres had a natural interest and affinity for the issues that Oscar Lewis was exploring. In addition, Parres's wife, Amparo, was trained as an anthropologist and archaeologist. It is also likely that the Parreses and Lewis met in New York City during the years that Ramón Parres was in psychoanalytic training there.[1]

That connection formed in New York City may explain why Lewis sought Parres out in Mexico City and, through him, the analysts who would soon found the APM. It is noteworthy that notwithstanding the fact that Erich Fromm and his group were already established in Mexico, Lewis engaged the APM psychoanalysts rather than the Frommians.[2] At first glance this is surprising. Like Fromm, Lewis felt a strong affinity for Marxist ideas (Harvey and Reed), so there was a natural ideological connection between the two men. In addition, Fromm was already a well-known figure within psychoanalytic circles in New York, Mexico, and elsewhere. Fromm had arrived in Mexico City in 1944. By 1950 he had begun training a group of Mexican psychiatrists in psychoanalysis. In fact, Fromm founded the Sociedad Mexicana de Psicoanálisis (SMP) in 1956, a year before the founding of the APM. Lewis was already conducting fieldwork in Mexico in Tepotzlán, which is very near Cuernavaca, Morelos, outside of Mexico City, where Fromm established a strong presence. There were many threads that might have linked Lewis to Fromm; however, Lewis appears to have avoided Fromm and his group, seeking out the APM instead.

The answer to this puzzle is likely to be found in the fact that by the time Fromm arrived in Mexico he had already run afoul of mainstream psychoanalysis. His criticism of Freudian theory—even if at times apposite—coupled perhaps with his marriage to Freida Reichman, who had been his personal psychoanalyst, led to his ostracism from New York psychoanalytic circles not long before Parres arrived for analytic training. The residues of those controversies were no doubt still in the air. Fromm was formally expelled from the New York Psychoanalytic Institute prior to his move to Mexico City. The APM, on the other hand, became an institute in good standing with the International Psychoanalytic Association (IPA), the accrediting body for psychoanalytic institutes at the time (the IPA immediately recognized the APM after its founding in 1957). Fromm's conflicts with the International Psycho-analytic Association—from which he was kicked out in 1959—likely had reverbera-tions in Mexico. In addition, when the foreign-trained Mexican analysts returned to Mexico, they were not accepted by the SMP, the Frommian association, leading to a schism between the IPA-trained analysts of the APM and the Frommian group.[3]

This was no doubt part of the context within Mexican psychoanalytic circles when, in 1956, Oscar and Ruth Lewis, who had been working intensively in Tepotzlán, as well as in Tepito, set in motion a series of meetings with the psy-choanalysts who were about to formalize the APM and receive its accreditation from the IPA. The format for these meetings was very much akin to that of a psy-choanalytic clinical case conference. Oscar Lewis presented detailed fieldwork material to which the Mexican psychoanalysts responded at some length. The only documentation found in the Oscar and Ruth Lewis Archive at the University of Illinois Urbana-Champaign pertains to six meetings that transpired between September and November of 1956. These meetings focused on the Martínez fam-ily of Tepotzlán, which is one of the families that comprise Lewis's *Five Families*. It is evident that the material gathered by Oscar and Ruth Lewis relating to at least some of the other families was similarly presented, given that, in the course of their reflections on the Martínez family, the Mexican psychoanalysts (or the Lewises) occasionally reference these other meetings.

The Leiwses either arranged for the recording and transcription of the meetings with the Mexican psychoanalysts or they obtained copies of the proceedings for their own files. In the Lewis's archive at Urbana-Champaign, there is a single file titled "Mexican Psychoanalysts." The file does contain the case material presented by Oscar Lewis, only typed transcripts of the analysts' discussion of the material. Oscar Lewis presumably drew from these to reflect on his interpretations. Some of the summaries are rather brief (6 double-spaced pages), while others are extensive (24 double-spaced pages).

Although occasionally there were additional panelists, it is clear that the five psychoanalysts referenced above, those who appear in the acknowledgments to *Five Families*, formed the core of the group to whom Lewis presented. As noted, these were all founding members of the APM. Ramón Parres was born in the poor and densely indigenous state of Chiapas. He studied medicine at the Universidad Autónoma de Mexico (UNAM), and then, as noted, went to New York to get his psychoanalytic training at Columbia. Although he was offered positions that would have allowed him to remain in New York, Parres chose to return to Mexico.[4] Santiago Rmírez and José Luis González also obtained their medical degrees at the UNAM and received their psychoanalytic training in Argentina before returning to Mexico to practice. It is clear that Ramírez had a strong interest in the impact of culture on personality. He would subsequently author *El mexicano: psicología de sus motivaciones.* José Remus was similarly interested in social issues and studied for a Master's degree in sociology along with his medical studies. In subsequent writings, he developed the concept of the class unconscious, a concept that was for the most part foreign to the psychoanalysis of his time, although a number of contemporary theorists, such as Lynne Layton, have developed related ideas regarding the relationship between society and the unconscious (Layton and Leavy-Sperounis). Remus also became interested in the psychology of social protest movements. Finally, Luis Feder, had studied medicine at the UNAM and been an analysand of Santiago Ramírez.

The "Mexican Psychoanalysts" file contains the following documents:

1 COMENTARIOS A LA PRIMERA CONFERENCIA DEL DR. LEWIS 22-IX-56 1956 (September 22, 1956–6 pages)
2 COMENTARIOS DE DR.PARRES, DR. RAMIREZ, DR. FEDER, DR. REMUS, DR. JOSE LUIS GONZALEZ. SOBRE EL CAPITULO . . . MARTINEZ" DEL LIBRO "DOS FAMILIAS CAMPESINAS MEXICANAS. OSCAR Y RUTH LEWIS ("no date, 24 pages—appears to be September 29)
3 Viernes 5 de Oct de 1956 (15 pages)
4 12 de OCTUBRE de 1956/SESION No. 4 Comentarios (20 pages)
5 Sesión del viernes 16-XI-56 (8 pages)
6 November 16, 1956 (handwritten date, 14 pages)

The transcripts of the meetings leave no doubt that the Mexican psychoanalysts had substantive interest in exploring the impact of social context on personality. Then following excerpts from what we believe is the September 29, 1956, gathering (which appears to be the second meeting of this series), captures the tone of the exchanges found in the six meetings:

> Dr. Ramón Parres -[referring to Oscar Lewis] What you've read has made me confirm some ideas that I had last time, especially that of the . . . important role of Esperanza, who is the mother, that . . . it might seem that her reasons

for hiding money is motivated by a wish for power, [but] in reality it is not; because when Esperanza is not present the family does not eat, and she uses the money that she saves to supply [food] throughout the year, because in reality she mistrusts the reliability with which Pedro and his children can give her money to feed [the family]; that is to say, there is an important piece of information that is mentioned as fact, a family of many men is a very difficult family because you have to take care of them, in reality men are not given a mature role, they are considered as children, actually . . . the woman does it all, she raises the children, she is the 'institution'. . . . Esperanza's presence is really the direct factor that gives the family cohesion which is a very important factor in this family.

(1–2)

A few pages later in the transcript Dr. Ramírez weighs in responding perhaps to Parres's characterization of the father, Pedro, as autocratic and as an "arrchaic" father figure who hasn't internalized the ideals of the Mexican Revolution (in which Pedro had fought as part of Emiliano Zapata's forces). Lewis, for his part, seemed to feel that Pedro sucked the air out of the psychology of the family to the point that it was difficult to discern their identities apart from that of their father:

Dr. Santiago Ramírez – Well, in some things I agree with what you have pointed out, and in other things I completely disagree, completely disagree, because of a series of egos, right? In other words, I believe that at a certain moment, defenses and tendencies are confused when describing the phenomenological picture. That is to say, I think that we are very frequently integrating [this material] and judging this family with our own models (or lines of thinking), rather than putting ourselves into the behavior patterns and motivations of this family and the life situation in which it is found, right? I think that Pedro [the father], for this type of family organization and for the town where he lives, is a guy with an enormous amount of constructive desires.

(13–14)

As a final example of the depth of information collected by Lewis and the depth of the psychoanalysts' exploration of its meaning, consider the following change: Lewis had presented one of Pedro's dreams in which he reported that he is before a man who is attacking him. Dr. Parres interpretets this dream as relating to a deeseated rage over the many abandonments he had experienced in his life, beginning with his father who left the family when Pedro was but three months old. Pedro's mother also abandoned him to be with her lovers when he was around eight, leaving him with an uncle who subjected him to recurrent beatings. These "may have been traumatizing" to Pedro, Parres speculates. The beatings and abandonments are followed by "a series of incidents in which Pedro always suffers," Parres notes. "All the world beats him. There is no situation in which someone doesn't do something to him. They even steal his girlfriend." (2). Later, when Pedro was employed at a hacienda, the foreman also beat him.

Parres then references a series of dreams in which Pedro reports that he cannot move his arms or in which his arms are very weak, suggesting that they represent the Pedro's difficulty accessing the internal rage born out of this childhood, filled as it is with abandonment, maltreatment, and neglect. Parres argues that Pedro's anger is "profoundly repressed" (2). The only place it finds expression is in the cruelty with which he treats his own children; victims of a wrath that had no other outlet.

"But there are positive elements," Parres continues. Esperanza saves Pedro because she brings strength and cohesion to their family. "Pedro never really had a mother," Parres concludes, so this relationship is profoundly important for him in psychological terms. This point appears to stir something in Lewis who responds to Parres: "After he'd been married 21 years, Pedro remembered that his mother died and he said to Esperanza, 'You are more of a mother to me than my own mother.' She actually rescued his 'Ego,'" Lewis concludes (2–3).

Conclusion

The aim of this contribution has been to document the role played by Mexican psychoanalysts in the work of Oscar Lewis as he was working in Tepoztlán and Tepito in the 1950s. The depth of this relationship has not been previously noted. Aside from a single sentence in his acknowledgments to *Five Families*, Lewis makes no mention of psychoanalysis and does reference psychoanalytic literature in his Mexico works. Yet there is no mistaking the depth of the exchanges that took place over the course of at least six meetings (perhaps more). Oscar Lewis presented his material in great detail to these psychoanalysts who would soon found the Asociación Psicoanalítica Mexicana. More generally, in places, it is easy to discern the language of Ego Psychology, and to see how psychoanalytic perspectives formed the scaffolding to Lewis's understanding of the psychological experience of the Tepoztecos he studied who were living in dire economic poverty in Tepoztlán and in Mexico City. This is even more true of the tools of Lewis's methodology: both the character, in tone and intent, of the interviews and in terms of the data collected via psychological tests and the collection of dreams. We believe this psychological voice is arguably the most important part of Lewis's contributions. While the culture of poverty has drawn the most interest (and controversy), it is Lewis's portraits of the Martínez and the Sánchez families—deep, complex explorations of the inner lives of people living at the bottom of Mexico's social structure, that stands the test of time. In Lewis's work, psychoanalysis is the voice, or at least one of the more prominent voices, behind the curtain—so very present yet unseen.

Notes

1 Personal communication from Juana Maria Parres Cook, Ramón Parres's daughter.
2 For more on the professional life of Ramón Parres, see www.medigraphic.com/pdfs/bmhfm/hf-2010/hf102k.pdf.
3 For an outline of the history of psychoanalysis in Mexico, see CARTApsi, Breve Cronología del Psicoanálisis en México, Psicoanálisis, Cultura y filosofía, see www.cartapsi.org/new/psicoanalisis-en-mexico/. For a description of the rejection of the returning foreign trained psychoanalysts by the Frommian group, see www.medigraphic.com/pdfs/bmhfm/hf-2010/hf102k.pdf.
4 Juanamaria Parres Cook, personal communication.

Works Cited

Freud, Anna. *The Ego and the Mechanisms of Defense*. International UP, 1968.
Harrington, Michael. *The Other America: Poverty in the United States*. McMillan, 1962.
Harvey, David L., and Michael H. Reed. "The Culture of Poverty: An Ideological Analysis." *Sociological Perspectives*, vol. 39, no. 4, 1996, pp. 465–495.
Layton, Lynne. *Toward a Social Psychoanalysis: Culture, Character, and Normative Unconscious Processes*, edited by Marianna Leavy-Sperounis. Routledge, 2020.
Lewis, Oscar. *Anthropological Essays*. Random House, 1970.
———. *The Children of Sánchez: Autobiography of a Mexican Family*. Basic Books, 1961.
———. *Five Families: Mexican Case Studies in the Culture of Poverty*. Basic Books, 1959.
Lomnitz, Claudio. "Bordering on Anthropology: The Dialectics of a National Tradition in Mexico." *Revue de Synthèse*, vol. 121, no. 3, 2000, pp. 345–379.
Los olvidados, directed by Luis Buñuel, 1959.
Morrison, Toni. *Paradise*. Aflred Knopf, 1997.
Moynihan, Patrick. *The Negro Family: The Case for National Action*. Office of Policy Planning and Research. United States. Department of Labor. Mar. 1965.
Parasite, directed by Bon Joon Ho, 2019.
Rainwater, Lee, and William L. Yancey. *The Moynihan Report and the Politics of Controversy: A Trans-action Social Science and Public Policy Report*. MIT Press, 1967.
Ramírez, Santiago. *El mexicano: psicología de sus motivaciones*. Grijalbo, 1977.

Index

Taylor & Francis Group
an **informa** business

Taylor & Francis eBooks

www.taylorfrancis.com

A single destination for eBooks from Taylor & Francis
with increased functionality and an improved user
experience to meet the needs of our customers.

90,000+ eBooks of award-winning academic content in
Humanities, Social Science, Science, Technology, Engineering,
and Medical written by a global network of editors and authors.

TAYLOR & FRANCIS EBOOKS OFFERS:

A streamlined
experience for
our library
customers

A single point
of discovery
for all of our
eBook content

Improved
search and
discovery of
content at both
book and
chapter level

REQUEST A FREE TRIAL
support@taylorfrancis.com

Routledge
Taylor & Francis Group

CRC Press
Taylor & Francis Group

For Product Safety Concerns and Information please contact our EU
representative GPSR@taylorandfrancis.com
Taylor & Francis Verlag GmbH, Kaufingerstraße 24, 80331 München, Germany

www.ingramcontent.com/pod-product-compliance
Lightning Source LLC
Chambersburg PA
CBHW070326270326
41926CB00017B/3773